SPATIAL PLOTS
VIRTUALITY AND THE EMBODIED MIND IN
BARICCO, CAMILLERI AND CALVINO

LEGENDA

LEGENDA is the Modern Humanities Research Association's book imprint for new research in the Humanities. Founded in 1995 by Malcolm Bowie and others within the University of Oxford, Legenda has always been a collaborative publishing enterprise, directly governed by scholars. The Modern Humanities Research Association (MHRA) joined this collaboration in 1998, became half-owner in 2004, in partnership with Maney Publishing and then Routledge, and has since 2016 been sole owner. Titles range from medieval texts to contemporary cinema and form a widely comparative view of the modern humanities, including works on Arabic, Catalan, English, French, German, Greek, Italian, Portuguese, Russian, Spanish, and Yiddish literature. Editorial boards and committees of more than 60 leading academic specialists work in collaboration with bodies such as the Society for French Studies, the British Comparative Literature Association and the Association of Hispanists of Great Britain & Ireland.

The MHRA encourages and promotes advanced study and research in the field of the modern humanities, especially modern European languages and literature, including English, and also cinema. It aims to break down the barriers between scholars working in different disciplines and to maintain the unity of humanistic scholarship. The Association fulfils this purpose through the publication of journals, bibliographies, monographs, critical editions, and the MHRA Style Guide, and by making grants in support of research. Membership is open to all who work in the Humanities, whether independent or in a University post, and the participation of younger colleagues entering the field is especially welcomed.

ALSO PUBLISHED BY THE ASSOCIATION

Critical Texts
Tudor and Stuart Translations • New Translations • European Translations
MHRA Library of Medieval Welsh Literature

MHRA Bibliographies
Publications of the Modern Humanities Research Association

The Annual Bibliography of English Language & Literature
Austrian Studies
Modern Language Review
Portuguese Studies
The Slavonic and East European Review
Working Papers in the Humanities
The Yearbook of English Studies

www.mhra.org.uk
www.legendabooks.com

ITALIAN PERSPECTIVES

Editorial Committee
Professor Simon Gilson, University of Oxford (General Editor)
Dr Francesca Billiani, University of Manchester
Professor Manuele Gragnolati, Université Paris-Sorbonne
Dr Catherine Keen, University College London
Professor Martin McLaughlin, Magdalen College, Oxford

Founding Editors
Professor Zygmunt Barański and Professor Anna Laura Lepschy

In the light of growing academic interest in Italy and the reorganization of many university courses in Italian along interdisciplinary lines, this book series, founded by Maney Publishing under the imprint of the Northern Universities Press and now continuing under the Legenda imprint, aims to bring together different scholarly perspectives on Italy and its culture. *Italian Perspectives* publishes books and collections of essays on any period of Italian literature, language, history, culture, politics, art, and media, as well as studies which take an interdisciplinary approach and are methodologically innovative.

APPEARING IN THIS SERIES

20. *Ugo Foscolo and English Culture*, by Sandra Parmegiani
21. *The Printed Media in Fin-de-siècle Italy: Publishers, Writers, and Readers*, ed. by Ann Hallamore Caesar, Gabriella Romani, and Jennifer Burns
22. *Giraffes in the Garden of Italian Literature: Modernist Embodiment in Italo Svevo, Federigo Tozzi and Carlo Emilio Gadda*, by Deborah Amberson
23. *Remembering Aldo Moro: The Cultural Legacy of the 1978 Kidnapping and Murder*, ed. by Ruth Glynn and Giancarlo Lombardi
24. *Disrupted Narratives: Illness, Silence and Identity in Svevo, Pressburger and Morandini*, by Emma Bond
25. *Dante and Epicurus: A Dualistic Vision of Secular and Spiritual Fulfilment*, by George Corbett
26. *Edoardo Sanguineti: Literature, Ideology and the Avant-Garde*, ed. by Paolo Chirumbolo and John Picchione
27. *The Tradition of the Actor-Author in Italian Theatre*, ed. by Donatella Fischer
28. *Leopardi's Nymphs: Grace, Melancholy, and the Uncanny*, by Fabio A. Camilletti
29. *Gadda and Beckett: Storytelling, Subjectivity and Fracture*, by Katrin Wehling-Giorgi
30. *Caravaggio in Film and Literature: Popular Culture's Appropriation of a Baroque Genius*, by Laura Rorato
31. *The Italian Academies 1525-1700: Networks of Culture, Innovation and Dissent*, ed. by Jane E. Everson, Denis V. Reidy and Lisa Sampson
32. *Rome Eternal: The City As Fatherland*, by Guy Lanoue
33. *The Somali Within: Language, Race and Belonging in 'Minor' Italian Literature*, by Simone Brioni
34. *Laughter from Realism to Modernism: Misfits and Humorists in Pirandello, Svevo, Palazzeschi, and Gadda*, by Alberto Godioli
35. *Pasolini after Dante: The 'Divine Mimesis' and the Politics of Representation*, by Emanuela Patti

Managing Editor
Dr Graham Nelson, 41 Wellington Square, Oxford OX1 2JF, UK
www.legendabooks.com

Spatial Plots

Virtuality and the Embodied Mind in Baricco, Camilleri and Calvino

Marzia Beltrami

Italian Perspectives 45
Modern Humanities Research Association
2021

*Published by Legenda
an imprint of the Modern Humanities Research Association
Salisbury House, Station Road, Cambridge* CB1 2LA

*ISBN 978-1-78188-302-0 (HB)
ISBN 978-1-78188-305-1 (PB)*

First published 2021

All rights reserved. No part of this publication may be reproduced or disseminated or transmitted in any form or by any means, electronic, mechanical, photocopying, recording or otherwise, or stored in any retrieval system, or otherwise used in any manner whatsoever without written permission of the copyright owner, except in accordance with the provisions of the Copyright, Designs and Patents Act 1988, or under the terms of a licence permitting restricted copying issued in the UK by the Copyright Licensing Agency Ltd, Saffron House, 6–10 Kirby Street, London EC1N 8TS, *England, or in the USA by the Copyright Clearance Center, 222 Rosewood Drive, Danvers MA 01923. Application for the written permission of the copyright owner to reproduce any part of this publication must be made by email to legenda@mhra.org.uk.*

Disclaimer: Statements of fact and opinion contained in this book are those of the author and not of the editors or the Modern Humanities Research Association. The publisher makes no representation, express or implied, in respect of the accuracy of the material in this book and cannot accept any legal responsibility or liability for any errors or omissions that may be made.

Trademark notice: Product or corporate names may be trademarks or registered trademarks, and are used only for identification and explanation without intent to infringe.

© *Modern Humanities Research Association 2020*

Copy-Editor: Dr Amanda Wrigley

CONTENTS

Acknowledgements		ix
Abbreviations and Translations		x
Introduction — Sketching the Borders: Spatiality, Plot Theory and Cognitive Approaches		1
1	Plot as Map: Alessandro Baricco's *City*, or Nothing to Do with the Metropolis	17
	A productive shift of perspective	19
	Moving through the plot	25
	Do you have it in mind?	36
2	Plot as Trajectory: Navigating Counterfactuals in Andrea Camilleri and the Crime Fiction Genre	59
	Spatiality cornered	63
	Possible worlds: a modally articulated narrative structure	68
	The dynamics of the investigation	74
	The multiple spaces of narrative understanding	85
3	Plot as Fractal: Calvino's *Se una notte d'inverno un viaggiatore*. A Vertigo of Variation and Repetition	101
	Patterns of order and disorder	104
	Calvino's obsession for 'the path not taken'	107
	Plot as fractal	129
	The space of narrative experience, fictionalised	152
Conclusions		171
Bibliography		175
Index		195

ACKNOWLEDGEMENTS

My warmest and sincerest gratitude goes first of all to my doctoral supervisors, Federico M. Federici, Katrin Wehling-Giorgi and David Herman: in their own way, each of them showed me that research can be both a passion and a profession and they taught me to keep my balance between the two. I will always be grateful to Federico for his steady support which began even before I officially started to work with him at Durham; to Katrin for her commitment, attention, and advice; to David for the model of calm rigour and intellectual energy he represented for me. I am indebted to Marco Bernini, Marco Caracciolo, Guido Furci and Mauro Senatore for their support through the revisions of this book, and to Richard Walsh, who kindly gave me some productive feedback on my reflections on fractality while he was an IAS fellow at Durham. I am grateful to the Department of Italian at Durham University for funding my doctoral research, and to Carlo Caruso, Olivia Santovetti, Simon Gilson and the two anonymous reviewers who, with their comments and notes, helped me improve this work and turn it into a book. I am also indebted to Amanda Wrigley for her careful copy-editing work. Revisions for the book were partially supported by the European Regional Development Fund and by the Estonian Research Council (MOBJD667 and PUT1481).

This research and then this book would not have been possible without the support of a number of people who have been close to me in many ways throughout these years. Many thanks to Giulia Crespi and Barbara Tanzi-Imbri for the countless conversations — academic and non-academic — and their generous and solid friendship; to Teresa Filizzola for the constant flow of positive vibes and to Anouska Munden-Zummo for introducing me to the tradition of Christmas cards; to Claudia Dellacasa for her intellectual passion; to Teo Manzo for the Milanese discussions on Calvino. Thanks also to the precious Moorlands family, to Elena Collaro, Finola Finn, Alexandre Burin, Giacomo Giannini, and Donal Khosrowi, whose presence greatly contributed to make a most enjoyable experience out of my years in Durham. A special acknowledgment goes to Emanuele, who has been at my side throughout the journeys of the past ten years, across England and beyond, and who has never stopped encouraging and stimulating me. Finally, my wholehearted gratitude goes to my family and especially to my parents, Gabriella and Claudio, who loved me and raised me to think that I could take my life in my own hands: there is no greater gift parents can give to a daughter.

M.B., January 2021

ABBREVIATIONS AND TRANSLATIONS

The following abbreviated references are used:

    Il ladro   ANDREA CAMILLERI, *Il ladro di merendine*
    Se una notte   ITALO CALVINO, *Se una notte d'inverno un viaggiatore*
    RRI, RRII, RRIII   ITALO CALVINO, *Romanzi e racconti*, 3 vols
    SI, SII   ITALO CALVINO, *Saggi: 1945–1985*, 2 vols

All translations from Italian are by the author except for the works indicated below. Excerpts from the following translations are offered immediately after quotations from these Italian works.

ALESSANDRO BARICCO, *City*, transl. by Ann Goldstein (New York: Vintage, 2001). [except blurb]

ANDREA CAMILLERI, *The Snack Thief*, transl. by Stephen Sartarelli (New York: Viking, 2003).

—— *The Shape of Water*, transl. by Stephen Sartarelli (London: Picador, 2004).

ITALO CALVINO, *If On a Winter's Night a Traveler*, transl. by William Weaver (London: Random House, 1993).

—— *Invisible Cities*, transl. by William Weaver (London: Secker & Warburg, 1993).

—— *Six Memos for the Next Millennium*, transl. by Patrick Creagh (Cambridge, MA: Harvard University Press, 1988).

—— 'From the Opaque', in *The Road to San Giovanni*, transl. by Tim Parks (London: Vintage, 1994).

—— *The Castle of Crossed Destinies*, transl. by William Weaver (New York: Harcourt Brace Jovanovich, 1977).

—— *Collection of Sand*, transl. by Martin McLaughlin (New York: Houghton Mifflin Harcourt, 2013).

—— 'Cybernetics and Ghosts', in *The Literature Machine*, transl. by Peter Creagh (London: Secker & Warburg, 1987).

—— 'The Count of Monte Cristo', in *Time and the Hunter*, transl. by William Weaver (London: Harcourt, Brace & World, 1983).

—— *The Baron in the Trees* in *Our Ancestors*, transl. by Archibald Colquhoun (London: Vintage, 1998).

INTRODUCTION

Sketching the Borders: Spatiality, Plot Theory and Cognitive Approaches

A first disclaimer for the reader: despite the references to spatial plots and virtuality in the title of this book, this is not a work on science fiction. It is about how we make sense of stories and, more specifically, how we manage to achieve the sense of 'a story' out of a series of bits and pieces — words in this case; movements, sounds and images in other narrative media. While most theories hold that causality and chronology are the fundamental principles through which we turn stories into meaningful wholes, I suggest that stories can be organised in a variety of ways, and that spatiality captures the logic underlying some of them. Far from designating stories set in far-away galaxies, therefore, spatial plots are designed to be understood like spaces.

This book explores the idea that plots can be spatial in nature through the discussion of Alessandro Baricco's *City* (1999), Andrea Camilleri's *Montalbano* series (1990–2019) and Italo Calvino's *Se una notte d'inverno un viaggiatore* (1979). To elaborate its theoretical underpinnings and illuminate some new angles opened up by this perspective, I employ concepts and models crafted in the broad field of cognitive literary studies, a field that arises from the encounter of cognitive sciences with the humanities. Loosely speaking, cognitive literary studies are characterised by the shared commitment to study the literary text through the cognitive processes scaffolding its production and comprehension.[1] My focus, more specifically, will be mostly on reception: by drawing on cognitive narratology and cognitive linguistics, literary criticism and narrative theory, I will seek to explain how certain verbal structures and narrative techniques can be used to design the production of certain effects and influence the ways in which we understand stories. In this introduction, I begin to illustrate how the debate on plot intersects the dimension of spatiality and why their interrelations can be fruitfully approached through the cognitive framework, a discussion that will continue throughout the book. A synopsis of the chapters will follow, presenting the three case studies I analysed.

The idea of spatial plots was initially sparked by an impasse I found myself in when confronted with Baricco's *City* — although the same could be said of quite different works such as Todd Haynes' film *I'm Not There* (2007) or David Mitchell's novel *Cloud Atlas* (2004). *City* is the story of an imaginative child who attempts to come to terms with his past traumas and social inadequacies by re-inflecting his experiences in a fictional form. However, it is not from the chronological reconstruction of the protagonist's adventures that such meaning can emerge. Similarly, while *I'm Not There* is presented as a biopic on Bob Dylan, the movie consists in fact of the stories of six unrelated fictional characters. Paraphrasing literary critic Hayden White, explaining 'why and how every event in the sequence occurred' was not leading me anywhere near grasping 'the meaning of the sequence considered as a whole' (1987: 50).

To address this issue, I turned to plot as the narratological concept that most aptly captures the global sense-making activity of a story. The problem is that, despite being one of the most commonly used concepts, plot is also a surprisingly elusive concept. On the one hand, it should indicate 'the way [in which] the story indicates its aim, purpose, meaning', the dynamic that turns sequences of events and states into a 'structured, closed, and complete whole' (Ronen 1990: 819, 828). On the other, the association of plot with action-structures dates back to Aristotle's *Poetics* and it runs so deep that causality has come to be widely regarded as the major, if not the only, structuring principle capable of ensuring the internal coherence of plot.[2] Yet, in this case, to reconstruct the plot as the unfolding of the chronological sequence of its events does not tell us much about how the narrative holds coherently. Causality, in other words, does not seem to be the type of logic underpinning Baricco's novel (or Haynes' movie). The suggestion I advance for *City*, and which I will articulate further through the book, is that the parts of this story are held together by analogical rather than causal relations. It is in the analogical nature of this organising principle that lies the key link to spatiality.

The concept of spatiality, in fact, will be engaged in a number of ways that range from abstract and metaphoric uses to others significantly more pragmatic and involved with the body. At a more abstract level, the idea of 'spatial form' of a text was first advanced by Joseph Frank (1945), who uncoupled it from the concept of narrative space which, instead, describes the setting where the story events take place. Building on the Leibnizian definition of space as 'order of possible coexistences', Frank argues that any type of formal pattern determined by any network of relations (be they semantic, phonetic or thematic) could be regarded as spatial. For these designs necessitate a synchronic perspective to be perceived, and synchronicity is associated with spatiality — as opposed to the association of diachronicity with temporality (Ryan, Foote and Azaryahu 2016: 6; Zoran 1984). In other words, whenever we have a pattern the meaning of which is better grasped by looking at its overall configuration (rather than by looking at how the individual parts are linked to one another), we may speak of a spatial phenomenon.

It is worth clarifying that, in order to be deemed as spatial, plots do not have to be completely devoid of chronological development nor should they programmatically subvert it. Spatial plots are plots whose parts make sense less because of their sequential, causal connections and more because of the overall pattern they progressively compose in the reader's mind. Reverting to my initial example, in Baricco's novel the storylines are not causally linked but they rather mirror and deform and reinterpret one another; in order to understand the story as a whole, the reader has to create a mental map of their internal analogical relations. Similarly, in crime stories an important part of the investigation consists of comparing and contrasting different possible scenarios which, I will argue, is a mental operation that has more to do with our sense of space than with our sense of time. Or, again, I suggest that the various chapters of Calvino's *Se una notte d'inverno un viaggiatore* are arranged like a fractal, an abstract geometrical form. With the due differences, all these designed sense-making processes endow the narratives with what I call a spatial plot.

As we move across the range of potential uses, we find that the notion of spatiality may be engaged with an increasingly embodied meaning. In this sense, the dimension of spatiality serves to account for narratives whose spatial form is elaborated in ways such that their readers are encouraged to think of it not only in terms of analogical relations but also as a space to be explored as if it were a physical space. In doing so, these stories arguably foreground the visibility of the embodied roots of our thought. For instance, both Calvino and Baricco indirectly stress the embodied nature of the mental operations underpinning story comprehension by marking narrative transitions such as changes of scene or perspective with sensorimotor verbs — that is to say, verbs usually employed to describe actual movements of the body. The more these mental operations are expressed in terms of physical movements through space, the more visible the reader's virtual body becomes. The concept of the reader's virtual body describes the projection of the reader's real bodily experience into the narrative world, and will be employed extensively through my discussion (Caracciolo 2014a).

As a matter of fact, this book rests on the assumption that narrative and literature are not abstract and disembodied phenomena. They are the outputs of cognitive practices which are not only historically and culturally situated but also, and importantly, biologically situated. The human minds that produce and consume literary works have developed within bodies which, in turn, are characterised by a specific bioevolutionary make-up shaped by experience of physical and social engagement with the environment. Since the mind is so irreducibly entangled with the body, we speak of embodiment of the mind.

The paradigmatic shift towards embodiment marked a turning point in cognitive sciences in the 1970s. Until then, extensive research on artificial intelligence had led to the formulation of a computational notion of mind as a software running on a 'brain-hardware', and to a view of reason as disembodied and literal. Second-generation cognitive scientists, instead, came to conceive cognition as situated in the body and dependent on its physical and emotional experience of the world. Experience does not simply provide cognition with its content: it affects its structure and shapes the way content is elaborated (Varela, Thompson and Rosch 1993; Wilson and Foglia 2011). Cognitive scientists who embrace a view of the mind as embodied thus share the belief that even abstract forms of thought are likely to be rooted in a more pragmatic type of knowledge, which is developed as human beings learn to make sense of the environment where they are situated, body and mind. Along these lines, neuroscientist Vittorio Gallese and cognitive linguist and philosopher George Lakoff (2005) argue that our conceptual knowledge — that is to say, our capability to elaborate abstract concepts — stems from perceptual knowledge, which, in turn, is deeply rooted in our sensorimotor system. Language, too, inasmuch as it is a high-level cognitive activity, is expected to make use of the same structures used in perception and action (Gallese and Lakoff 2005: 473). From an evolutionary perspective, it only makes sense that our abstraction skills should develop from pre-existing and more basic forms of knowledge rather than from the creation of an entirely separate neuronal system.

Mind embodiment and the subsequent claim that mental processes are rooted in perception are critical to my approach because they establish a clear connection between bodily experience and abstract ideas. In this view, human thought is built up metaphorically from the basic kinesthetic experiences of living in a body. Metaphorically — because the link between sensorimotor knowledge and conceptual (abstract) knowledge relies on a process of 'mapping across conceptual domains, from a (typically) sensory-motor source domain to a (typically) non-sensory-motor target domain', which is the basic relation typifying metaphors (Gallese and Lakoff 2005: 469–70). In other words, individuals derive from their sensorimotor knowledge and experience general inference patterns of comprehension that can be applied to a wide range of forms of reasoning. Returning to narrative studies and to plot understanding, we may thus argue that also abstract and high-level cognitive activities such as making sense of a story as a whole are ultimately likely to rely on patterns — or 'image schemata', as I will call them later on — that are rooted in our sensorimotor system. As Richard Bjornson puts it, 'people seek coherence and consistency in textual images in the same way as they do in their cognitive maps of actual spatio-temporal environments' (1981: 58). My suggestion is that, if causality might even be the most common strategy to ensure such coherence, it is not the only one. Spatiality is a complex dimension of experience that can provide patterns and templates equally capable of making sense also of fictional experience.

It should be increasingly clear to the reader that, while the comprehension strategies on which I draw are developed through real experience, the spaces to which they are applied are not fictional places traditionally explored and moved through by characters, places that Marie-Laure Ryan, Kenneth Foote and Maoz Azaryahu (2016) would call narrative space. In fact, it is rather a matter of virtual spaces, which is why virtuality, together with the embodied mind, is one of the key concepts transversally employed in this work. In its broader sense, the concept of virtuality includes several meanings and applications. Cybernetics, for instance, refers to virtuality as juxtaposed to reality and uses this notion to describe things that look or work *as if* they were real (M.-L. Ryan 2005). By contrast, in the present discussion the concept of virtuality will be used in juxtaposition to actuality:[3] while actuality comprises what actually and certainly happens in the fictional world, the dimension of virtuality encompasses anything other than actual, which includes possible (or potential) and impossible (or counterfactual) states or scenarios prompted during reading.

To usher in virtuality, therefore, means to embrace a view of the world that is modally-articulated — that is to say, that its characters, events and states of affairs may be characterised by different modes of existence, whether actual, possible or counterfactual.[4] As we will see in Chapter 2 when discussing Ryan's possible-world theory, it follows that the ontological structure of the *storyworld* is made more complex by the private worlds of characters which include their thoughts, expectations, and beliefs. Building on the philosophical notion of 'world' (Lewis 1986; Ronen 1994; Werth 1999), the term *storyworld* was coined by David Herman (2002) to describe the holistic and in-progress representation of the narrative world, mentally co-constructed by the reader through textual clues and inclusive of characters, settings, states of affairs and events.[5] For the purposes of my discussion, the notion of *storyworld* is to be privileged over *story* because it 'better captures what might be called the ecology of narrative interpretation. [...] More generally, *storyworld* points to the way interpreters of narrative reconstruct a sequence of states, events, and actions not just additively or incrementally but integratively or "ecologically"' (2002: 13–14).

Herman's conceptualisation, in particular, addresses the extent to which this mental activity is informed by real-life experience and draws attention to the fact that, if stories are conveyed linguistically, what is retained and manipulated in the readers' minds is not necessarily verbal anymore. This means to acknowledge that language is the main but not the only vessel for narrative understanding, and that what readers mentally re-construct is certainly prompted by the text but is also affected by types of knowledge conveyed or stored not only propositionally.[6] On the one hand, to adopt a view of the storyworld as not entirely verbal implies a certain stance on current debates on the nature of cognition and therefore the idea that meaning can be produced from means other than verbal — namely, through patterns of sense-making rooted in sensorimotor and perceptual knowledge. On the other hand, remaining on the construction of storyworld, it also presupposes that background knowledge as well as internal states of characters can be evoked and can impinge on the understanding of a text without being necessarily structured into propositions. As I explore in Chapter 1, this is significant to my argument because it foregrounds the importance of context in narrative comprehension and, in doing so, serves to explain how the storyworld can be regarded as a conceptual space open to potential exploration on the reader's part. It should be clarified that a non-fully propositional approach does not deny the importance of language. It posits mental spaces and mental relations as alternative carriers of meaning — as other than propositions — on which our cognition primarily relies. 'When approached in this way', Gilles Fauconnier (1997: 38) explains, 'the unfolding of discourse is a succession of cognitive configurations', conceptualised in terms of mental spaces, which can be locally manipulated and derive from a progressive re-arrangement of the mental space initially conjured up at the beginning of a text.

This consideration brings me to another implication of welcoming virtuality in our approach to narrative comprehension.[7] Virtuality, in fact, includes characters and states of affairs typified by different modes of existence, but it also indicates what possesses the force of coming into existence (M.-L. Ryan 2019), which becomes particularly interesting in relation to postclassical views of plot.[8] Overcoming the structuralist notion of plot as linear and grasped retrospectively, Karin Kukkonen's definition of plot as 'progressive structuration' (2014: section 3.3) not only recognises the scaffolding function of plot but also highlights the work in progress that is plot comprehension, which is conceived as a delicate interplay between construction of expectations, building up of semantic content, revision and adjustment of the relationships connecting the parts with the whole.[9] In this light, to see plot understanding as an ongoing process that happens during reading means to reshape the structure of plot — and not only the structure of the storyworld, synchronically — so that it is capable of accounting for actual events as well as for scenarios that are aroused and then modified or even totally discarded. Even if they are unrealised, these scenarios, alongside other unfulfilled predictions, still exert a fundamental influence on the reader's narrative experience.[10] In other words, while storyworlds include virtual elements attached to their characters, plot, too, can be modally-articulated. It can be thought of as a space to be navigated and explored, a complex network of actual, counterfactual and possible scenarios that have to be mentally manipulated by the reader in more nuanced ways than being linked, or reconstructed, in a linear temporal-causal chain. When virtuality as a mode of fictional existence enters the picture, the cognitive structure of the plot is enhanced, because the reader is required to keep track of both syntagmatic connections among narrative events and paradigmatic interactions with virtual information. To put the same concept differently, the reader has to remain aware of the reciprocal relations between things that actually happen as well as of how these relate to things that at a certain point they thought could have happened. The hypothesis I explore in this book is that, in order to be negotiated, this more complex scenario demands navigation strategies that are cognitively more akin to our capability of making sense of space than of time. In some instances — as we will see with Baricco and Calvino — this navigation process is also developed in a metanarrative fashion, by staging fictional characters who can uncannily move through different narrative levels.

It goes without saying that the virtual dimension of a text does not include everything that does not take place in the narrative. The virtual events and hypotheses I consider in my account are those prompted or suggested through various techniques by the text itself, and whose virtual presence is designed to impinge to some extent on readers' understanding and on the reading experience. In Camilleri's stories, for instance, the various explanations Montalbano entertains throughout the novel do impact on the different angles we hold on the characters and their behaviours, even if they may not have happened: yet these are inscribed in the text. In fact, it will be argued that the thorough exploration of the virtual dimension of counterfactuality may be regarded as the purpose of the investigation process — one of the distinctive practices of crime fiction novels.

My previous reference to the mental manipulation of storyworlds and plots on the reader's part leads to another aspect closely related to the cognitive framework, which is enactivism. The enactivist perspective is closely linked to the embodied view of the mind, and focuses on the impact of the relations of the body with the world on cognitive activities.[11] Launched by the research of Francisco Varela, Evan Thompson and Eleanor Rosch (1993), enactivism is grounded in the principle that perception is something we do — and thus something that we 'enact' — rather than something that happens to us. The main contribution provided by enactivism to the theoretical account advanced in this book is the way it bridges between the cognitive framework and reception theories. In his examination, philosopher of perception Alva Noë places at the centre of his way of looking at the environment the necessarily active engagement of individuals, who cannot avoid interacting with their context in order to make sense of it. In the same way, in narrative the process of co-construction of the storyworld entails the active engagement of readers. Herman attributes so great an importance to this active participation that he conceptualises narrative itself as a discourse genre that aims at the production and co-construction of storyworlds, that is to say mental models, by means of textual cues (Herman 2002: 6). Crucial to his model, Noë offers a view of environment — as Marco Caracciolo does of narrative storyworlds — as made up not only of objects and surfaces but also of 'affordances'. In James Gibson's coinage of this term, affordances are things or properties of the environment which are not only available for use but also shape the environment by enabling human use. Noë suggests that 'to perceive is (among other things) to learn how the environment structures one's possibilities for movement and so it is, thereby, to experience possibilities of movement and action afforded by the environment' (2004: 105).

To think of narrative as a system of affordances endorses its conception as something that is constructed by an author but also co-constructed, actualised and actively shaped by its recipients. Furthermore, the enactivist-based view of the storyworld as a system of possibilities can be productively put in relation with the foregrounding of virtuality on the one hand and of readers' expectations on the other. Indeed, in her overview of the applications of virtuality in narrative studies Ryan describes virtuality as the cloud of affordances of an object, 'what this object can become and what can be done with it' (M.-L. Ryan 2019: 336). The enactivist view helps to explain how virtuality can be textually encoded and thus enter narrative comprehension, for it can be argued that certain propositions act as affordances through which the reader is invited to engage with other mental scenarios that thus become present to variable degrees, potentially accessible, potentially manipulatable. Establishing an analogy with Noë's argument that '[y]ou enact your perceptual content, through the activity of skillfully looking' (2004: 73), we could say that readers enact narrative content through the activity of skillfully reading.

Generally speaking, therefore, spatial plots designate stories that engage with our spatial experience and prompt us to contemplate the possibility for interaction among parts of the narrative, and to implement specific navigation strategies. The concept of spatial plot, as discussed above, is concerned less with fictional spaces (although stories that significantly rely on the narrative space may foster the visibility and therefore determine a stronger role of spatiality at large)[12] and more with the idea that spatiality may function as organising principle for certain narratives, as an alternative to the principle of causality. Naturally, since Albert Einstein and Mikhail Bakhtin have irreversibly demonstrated that time and space are complementary and interdependent dimensions that shape our way of approaching the world both in the real universe and in theories of narrative, to privilege one never means to exclude the other. In a sense, it could be argued that spatiality is always involved to some extent in any act of thought and, more narrowly, in any instance of narrative comprehension. In the same way, we could say that plot apprehension is always chronological because reading needs and takes place in time. Also, we should not forget that reading narrative is not a neutral, unmediated experience, and we never completely forget that the text is an artefact that has been designed to be read. According to Jerome Bruner's (1991) principle of hermeneutic composability, whatever the elements in the narrative, as long as the reader 'has' the rules — which are partly cognitive and partly culturally-based — she will make sense of the whole by using the elements at her disposal. Since the reader knows that *she is expected to* find a meaning in the whole, she will arrange the interpretive grids at her disposal in order to *make them* fit for endowing with sense the elements to which they are applied. In fact, the human mind is characterised by such a strong 'representational hunger' that it tends to identify intentions and plans — to find a pattern — even when there is no actual mind behind it (Clark 2001: 167). In fact, this happens with fictional narratives as well as with other human phenomena such as history and even with natural environments. A telling example is provided by the Runamo rock in Sweden: its naturally produced markings were interpreted for centuries as runic writings (Herman 2013b: 25–37).

My point is that stories can capitalise on the engagement of spatiality (or temporality) in different ways and the embodied mind can be emphasised to various degrees. Spatial plots are specific of narratives which display significant pro-spatiality markers at the structural level and reinforce them through their content, literary conventions or rhetorical strategies. Together with advancing the notion of spatial plot and discussing it from both a theoretical and applied perspective, this book highlights and addresses some general features that recur across different types of spatial plots and support a spatially-oriented narrative understanding. These features — which will be explored in depth through the case studies — are criteria that critics may use, in a preliminary way, to identify other narratives that could benefit from a specific focus on spatiality and that, perhaps, could be regarded as spatial plots. The book will pinpoint five potential criteria: (a) engagement of virtuality; (b) semantic references to spatiality; (c) embodiment of comprehension strategies; (d) self-reflexivity; (e) engagement of the reader's virtual body.

These criteria, however, are neither necessary nor sufficient conditions for a plot to be regarded as spatial. Their implementation is a matter of gradience rather than all-or-nothing. If a narrative significantly engages with space from a thematic perspective and, in addition, also adopts spatially-oriented comprehension techniques in its structuring, then these formal features may resonate with the content, enhancing the overall spatial quality of the narrative. Moreover, they may be expressed through different textual devices and aim to achieve different effects on the reader. The narratives of Baricco, Camilleri and Calvino variously combine and implement these criteria, hence resulting in three different ways in which spatiality operates as organising principle of the narrative. Each case study represents a plot *type*, and these three types are captured by the image schemata of the map, the trajectory and the fractal — also used as titles for the book chapters. In its broader cognitive sense, an image schema is 'a recurring, dynamic pattern of our perceptual interactions and motor programs that gives coherence and structure to our experience' (Johnson 1987: xiv). They are instances of those aforementioned cognitive patterns, borrowed from experience and then re-employed to make sense of something else — narrative, in this case. Indeed, these images have been chosen less because of the object they identify and more because of the process, the procedural strategies they entail.

The image of the plot as map (represented by Baricco's *City*) epitomises narratives in which the cognitive activity of spatially mapping out storylines and their reciprocal connections is more relevant to their overall understanding than the chronological apprehension of fictional events. Arguably, stories that are meant to portray situations of dynamic equilibrium would be included in this plot type. By contrast, the image of plot as trajectory typifies narratives that are strongly teleological in nature (for example, crime fiction stories such as Camilleri's *Montalbano* series) and embodies the goal-oriented attitude of readers as they make sense of the plot while it unfolds. The trajectory represents a virtual structure that guides readers in their navigation through counterfactual scenarios. As we shall see, its virtual presence is ensured by readerly expectations, on account of the conventions of the genre. Finally, the geometric figure of the fractal is more specific and particularly suited for Calvino's *Se una notte*. While this may reduce the broader application of this figure to other narratives, the fractal may be still used to epitomise stories that variously adopt geometric forms to guide their structuring. Typified by self-reflexivity and by a pattern of variation within continuation, the fractal productively describes the strategies of comprehension designed in *Se una notte*. To privilege the concept of fractal over that of labyrinth, frequently discussed in Calvino studies, helps us to understand the difference between metaphoric use and implementation of an image schema: the image schema does not simply suggest an overall quality, but primarily renders the dynamic nature of the process of plot understanding and the peculiar relationship in the novel between its parts and the narrative as a whole. Unlike the labyrinth, the fractal both captures the sense of disorientation produced by Calvino's novel and hints at the underlying regularities that ultimately prevent the reader from getting lost.

The spatial approach to plot understanding discussed in this book proposes a novel way of examining and identifying similarities among narratives whose structures cannot be satisfactorily described in terms of causal or chronological relations only. A variety of theoretical inputs — from Herman's narratology to Ryan's possible worlds theory to Caracciolo's enactivist hypotheses concerning readers' engagement — are integrated within a cognitive-oriented framework that relies on the view of cognition as embodied and non-fully propositional. To think of the mind as embodied allows to explain why and how perception and experience crucially shape high-level mental activities, including narrative understanding, which operate by recycling mental processes we have learnt to perform by living in the world as a space to interact with and move through. At the same time, to replace the focus on language with a focus on the mind as pilot-notion for narrative theory allows for a view of thought which admits that story comprehension is certainly anchored to textual propositions, but can also be enriched by a range of inputs which may not have verbal form.

The cognitive approach is called for by the fact that the explanation I advance depends on the assumption that these narratives — which I call spatial plots — are not necessarily characterised by a specific theme, form or medium, but rather by the foregrounding of certain cognitive mechanisms and by the encouragement to their readers of making sense of experience in certain ways. In this sense, cognitive sciences and literary theory may productively illuminate each other: on the one hand, narrative requires complex cognitive activities whose study could certainly benefit from a better understanding of the workings of the mind. On the other, storytelling (across all media) is a specific type of activity deeply governed by cultural conventions, which literary studies are best equipped to explore. A spatially-oriented approach to plot comprehension concerns textual elements as much as reception strategies, as the two aspects are irreducibly interdependent. Since readers' cognitive processes are triggered by strategies that are textually encoded, narratives can be designed to encourage a certain way of co-constructing a storyworld. As Herman (2002) often observes, we can speak of 'co-construction' because the storyworld is firstly constructed by the author by means of a specific text. Then, through the text, the reader is expected to re-construct the storyworld by relying on her own knowledge and experience but also on a set of rules and conventions arguably shared with the author. This makes it possible to design (and explain) specific readers' reactions through specific narrative techniques. In this light, the various interpretive hypotheses that I will advance build on established narrative theories that link determinate psychological and cognitive responses to certain textual patterns — which can emerge at syntactic, rhetorical or discourse level. The interpretations will be placed in relation to the extant scholarship in literary criticism on those works and authors.

★ ★ ★ ★ ★

The narratives analysed in the following chapters aim to illustrate the theoretical plausibility, interpretive potential and flexibility of the spatially-oriented approach. Each case study marks a step further in the elaboration of the central idea that spatiality can function as a narrative organising principle and that plot understanding can be therefore spatial in nature. My argument will unfold by combining bottom-up and top-down approaches: theoretical questions arise from critical problems sparked by specific narratives, and ensuing theoretical hypotheses are tested, expanded and enriched in dialogue with new texts. The three case studies share a research perspective (focus on plot and on reception), a set of theoretical premises (non-fully propositional view of thought and mental processes as embodied) and some recurring concepts (such as storyworld and virtuality), with a view to isolating in each narrative the specific logic that turns their elements into a coherent and integrated whole.

In Chapter 1, I show how looking at Alessandro Baricco's *City* from a spatially-oriented perspective allows one to go beyond established readings and opens a window into the workings of this well-crafted narrative machinery. While previous interpretations of the novel as a portrayal of the postmodern metropolis raised a number of unanswered issues, I argue that the city is not a theme but a cognitive metaphor pointing at the narrative structure rather than at its content. Tapping into contextual frame theory (Emmott 1997) and phenomenology of reading (Caracciolo 2014a), I illustrate how Baricco draws on strategies rooted in our sensorimotor knowledge to facilitate the reader's comprehension throughout the numerous shifts between the storylines that compose the novel. The framework of enactivism is used to explain how virtuality impacts on readers' understanding in the form of world knowledge that is only hinted at by means of scripts (Herman 1997 and 2002; Schank and Abelson 1977). This chapter also contains an overview of the array of spatial conceptualisations exhibited by Baricco in the novel. All these elements converge to demonstrate how the spatially-oriented perspective reorients the way of looking at *City*'s structure, content and rhetorical techniques, providing the framework to produce a fresh reading of this story.

My second case study in Chapter 2 makes two main contributions. The first one consists of a theoretical re-description of the genre of crime fiction as typified by competing counterfactual scenarios. Particularly when its conventional features are foregrounded — namely, the teleological character and the centrality of the investigation process — I suggest that the management of counterfactual hypotheses on the detective's and on the readers' part constitute a major phase of the process of narrative understanding. Spatiality is identified as a protean *fil rouge* that runs throughout the genre, as it connects early elaborations which emphasised space as a dimension which is knowable through order and geometrical plots (in the nineteenth- and early-twentieth centuries) to more recent developments marked by a distinctive interest in space as network of sociological relations, starting from the hardboiled genre in the 1920s. This chapter explores virtuality especially in its counterfactual dimension. Possible-worlds theory (Ronen 1994; M.-L. Ryan 1991 and 1985) and research on counterfactuality in plot (Dannenberg 2008) provide the principal theoretical background for reformulating crime fiction as an epistemological genre that capitalises on a modally-elaborated (in other words, including possible and impossible alongside with actual elements) and ontologically complex notion of storyworld. Building on the critical premise that the investigative practice is the indispensable component for narratives to be labelled as crime fiction, the chapter also argues that the investigation represents a perfect implementation of Ryan's argument, as it indeed consists in the navigation through the private worlds of characters and counterfactual scenarios. In this instance, my use of the spatial perspective is less a matter of providing new interpretive insights on the novels and more of a contribution to the genre-related criticism and theory. While crime fiction is often regarded as a 'lowbrow' and less-demanding type of literature, my reading suggests that, from the cognitive perspective, it is in fact a complex genre which demands a flexible management of counterfactuals and a particularly good acquaintance with its internal literary conventions. In fact, it might be said that its success with the public partly resides precisely in the promise of such a steady, enticing engagement of virtuality. Furthermore, by emphasising the impact of spatiality on the comprehension process I bring into focus the relationship recently established by geocriticism between crime fiction and cultural geography.

The second contribution considers specifically Andrea Camilleri's work, where the adoption of the privileged focus on spatiality allows me to identify a distinctive structural feature of the *Montalbano* stories. Reflecting and reinforcing the general propensity of crime narrative to rely on the proliferation of counterfactual scenarios, I argue that Camilleri's plots are systematically organised as systems of interacting narrative inputs, which bear on the investigation and cause the novel to convey a meaning that slightly diverges from the outcome of the main case. These complementary narratives usually include extra-textual literary works, theatre-like '*messinscene*' organised by Montalbano himself, dreams and secondary cases. This hypothesis seeks to contribute to the scholarship that so far has mostly examined the content of the *Montalbano* series (for example, the emotional and psychological profile of the Inspector, the Sicilian setting, or Camilleri's imaginary linguistic *patois*).

The twofold focus on a set of novels as well as on the whole crime-fiction genre is adopted because of the belief that the active engagement with virtuality and the involvement of spatially-based cognitive strategies are partly due to features that specifically pertain to Camilleri's work and partly rely on features that, in fact, conventionally typify the crime fiction genre more broadly. As we have already stated, plot understanding ought to be theorised as a process that takes place during reading through constant re-assessment and involves both textual and extra-textual cues, such as expectations stemming from genre affiliation. To realise that engagement of the virtual dimension is triggered by the investigation process is important because it helps to situate the case study within a wider category (a genre). It takes a step in the direction of demonstrating that a spatially-oriented approach could identify plot types not only on the basis of the specific cognitive style of an author but also on the basis of sets of conventions, provided that they are sufficiently culturally defined to reliably impact on readers' expectations. To extend the observations on the procedural dynamics of plot comprehension from the specific case study of Camilleri to the broader genre is arguably possible because crime fiction is traditionally characterised by a certain rigidity of its conventions, which allows one to infer a general model of narrative comprehension (Cawelti 1976; Hühn 1987). Conventions generate expectations, and it is necessary to manage readers' expectations, irrespective of whether they are ultimately met or disrupted, in order to ensure narrative understanding. If certain expectations are generally to be avoided — for an excessive predictability could undermine curiosity — expectations stemming from the affiliation to a certain genre play a crucial role in plot understanding. Ellen Spolsky even argues that the decision of the author to present content through a specific literary genre is the 'foundational step in the making of literary meaning' (2004: 52). This depends on the fact that 'narrative genres are distinguished by different preference-rule systems prescribing different ratios of stereotypic to nonstereotypic actions and events' (Herman 2002: 91), which means that narratives belonging to different genres will be understood by readers in different ways on the account of different operating expectations of how textual cues should be anchored to stored world knowledge (Herman 1997). It goes without saying, expectations and preference-rule systems are not absolute and can be negotiated: crime fiction is indeed what Spolsky describes as a functional genre, that is a template which is 'culturally produced and learned' (2004: 52).

The third and final chapter opens up a fresh perspective on Calvino studies as it proposes to view his cognitive style as strongly rooted in spatiality (as is Baricco's style, although the latter does not problematise it as much), illustrating how several features of his fictional and nonfictional work exhibit an ongoing reflection on the spatial nature of this thinking style. While counterfactuality was the virtual dimension in the spotlight for crime fiction, this chapter explores two additional articulations of virtuality (potentiality and absence) and considers under a new light two strategies already pinpointed in relation to Baricco: the fictionalisation of the readers' virtual body and the embodiment of comprehension mechanisms. This chapter makes use of familiar theoretical tools including the focus on virtuality and the concept of the reader's virtual body as a framework to embrace a set of features of Calvino's oeuvre that have been acknowledged but have not received a unified critical interpretation. Thus, for instance, framing Calvino's exploration of possibility and combinatorics under the aegis of a broader and deeper interest in virtuality helps us to disclose new distinctive patterns to be used by scholars to chart his richly varied production. Self-reflexivity, briefly mentioned in Chapter 2, is the distinctive criterion examined here. This exploration leads us to recognise the centrality of patterns of repetition and variation in Calvino's works and in particular in *Se una notte*. This chapter discusses in detail this specific type of plot as fractal. Along with the notion of fractal, I introduce the analogy between metanarrative text and complex system, and carry out a close reading of the novel according to this organising principle. The notion of virtual body, borrowed from Caracciolo's theory, is used to foreground the importance of bodily engagement in the reading process designed by Calvino and, consequently, to endorse a more nuanced view of the author as a strongly mind-centred writer (Hume 1992) who, yet, is also crucially concerned with the role of corporeality.

The questions discussed in this book are both theoretical and critical. The theoretical line of inquiry investigates the hypothesis that plot can be spatial in nature and explores a range of frameworks and concepts that may give these insights greater coherence in the field of narrative studies and allow them to be applied to texts that have been explored above all by literary scholars and critics.[13] It is my hope that this book will be able to speak to both readerships: scholars in narrative studies interested in a new spatially-oriented model of narrative understanding, and Italianists working on these authors and curious to explore cognitive approaches to literature that to date remain relatively underutilized in Italian studies. By proposing a set of criteria that may help recognise other plots as spatial, I hope that this approach will offer useful tools for the exploration of other narratives as well as foster theoretical speculations on the dynamics of how we make sense of stories.

Notes to the Introduction

1. For an overview of the relationships between cognitive sciences and literary criticism and theory, see Adler and Gross (2002), Bernaerts et al. (2013), Burke and Troscianko (2017), Eder (2003), Garratt (2016), Hart (2001, 2004), Herman (2013a), Jaén and Simon (2012), Nünning (2003), Olson (2011), A. Richardson (2004), Richardson and Steen (2002), M.-L. Ryan (2010), Spolsky (2003), Stockwell (2009), Turner (1994).
2. See Bremond (1966/1980), Chatman (1978), Dannenberg (2005b), Greimas (1977), Prince (1982), Propp (1958 (1928)).
3. Both actuality and virtuality may pertain to the realm of fiction, which is, in turn, distinct from reality. To refer to 'fictionality' implies the definition of a domain on its own, which usually overlaps with but is theoretically distinct from that of narrative. Speaking of fictionality means to assume that the approach to an artefact as fictional is regulated by a set of conventions and attitudes that stem specifically from its fictional (rather than narrative, or literary) nature. For further detail see Cohn (1990), Doležel (1998), Hrushovski (1984), and Ronen (1988; 1990; 1994).
4. Ronen (1990) notes that modal categories had already entered structuralist theories but remained on the fringes: i.e. Bremond's description of plot as a mechanism of *choices among alternative* narrative sequences (1966/1980: 405); Algirdas Greimas' *modal* utterance as sub-typology of narrative utterances (1977: 30 ff.); Todorov's grammar's *mood* (1971/1977).
5. The concept of storyworld adopted here is philosophically elaborated by Ronen, refined by literary theorist M.-L. Ryan and narratologically employed by Herman. While he builds on Ronen's and Ryan's theories, Herman coins the term 'storyworld' which was previously referred to as possible or fictional 'world'.
6. For a discussion of non-propositional forms of thought and of mental models *versus* textual models, see Johnson-Laird (1981, 1983, 1993), Fauconnier (1997), Ferstl and Kintsch (1999) and Schank and Abelson (1977). In the narrative studies context, M.-L. Ryan praises a non-propositional view of thought as it 'opened up to many possible forms of thinking in addition to verbal, including visual or musical, and admits the possibility to favour either spatial or temporal dimension' (2003: 334).
7. It is not the first time that virtuality is called upon in reader-response theories: Roman Ingarden (1973), for instance, relies on the notion of virtuality to explain his understanding of the text as incomplete in his phenomenology of reading. The view adopted in this book, however, differs from Ingarden's because it holds that, in spatial plots, virtuality constitutes a liminal cognitive space of the reader's mind but is nonetheless fully encoded in the text. Methodologically, this is an important difference. Whereas for Ingarden the virtual contribution of the reader is based on their individual experience and therefore its content is ultimately unpredictable, in my argument I aim to discuss cues that prompt the reader to construct or recall virtual elements by means of specific textually encoded strategies.
8. Postclassical narrative theories encompass approaches that develop from but move beyond the structuralist poetics of classical narratology, reinterpreting and supplementing it through disciplines that were either neglected or unavailable to structuralist scholars, such as gender theory, philosophy of language, sociolinguistics or, as in this case, cognitive sciences (Alber and Fludernik 2010; Herman 2009). The present study is especially concerned with cognitive narratology and hopes to contribute to embodied narratology, which considers the impact of embodiment on narratological issues (Kukkonen and Caracciolo 2014; Caracciolo et al. 2017; Kuzmičová 2014; Polvinen 2016; Popova 2015). The passage from classical to postclassical narratology brought about not only a substantial innovation in terms of available frameworks, but also a change in method. Compared to early structuralist perspectives, postclassical approaches register a stronger tendency to carry out theoretical discussions in dialogue with the critical interpretive practice rather than in the abstract (Todorov 1969). Aligning with this trend,

this study integrates cognitive narratology and cognitive literary criticism, seeking to combine insights from both perspectives.

9. Paul Ricoeur states something similar when he talks of *emplotment* as a 'configuring act' and a key manifestation of narrativity (1982/1984: 102). White (1987: 44–45), too, speaks of emplotment as a mode of discourse that is able to produce meaning through the formal arrangement of its elements.
10. Following an analogous line of argument, in *Lector in fabula* (1979) Umberto Eco posits the idea of plot structure as a process of activating some semantic possibilities while narcotising others. For early suggestions in favour of integrating modally-oriented plot models in narrative semantics, see Pavel (1980) and Perry (1979).
11. Recent research around cognition usually articulates along four main axes, which focus respectively on the mind as embodied (developed through bodily experience), embedded (depending on the interactions with the environment), enacted (happening through action) and extended (distributed among other agents or tools). All together, these are also referred to as 4E approaches to cognition (see Menary 2010; Newen, de Bruin and Gallagher 2018).
12. For an updated discussion of narrative space and of the intersections of space and narrative, see Ryan, Foote and Azaryahu (2016).
13. The number of three case studies is intended to strike a balance between variety of narratives and the in-depth argumentation required by an engagement of the critical scholarship on the authors and works considered. Perhaps because of the difficulty in combining the theoretical and applied focus, it is worth noting that there are still very few organic applications of cognitive models to the interpretation of specific authors, among which it is worth noting Bernini (forthcoming), Calabrese (2017), Hogan (2014), Lau (2018) and Troscianko (2014).

CHAPTER 1

❖

Plot as Map: Alessandro Baricco's *City,* or Nothing to Do with the Metropolis

Over the last thirty years, Alessandro Baricco (b. 1958) has grown to be a well-known and multifaceted figure in the contemporary Italian cultural landscape. Displaying a long-standing taste for communications and a strong belief in the accessibility of art to the broader audience, Baricco started his career as music reviewer for magazines and radio programmes (*Radio Tre Suite*) and then as host for television broadcasts on opera (*L'amore è un dardo*, Rai Tre, 1993) and literature (*Pickwick, del leggere e dello scrivere*, Rai Tre, 1994). In addition to contributing regularly to *La Repubblica* and *La Stampa*, in 1994 he co-founded in Turin the Scuola Holden, a school of creative writing and storytelling. Baricco's literary debut with *Castelli di rabbia* in 1991 initiated a narrative production that has resulted in eleven more novels, but his explorations in storytelling have seen him experiment also with plays (*Davila Roa*, 1996; *Novecento, un monologo*, 1998), re-writings of classics (*Omero, Iliade*, 2004), screenplays (*Novecento*), advertisements, and more hybrid projects combining performance, visual arts and writing, such as *Totem* (1998–99) and *City Reading* (2003). His contributions to newspapers, mostly focusing on contemporary culture and its developments in relation to latest technologies and lifestyles, have been collected in various thematic volumes. In the second part of this chapter, particular attention will be paid to the essay *I barbari* (2008), where Baricco expands on some ideas that are interestingly implemented in his narrative works.

Perhaps partly because of his commitment to projects aiming to popularise culture, Baricco has not been free from criticism.[1] His purported affiliation to 'middle-culture' (Macdonald 1963; cf. Coccia 2014) stems from a certain deliberate combination of naivety, a sensationalism rich in pathos and a pleasurable lightness in his approach to fundamental existential questions — and from a perhaps excessively self-satisfied compliance with the alleged desires of the reader. On the other hand, precisely as a result of his cultivated attention to the response of readers, Baricco's mastery of the narrative medium and its strategies is hard to deny: irrespective of an evaluation of the content of his oeuvre, it is on his implementation of certain narrative techniques that this discussion focuses. In contrast with the number of almost divinely inspired and unnaturally gifted characters who inhabit his stories, from Novecento to Gould to Mr Gwyn, Baricco's commitment to teaching creative writing speaks significantly of his belief in storytelling as a craft that one gets to master primarily through learning and practice. As little as possible is left to chance; the feeling of straightforwardness and recurrent praising of genius are in fact the results of carefully designed effects.

My analysis will specifically focus on Baricco's fourth novel, *City*, published by Rizzoli in 1999. And yet, while this work foregrounds spatiality in a particularly effective and productive way, I believe that it is not only *City* but Baricco's own cognitive style — that is to say his way of making sense of things and communicating abstract ideas — that is strongly spatial in nature. Successfully welcomed by the public,[2] *City* has been generally understood by scholarship as a critique of the postmodern metropolis. In this chapter, however, I argue that the cognitive perspective provides suitable analytical tools and concepts to emphasise certain features of *City* that shed new light on its inner workings and open it up to a convincing interpretation according to which spatiality concerns the structure of the novel rather than its theme.

To recount what *City* is about is not as straightforward a process as it might seem. It is the story of thirteen-year-old child prodigy Gould who, after graduating in theoretical physics, is attending college to receive the education that is expected to gently lead him in a few years to his destiny: the award of the Nobel prize. Being a genius, however, has major side-effects: with his father living away at a military base, Gould is an extremely lonely and isolated boy, who spends his free time wandering around with his two imaginary friends, the giant Diesel and the mute Poomerang. The narrative focuses on a span of roughly two years, between 1987 and 1989, which corresponds to the period when he makes friends with a young woman, Shatzy Shell, and employs her as his governess. Over the final pages, the narrative stretches six years into the future, accounting for Gould's whereabouts following his sudden disappearance. The boy, after deciding to flee his own destiny, has abandoned an academic career, now working as a cleaner in a shopping mall and being presumably happier than he would have been had he pursued the life originally set out for him. As to the narrative format, the novel is subdivided into thirty-five numbered chapters of variable length spanning from a couple of lines to twenty-something pages, preceded by a Prologue and closed by an Epilogue.

This is a fairly reliable summary of *City*. And yet it does not grasp what typifies the narrative the most, nor does it account for the majority of events actually recounted throughout the narrative, which mostly consists of episodes and digressions that do not directly concern the plot as summarised above. In order to summarise *City* coherently, we would have to read through the actual matter of the narration which includes the assemblage of excerpts of the Western authored by Shatzy, imaginary conversations between Diesel and Poomerang, the story of Larry the boxer that Gould invents on the toilet, and the lectures delivered by his college professors.

My investigation into the spatial dimension of plot breaks new ground in the scholarship on Baricco because it lays stress on features that have thus far been neglected by extant criticism. The results presented in this chapter arguably demonstrate that *City* is designed according to narrative strategies that aim at keeping the reader's engagement alive, and work to ensure its readability at various levels. Starting from how readers are guided through the numerous shifts of context and perspective staged in the novel to the way the text engages readers' background knowledge (that is, knowledge that is not conveyed directly by the narrative), my discussion illustrates how *City* consistently provides readers with affordances (Gibson 1979) to co-construct the narrative storyworld successfully. Caracciolo's enactivist framework, Emmott's cognitive theory of discourse comprehension, and script theory as elaborated in post-classical narratology enable one to foreground these strategies and explain how they impact on the reader's understanding. It is my contention that the 'narrative machinery' (Eco 1979) of *City* works precisely because its textually encoded strategies operate synergistically to convey the view of the narrative as something to be explored as a space. The considerations emerging from the application of these frameworks will be supplemented and confirmed through the close reading of narrative and paratextual elements of *City*, but also by drawing on Baricco's own critical production aimed at a popular audience, collected in *I barbari* (2008).

In turn, Baricco's novel offers interesting insights for theoretical reflection. It provides the terrain to productively test the hypothesis that some narratives prompt a spatially-oriented understanding of plot, where spatiality works as main organising principle and causality mostly operates locally. Building on a re-interpretation of the novel, my reading argues that, instead of designating a narrative about urban reality, the image of the city works as a cognitive metaphor. As such, the title does not refer to a theme but to a set of comprehension strategies that should be used to understand the narrative as a whole. *City* offers a suitable starting point for attempting to isolate the textual strategies through which a plot could be deemed as spatial. The analysis will suggest ways in which the text could encourage readers to tap into their sensorimotor knowledge and into the cognitive processes involved with making sense of spatial relations. More specifically, I will look into how textual information is managed and how extra-textual information is integrated — both crucial phases of narrative understanding. The examination builds on the finer-grained analysis of the Prologue of *City*, which displays a number of mechanisms and prompts strategies that are then reproduced on a larger scale throughout the whole novel.

A productive shift of perspective

The city as theme: the postmodern metropolis

In their examination of Baricco's work, to date scholars have mainly focused on linguistic and discursive features (Bellavia 2001; Scarsella 2003), on social and thematic aspects (Bonsaver 2001; Tarantino 2006), or on traits which have been variously linked to the postmodern, from kitsch to intertextuality (Casadei 2002; Giannetto 2002; La Porta 1999; Scarsella 2003). Within a scholarship that is not extensive, there are very few works that have attempted to look at the macrodesigns governing the narrative of *City* and to account for what I referred to in the introduction as the logic underlying the narrative: in other words, to look for that potential set of features — be they mimetic, or thematic, or synthetic (metanarrative) — that may work as general principle(s) giving coherence to the narrative.

Attempts in this direction have been advanced by Ewa Nicewicz (2009), Laura Rorato (2001), Rorato and Simona Storchi (2004), and Giovanni Piazza (2007),[3] whose readings of *City* stress the centrality of the postmodern metropolis. Rorato argues that *City* is entirely devoted to the representation of the postmodern metropolis through the bodies that inhabit it (2001: 245). Similarly, in her follow-up article co-authored with Storchi, they suggest that *City* aims to represent a new 'globalised habitat', juxtaposed to the 'traditional concept of *città*, where space and time form a harmonious and meaningful entity, [which] is no longer suitable to express the globalized, metropolitan reality of many Italian cities' (2004: 251 — de-italicised). According to Piazza, *City* portrays the metropolis as a space staging people in transit (2007: 121). Alessandro Scarsella recognises in the adoption of a metropolitan frame a programmatic choice (2003: 94). Nicewicz suggests that *City* is a metropolitan work par excellence, whose true protagonist is indeed the city (2009: 161). However, if we look at the summary of the novel, it would appear that the story recounted in *City* is hardly about urban life at all. In fact, in the whole novel there is only one scene set in a typically urban context (23–28 [17–21]). It is my contention that the alleged identity between the title of the novel and its thematic core stems from a hermeneutic *faux pas*, and the number of problematic ambiguities resulting from pursuing a reading of *City* as a novel about the contemporary metropolis seems to endorse this interpretation.

Critics defended their point by stressing the polarisation between *città* and *city*, and with it the features that allegedly typify the postmodern metropolis. In order to highlight the sense of loss and displacement assumed to be prototypical of the postmodern metropolis, scholars overemphasised the indeterminacy of time and space to the extent that some critical observations even seem to stand in contradiction to the text. Rorato and Storchi observe that Baricco's representation of the city corresponds to a process of 'etherealisation', and that 'no indications of space or time are provided' (2004: 252). However, even though the narrative is not set in a real city, it is undeniably a verisimilar one, reminiscent perhaps of a North-American town: the protagonist Gould goes to college and is supposed to go to Couverney University; his father works at the Arpaka military base; most of the names would not look out of place in an American context. The fact that the location is fictional does not imply per se any geography of 'loss and displacement', as instead it has been argued. Also, temporal signposts are clearly offered: on the very first page it is specified that the narrative begins in October 1987, while halfway through the story the narrator points out that it is now September 1988 and Gould is celebrating his fourteenth birthday; a few pages later, the narrative recounts of an important academic achievement of Gould, dating it February 1989. It follows that, although interspersed with many conversations that may indeed make the reader lose track of time, time is definitely not annihilated.

Along similar lines, Nicewicz and Rorato and Storchi refer to the notion of 'non-place' elaborated by anthropologist Marc Augé, closely linking its use to the sense of identity — or better, the lack thereof — conveyed by a certain space in relation to its users and inhabitants. They argue that:

> In *City* the urban imagery is constructed through an accumulation of 'non-places', or places whose identities (and consequently the identities of the human beings transiting those places) are blurred, distorted, artificial: motorway restaurants, shopping malls, the 'Ideal Home Exhibition', fast-food restaurants. [Rorato and Storchi 2004: 253]

According to Augé, the non-place is the typical product of contemporary age, which he calls 'supermodernity'. As a matter of fact, examples of non-places include several settings that also feature in Baricco's novel and, as this concept complies with the sense of displacement advocated by many scholars, it is not surprising that they should draw on it in their critical readings. It could also be well argued that, on some occasions, Baricco employs certain places (such as the diner) to express a criticism of the isolation of the individual in contemporary Western society.[4] Yet, Rorato and Storchi themselves admit that the attitude toward these non-places in the novel appears, at best, ambiguous (2004: 253). My suggestion is that, by stressing the notion of non-place, previous readings have perhaps accorded a disproportionate relevance to features which are usually associated with this concept and which risk not to give a fair representation of the way in which these settings are arguably used in this novel.[5] In what follows, I shall build on the notions of script and contextual frame to demonstrate how Baricco capitalises on the recognisability of these fully-fledged, if fictional, places in order to enhance the narrativity of the story.

Finally, the novel is surely characterised by a fragmentary structure. Different discourse types and styles are juxtaposed according to modalities and with designed effects that I shall thoroughly explore. Yet, the majority of the extant scholarship has drawn on the multilinearity of the narrative to reinforce the comparison with the postmodern metropolis which, described as a 'collage' made of fragments and juxtapositions among different cultures, arguably embodies a reality 'dove tempo e spazio sono compressi e privati di significato: nella città nuova tutto è presente e contemporaneo in quanto non esiste più il passato e non esiste più la distanza' ([where time and space are compressed and deprived of any meaning: in the new city everything is present and contemporary inasmuch as there is no past nor any kind of distance] Amendola 1997: 50). Again with a view to endorsing the claim of a collapsing temporal and spatial dimension, Nicewicz observes that in *City* images and situations follow one another like in a stream of thoughts, with no logic (2009: 163). If we look at these 'pieces of stories', though, we see that they belong to a limited number of intertwined narrative strands, linked to one another in a way that can be hardly described as devoid of logic.

One of the main elements that might confuse the reader is the fact that *City* is made of several storylines, some of which do not even directly interact with the others. As a further complication, not all the characters belong to the same ontological storyworld, and this information is ingeniously retained from the reader, who is given only increasing clues of the truth throughout the narration. As the narrative proceeds, the reader realises that some characters surely belong to the actual (fictional) storyworld, including the protagonist Gould, his parents, his professors (Dr Martens, Mondrian Kilroy, Professor Taltomar), and his governess and friend Shatzy Shell. Most of these entities originate, in turn, other departing narrative strands. Shatzy records on tape passages of a Western story centred on the fictional deserted city of Closingtown, while the professors recount lectures and anecdotes. The main source of virtual storyworlds, however, is Gould himself: he has two imaginary friends constantly interacting with him, the giant Diesel and the mute Poomerang, and he is used to entertaining himself while he sits on the toilet by imagining the adventures of boxer Larry Gorman and his coach Mondini. These narratives or imaginative acts instantiate embedded storyworlds which are virtual inasmuch as they are not actual, in the sense that they and their entities do not belong to the same ontological level, or degree of existence, of the main characters. Unlike traditional framed narratives, the ontological boundaries between the various storyworlds in *City* are sometimes porous: Gould interacts with Diesel and Poomerang in a way that tricks readers into believing that they are (fictionally) actual characters; the boxing matches are narrated via a running commentary that is produced by Gould himself, although this is not immediately clear to the reader. As she proceeds, the reader is given more and more clues to distinguish what stories and characters are imagined by Gould or Shatzy and what events and conversations are real instead ('Lei non trova spaventoso che un bambino giri tutto il tempo con due amici che non esistono?', 250 [You don't find it frightening that a child spends all this time with two friends who don't exist?, 253]). All doubts are ultimately swept away, so that the reader is not left dealing with an ontologically subverted narrative world. If the quick shifts from one narrative strand to another seem initially confusing, they are definitely not without logic. More interestingly, I shall argue that the logic underpinning the connections among narrative excerpts resides precisely in the strong recognisability of narrative places and contexts. Far from triggering a sense of displacement — which is the view critics largely supported through stressing their nature of non-places — these settings work instead as crucial signposts to engage and direct readers' comprehension.

In conclusion, building on the assumption that *City* is meant to convey thematically a critique of the modern metropolis, scholars are formulating not fully convincing interpretations of the alleged indeterminate nature of its settings: a significant game-changer could be the hypothesis that *City* may *not* be primarily meant to represent a metropolis in the first place.

The city as cognitive metaphor: a map for the reader

Let us take a closer look at the paratextual passage on the back cover of the novel as it appears in the first edition published by Rizzoli in 1999. In addition to the seemingly obvious hint of the title, many critics rely on this excerpt to support the position previously outlined, that *City* is meant to represent our lived urban environment:

Questo libro è costruito come una città, come l'idea di una città. [...] Le storie sono quartieri, i personaggi sono strade. Il resto è tempo che passa, voglia di vagabondare e bisogno di guardare.

[This book is built like a city, like the idea of a city. [...] Its stories are neighbourhoods, its characters are streets. All the rest is time passing by, a desire to wander and a need to look around. — my translation]

The first line is crucial to my argument: the narrative is *constructed like* a city. It does not *represent* a city. The connection stressed here concerns the macrodesign, not the object, of narrative representation. My suggestion is that the reference to the city is not to be intended as a thematic pointer but rather as a cognitive metaphor. In other words, the idea of city is offered to the reader to provide her with the best way to make sense of the narrative as a whole, as a mental image to guide the process of connecting the parts of the narrative together. The city works as metaphor because comprehension is enabled by a 'conceptual cross-domain mapping' that is proper of this technique (Lakoff and Johnson 1999: 70); the metaphor is cognitive because it concerns the way the narrative is cognized, that is to say it is made sense of. The metaphor, in this case, does not express a similarity between entities but rather a similarity between modes of sense-making. To put the same concept another way, the reader should make sense of the narrative in the same way the traveller/walker makes sense of a city. Hence, it is no longer a matter of words, words that would belong to a domain but can be used to describe another, but of forms of reasoning, which are normally used to reason about the city (that is, about a space) and whose use is now prompted to reason about a narrative.

In advancing the notion of cognitive metaphor, I refer to the theoretical framework of phenomenological embodiment, firstly posited by Varela, Thompson and Rosch (1993) and hereby adopted in the further elaboration by Lakoff and Johnson (1999). By introducing the notion of conceptual metaphor, Lakoff and Johnson intend to challenge the idea, substantially ingrained in most of Western thought and epitomised by the Cartesian *cogito ergo sum*, that our reason exists independently from our body.[6] By contrast, they argue for a notion of reason as embodied (or mind as embodied), a view that aims to account for the fact that the human cognitive ability to elaborate abstract concepts — as, for example, understanding a narrative as a whole, which is quite a high-level cognitive operation — ultimately builds on our sensorimotor experience, which in turn shapes the way we elaborate these abstract concepts and our subjective experience.[7] Conceptual metaphor is the general expression that Lakoff and Johnson use to indicate the fundamental link that enables our cognition to move from sensorimotor knowledge to any superior kind of abstract knowledge. In this chapter, I adopt the term cognitive metaphor to describe the metaphoric connection between narrative sense-making strategies.[8]

The image of the city fits the specific use Baricco makes of it, firstly because he arguably taps into the readers' background knowledge not only of a generic space but of a familiar environment — as an urban environment is likely to be, at least for the Western reader. Secondly, because the city represents an inherently composite and diverse environment, which evokes a closer analogy with a composite novel made of multiple storylines. Thirdly, although I advocated that this is not his main point, Baricco does take up some opportunities to portray aspects of contemporary society, and this, at least in the Western world, is characterised by a typically urban setting.

In using the description of 'plot as map' as the overarching image for this chapter, my purpose is to draw on the particular case of the city — and of this novel — to build a more general case and to indicate with this label a broader category of narratives. If the city is the cognitive metaphor offered to the reader to make sense of the narrative as a whole, the process of plot understanding amounts to the process of exploration of the city-narrative; in other words, to the elaboration of a mental map. Plot, intended as the constantly re-assessed outcome of narrative understanding, is the product, while the mapping process conceptualises the reader's narrative experience in spatial terms.

The term 'cognitive map' was first employed in 1948 by psychologist Edward Tolman and refers to 'an individual's knowledge of spatial and environmental relations, and the cognitive processes associated with the encoding and retrieval of the information from which it is composed' (Kitchin and Blades 2002: 1). The concept of map is particularly useful here because maps capture the way individuals cognize the relation between the whole and its constituents, its 'structural inter-relatedness' (Moore and Golledge 1976: xii). In this sense, maps and plots share a fundamental property: far from duplicating reality (as this would make it pointless), a map provides an orienting mechanism and an interpretive grid (Bjornson 1981; Muehrcke and Muehrcke 1974) in the same way as plot emerges from the story as a whole and should convey its organising principle, on the basis of which readers understand the narrative.

In this light, it might be argued that the process of narrative understanding could be always described as a mapping process, irrespective of the type of narrative analysed. In their work on cognitive mapping, Roger Downs and David Stea — a geographer and a psychologist, respectively — point out that the mental abilities that enable us to understand and navigate a spatial environment are the same ones we use, more generally, to 'collect, organize, store, recall, and manipulate [any kind of] information' (1977: 6). Individuals, for instance, employ cognitive mapping abilities in order to make sense of personal experience. The comparison between plot understanding and cognitive mapping surely points toward a fascinating direction for research; however, it is beyond the scope of this book to investigate its full impact and I shall limit the use of the concept of map in relation to plot only to indicate a specific, if negotiable, category of plot types, epitomised by the novel analysed in this chapter.

By advancing the analogy of plot as map, my purpose is less to focus on the process of plot understanding as cognitive mapping of a narrative than to outline a category of narratives which aim to portray a state of affairs or a situation that could be broadly deemed as static. This category is expected to include narratives, such as *City*, that are designed to guide their readers through an exploration of their conditions of narrativity, rather than their evolution. The plot is described as a map because to understand the plot means for readers to map out those states of affairs and issues that typify a certain storyworld in its dynamic equilibrium. As M.-L. Ryan points out, '[t]he association of the concepts of map and narrative presupposes that we expand the widely accepted definition of narrative as the expression of the *temporal* nature of human experience into a type of meaning that involves the four dimensions of a space-time continuum' (2003: 335).

Moving through the plot

Framing the story

As anticipated in the introduction, recent work in narrative theory draws on a cognitive perspective and a non-propositional view of thought to advance the hypothesis that 'grasping the *when, what, who,* and *where* of events being recounted is a matter of actively building and updating the mental representations', or storyworlds (Herman 2002: 270). Such an approach entails an understanding of events not in terms of transient entities running along a chain of facts temporally conceived, but rather in terms of progressive modifications of a storyworld and of the interrelationships connecting its entities, namely objects or characters. I have already pointed out that embracing a non-propositional view of thought does not deny the impact of language: in fact, as one reads, any additional linguistic specification modifies the discourse model and, by doing so, also modifies the mental model of the storyworld, either by actively changing its fictional configuration or by changing the perspective from which it is mentally represented.[9]

The reason why *City* represents a case study worth further investigation is that its overall storyworld does not go through major changes, or at least not significant enough to cause Gould to break free from his existential impasse until the very end of the narrative. The narrative is designed as an exploration for the reader to undertake, an encouragement for interpreters to map out the fictional state of affairs: things do happen, but the point of the narrative is less in their chronological unfolding and more, if anything, in their accumulation. In my case study analysis of *City*, in the same sense, I evaluate whether the tellability of a story may stem from the exploration of a static state of affairs.

In this light, the cognitive aspects usually relied on to make sense of a space may play a more relevant role than the one they would have had if chronology had occupied a pre-eminent function. Yet, if the state of affairs portrayed in *City* is relatively static, its narration is, on the contrary, quite lively. This dynamism is arguably ensured by the swift changes of perspective (and storyline), and I suggest that the cognitive mechanisms underpinning the maintenance of coherence in plot understanding are well described by Emmott's (1997) contextual frame theory. Contextual frame theory productively fits within my work not only because its theoretical premises are compatible with the other theories I build on, but because it provides suitable tools to parse those cognitive operations prompted by the narrative understanding designed in *City*. The concept of contextual frame is not usually included among the traditional narratological components, and its visibility is granted precisely by theories that adopt a cognitive lens and foreground processes taking place in the mind as response to the narrative. Plot emerges as the reader understands the mechanisms that regulate these configurational changes affecting the storyworld. As Hilary Dannenberg (2008: 12) observes in her endorsement of a cognitive approach to narrative studies,

> [p]recisely because the cognitive research explores the overall sense-making patterns that the human mind within the human body uses to negotiate its way through the spatial and temporal environments of life, it can be used to study plot by investigating how narrative fiction simulates both the experience and the conceptualization of time and space.

While not laying any claim to sorting out the inherent theoretical instability of the notion of plot — in fact, embracing it — Dannenberg argues that coming to terms with the plot actually represents the 'attempt to make sense of a larger, unorganized entity' (2008: 13), and that therefore plot understanding as a process that unfolds throughout reading becomes an active cognitive operation that capitalises on a range of cognitive connecting patterns.

Emmott's theory of contextual-frame shifts aims to explain how narrative comprehension takes place and specifically, to put it in Herman's words, 'how readers of written narratives supplement text-based or propositional information with situation-based information' (2002: 270). Emmott individuates its key processes in the interrelations between text and reader's knowledge, inference-making, and referencing. Building on an approach hinging on mental representations as formulated by Philip Johnson-Laird (1981; 1983; 1993) rather than on a propositional approach,[10] Emmott posits the notion of contextual frame as 'a mental store of information about a particular context', which includes '"episodic" information about a configuration of characters, location, and time at any point in a narrative' (1997: 132 and 104). While context is thus the overall mental space against which the meaning of a certain proposition is projected, and as such it affects the way that proposition is understood (Emmott 1997: 58), contextual monitoring is described as an active form of memory which expresses the reader's awareness of the narrative configurations — namely, groupings of characters, objects and relations among them — 'located at specific space-time coordinates in the storyworld' (Herman 2002: 270), in terms of continuity and change (Emmott 1997: 104 and 112–15). Emmott points out two main types of contextual monitoring: *binding*, which defines processes related to the establishment of episodic connections among narrative entities, and *priming*, which describes changes in the attentional focus of the reader (Chilton 2014).[11]

Also relevant for an investigation of *City* are Erving Goffman's (1974) ideas on frame analysis, considering that Baricco's novel decidedly attempts to reproduce the rhythms and features of orality. Unlike Emmott and Herman, who conceive frames in terms of mental representations, Goffman deploys the notion of frame with the meaning of 'boundary', to indicate the 'brackets' that delimit parts of discourse characterised by different reality statuses. He pinpoints eight types of frames, which serve to separate a story within a conversation:

Conversation
 [Preface
  [Opening
   [Orientation
    [Beginning
     [*Story*]
    End]
   Closing
  Evaluation]
 Coda]
Conversation

As Katharine Young (2005) aptly summarises in her entry on 'Frame Theory' in the *Routledge Encyclopedia of Narrative Theory*, beginnings and ends frame events for stories and therefore belong to the storyworld; openings and closings frame stories for conversations and therefore belong to the storyrealm (Young 1986);[12] prefaces and codas are part of the realm of conversation and are indeed responsible for soliciting permission to suspend and reinstitute turn-taking, respectively. The orientation section preceding stories usually provides readers with information useful to follow the narration and at the same time directs the hearers' attention toward the storyworld, while the evaluation section comprises the hearers' expression of their emotional response and frames storyworld and storyrealms as potential aesthetic objects. In order to avoid terminological confusion, whenever I use the term 'frame' I do so in Emmott's sense; when I use it to refer to Goffman eight types of frames, I will adopt from now on the disclaimer expression 'B-frame' (boundary-frame). By providing a close reading of *City*'s Prologue through the occurring frame shifts, my purpose is to demonstrate how consistently and extensively the narrative capitalises on them. To ensure readability, I devote the next section to the description of the contextual-frame shifts and I postpone the ensuing considerations and comments to the following section.

In his monograph, Scarsella identifies the alternation of different discourse styles — short story, anecdote, lecture, stream of consciousness — as the principle and driving force of Baricco's narration (2003: 92). This isolated insight should indeed be taken seriously, and by framing it within a cognitive approach it gains its full theoretical potential. The alternation acknowledged by Scarsella is not simply a matter of style. It rather mirrors a process that affects the narration at a more structural level and could be better described in terms of alternation of contextual frames. Emmott's theorisation allows for a reformulation of the issue in terms not of how a certain content is expressed, but of how the various parts are connected, how the narrative proceeds and how it maintains the reader's engangement — namely, a set of processes that fall within the scope of the notion of plot.

The Prologue: a description of the contextual-frame shifts

  — Allora, signor Klauser, deve morire Mami Jane?
  — Che vadano tutti a cagare.
  — È un sì o un no?
  — Lei che ne dice? [9]

["So, Mr Klauser, should Mami Jane die?"
"Screw them all."
"Is that a yes or a no?"
"What do you think?"] [3]

The narrative opens with four lines of direct speech (initially not recognised as a phone call) that already set up a first contextual frame into which at least two fictional interlocutors (as yet unidentified) are bound. After these four lines, the narrator takes on the narration, performing a frame switch from the direct-speech frame. In a retrospective way the narrator outlines the Orientation B-frame, informing the reader of the identity of Mami Jane and of the context of the telephonic poll, in the course of which the direct speech — now understood to be a sample phone call — had taken place. The narrator also isolates an expectedly relevant character by introducing, and thus priming, the figure of Shatzy Shell among the eight secretaries in charge of performing the poll. If the Orientation for the first call is offered retrospectively, the next contextual frame is introduced by means of a proper Opening instead, 'Ne seguì la seguente conversazione' (10 [The following conversation ensued, 4]).

Within the broader contextual frame that binds in the CRB office as the location where Shatzy Shell is working with other seven secretaries, the more specific contextual frame of the phone call is now primed, binding in the character of Shatzy and the other interlocutor, a thirteen-year-old child named Gould. During the conversation, Shatzy herself performs a narrating task, thus triggering another frame switch from the phone call frame to that of the diner, a different contextual frame that binds in a different setting and an array of other fictional entities. Shatzy's story is introduced by a Preface and signalled by a proper Beginning ('Una volta ero in una tavola calda, sulla Statale 16, appena fuori città', 13 [Once I was at a cafeteria, on Route 16, just outside of town, 7]). Later on, the reinstitution of turn-taking is properly signalled by means of a Coda ('Assurdo, no?', 14 [Absurd, isn't it?, 8]), which ends Shatzy's story, unprimes the diner contextual frame, and recalls the telephone conversation frame, thus bringing the reader's attentional focus back onto it. The following shifts from the telephone conversation between Shatzy and Gould and to the verbal interaction between Shatzy and her boss, are easily understood thanks to diacritic markers.[13] Once the call is finished (B-framed by phatic expressions that amount to a Closing in Goffman's model), the narrator describes Shatzy as she leaves the office after being fired and mentions a few details, such as that Shatzy changes her tennis shoes into high heeled shoes and that she collects in her bag two framed pictures, portraying Eva Braun and Walt Disney respectively.

Here the reader experiences an unexpected shift: the contextual frame of the office is suddenly unprimed and a new unidentified contextual frame is instated, marked by an Opening in the form of a direct speech ('"Capito?" / "Più o meno."', 20 ["Get it?" / "More or less", 14]) that leads straight to the Beginning of a new story: 'Faceva il pianista in un enorme centro commerciale' (20 [He played the piano in an enormous department store, 14]). Since the story tells the reason why someone should carry around the portrait of Eva Braun, the reader is prompted to identify the narrator of the story as Shatzy. The frame switch is signalled by a change in the use of diacritic signs — inverted commas rather than the dash, previously used for reporting the phone call — and by a clear change of topic. Once again, a Coda signals the reinstitution of turn-taking and the End of the 'Eva Braun's picture' story. The two following lines of direct speech bind the character of Shatzy to the setting of a diner ('Buono l'hamburger?', 23 [Is the hamburger good?, 17]) and thus trigger the preliminary hypothesis that the interlocutor may be Gould, since during the phone call he had invited Shatzy to celebrate his birthday at the diner of her story. However, the reader's wondering is interrupted soon enough by another contextual-frame shift, performed by the narrator overtly taking the storytelling floor: the narrator unprimes the contextual frame of Shatzy and (possibly) Gould, and primes instead the contextual frame binding Diesel and Poomerang on their way to the CRB office, as anticipated by Gould's warning phone call ('Finì, comunque, che Diesel e Poomerang non arrivarono mai alla CR', 23 [Diesel and Poomerang never made it to the offices of CRB, anyway, 17]).

The following five pages display a complex interaction of overlapping and shifting frames. The contextual frame introduced by the narrator — binding in the street setting, Diesel, Poomerang, and the stiletto heel of a black shoe — remains primed, but the attentional focus of the reader zooms in onto the detail of the heel. In turn, this detail prompts the priming of a new contextual frame that nonetheless seems characterised by a weaker ontological status: through looking at the stiletto heel, Diesel and Poomerang are described in the process of *seeing* the scene that had led the woman to break and lose the heel. This happens in a continuous switching from the hypothetical contextual frame binding the woman to the contextual frame binding Diesel and Poomerang. The impression of a weaker status of the former frame is enhanced by the fact that, even though it looks like a flashback, it is actually a *present* imaginary reconstruction:

> Fissavano quel tacco nero, a spillo, e fu un niente vedere — un attimo dopo l'inevitabile flash di una caviglia in nylon scuro — vedere il passo che l'aveva perso, esattamente il passo [...]. [i] capelli — corti neri, pensò Diesel — corti biondi, pensò Poomerang — lisci e sottili [24]

> [They stared at the black heel, a spike heel, and it took no time to see — a moment after the inevitable flash of an ankle in dark nylon — the *step* that had lost it, the exact step [...]. The hair — short and black, thought Diesel, short and blond, thought Poomerang — smooth and light] [17–18]

What follows poses an even more unexpected challenge to the reader's activity of contextual monitoring. While the frame with the woman is primed, the other one binding in Diesel and Poomerang is never fully unprimed and, despite being in the background, it remains active because it contains the focalisers to which the foreground frame is attached. Once again, the zoom on a detail of the reader's (along with Diesel's and Poomerang's) attentional focus works as a bridge to trigger another frame shift: the glimpse of the woman's thigh entering a taxi is randomly spotted also by an unknown man, and the moment of joint attention with the main frame's focalisers causes the bystander to get bound into the frame. The woman is bound out, determining a rearrangement of the central directory, that is the set of characters bound in to a frame.[14] The bystander becomes the object of the attentional focus of a newly primed contextual frame:

> Quel che successe fu che Diesel e Poomerang rimasero impastoiati nell'uomo in scuro, in verità, risucchiati dalla composta scia del suo turbamento, che li commuoveva, per così dire, e che li spinse lontano, fino a vedere il colore del suo scendiletto — marrone — e sentire il puzzo della sua cucina. [25]

> [What happened was that Diesel and Poomerang stayed with the dark-suited man, sucked in by the quiet wake of his distress, which moved them, so to speak, and pushed them on, until they saw the color of his bathrobe — brown — and smelled the odors of his kitchen.] [19]

> Stavano rovistando tra la biancheria intima della signora Mortensen quando, per banale e volgare associazione di idee, gli risalì nel sangue il ricordo del compasso femmina smaltato nylon scuro — scossa feroce che li costrinse a precipitarsi indietro fino al taxi giallo, e a farli rimanere lì, sul bordo della strada, un po' inebetiti dalla rovinosa scoperta — rovinosa scomparsa del taxi giallo nelle viscere della città — tutto il viale pieno di macchine, ma vuoto di taxi gialli e leggende accomodate sul sedile posteriore.
> — Cristo — , disse Diesel.
> — Sparita — , nondisse Poomerang. [26]

> [They were rifling through Mrs Mortensen's intimate lingerie when, by a banal and vulgar association of ideas, in their blood rose the memory of the woman dark metallic nylon compass — a violent shake that compelled them to rush all the way back to the yellow taxi, and remain there, on the edge of the street, a little dazed by the disastrous discovery: the disastrous disappearance of the yellow taxi into the bowels of the city — a whole avenue full of cars but empty of yellow taxis with heroes making themselves comfortable on the backseat.
> "Gone", Poomerang didn't say.
> "Christ", Diesel said.] [19–20]

Let me continue with the description of the few remaining frame shifts, before advancing a few considerations. The primed frame is now, once again, the frame that binds in Diesel, Poomerang, the stiletto heel, and the street setting, from which the woman has just been bound out. Displaying an unnatural — but no longer surprising — ability to navigate within and among contextual frames, Diesel and Poomerang deduce where a woman who has just broken her shoe could be and find her in a shoe shop, binding her back to the frame: 'Allora non la persero più. Per un numero imprecisabile di ore catalogarono i suoi gesti e gli oggetti intorno a lei, come se testassero dei profumi' (27 [They never lost her again after that. For an indeterminate number of hours they catalogued her gestures and the objects around her, as if they were testing perfumes, 20]). The focalisers remain bound in to the contextual frame to which the woman is bound in, until she leaves the house of the man she spent the night with. As soon as the woman is bound out, the frame revolving around her dissolves: the attentional focus returns on the initial frame containing Diesel, Poomerang, and the stiletto heel. A change of focalisation, from Diesel's and Poomerang's to the narrator's perspective, subtly modifies the contextual frame, enlarging it to contain the two characters, who are no longer the focalisers. The reader's attention is drawn to the act of storytelling of the narrator by the presence of a nominal sentence that works as Closing by pulling the reader away from Diesel, Poomerang, the stiletto heel, and the setting of the street pavement:

> L'uno e l'altro, vicini, e poi pezzi marci di città sulla strada di casa, luci liquide di semafori, auto in terza a far rumore di sciacquone, un tacco per terra, sempre più lontano, occhio bagnato, senza più palpebre, senza ciglia, occhio finito. [28]
>
> [The one and the other, close together, and the soaked stretches of the city on the way home, the liquid lights of traffic signals, cars in third that sounded like toilets flushing, a heel on the ground, farther and farther away, the eye wet, without, any longer, an eye-lid, without a brow, finished.] [21]

Graphically stressing the frame switch with a new paragraph, the narrator mentions the second portrait owned by Shatzy, that of Walt Disney. The re-priming of the picture recalls the contextual frame to which both pictures are bound; it is a particular contextual frame, conceptually rather than physically instantiated, since its priming does not determine the priming of any specific topological setting. The connection between the pictures of Eva Braun and Walt Disney is established in the office scene but, since both pictures are Shatzy's belongings, this connection is stored by the reader as a non-episodic relation (Emmott 1997: 128) — namely, a relation that remains true beyond specific contexts (unless otherwise specified). The return to a previous moment of the narrative is further emphasised by the fact that Disney's picture is introduced by means of a variation modelled on the previous description of Eva Braun's photograph:

> La foto di Eva Braun aveva una cornice di plastica rossa, e un piedino dietro, foderato di stoffa, e pieghevole: per tenerla su, all'occorrenza. [20]
>
> [The photograph of Eva Brow had a red plastic frame, and a foot that folded out from the back, covered in fabric: to hold it up, if necessary.] [14]
>
> La foto di Walt Disney era un po' più grande di quella di Eva Braun. Aveva una cornice di legno chiaro, e un piedino dietro, pieghevole: per tenerla su, all'occorrenza. [28]
>
> [The photograph of Walt Disney was a little bigger than the one of Eva Braun. It had a pale wood frame, and a foot that folded out from the back: to hold it up, if necessary.] [21]

Immediately after this passage, the contextual frame binding in Shatzy and Gould in (presumably) the diner is recalled by the reappearance of the inverted commas as diacritic signs marking the direct speech, and by an actual repetition of the first two phatic lines (" "Capito?" / "Più o meno." ', 20, 28 ["Get it?" / "More or less.", 17, 22]). After having opened the story of why Shatzy is keeping a portrait of Eva Braun in her bag, now the same lines open the explanation of why she has Disney's. The final shift is triggered by the very last line of the Prologue, where the narrative voice reassesses the framed status of the dialogue, circularly closing the narration and the Prologue:

[Shatzy]	"Andiamo?"
[Gould]	"Andiamo."
	Andiamo? Andiamo. [29]
[Shatzy]	["Shall we go?"]
[Gould]	"Let's go."
	Shall we go? Let's go.] [22]

The space of narrative experience

The description outlined above suggests that a deliberate design informs the structural and cognitive configuration of *City*'s narrative. Over the nineteen pages of the Prologue, Baricco prompts the reader to keep track of at least twenty frame shifts: given their frequency and prolonged use throughout the narrative, it does not seem out of place to argue that these rapid shifts in focalisation constitute a critical strategy in the novel.[15] This strategy aims at keeping the reader's attention alive by maintaining the narration lively but, at the same time, taking care to provide enough affordances to ensure orientation. From typographic devices (for example, differentiation of diacritic marks) to rhetoric and discourse comprehension strategies (in other words, repetitions and parallelisms, the use of B-frames), Baricco makes sure that the surface impression of quickness does not actually hinder narrative comprehension.

The fact that the linking strategies employed in the Prologue do not pre-eminently include chronology already partly proves that plot understanding does not necessarily have to be rooted in the temporal dimension. Chronology is not annihilated and should be reconstructed, but the reader cannot make sense of the story by relying on the re-composition of the events as ordered in the *fabula* starting from their order in the discourse. It is thanks to strategies of contextual monitoring that readers are encouraged to understand the Prologue and the whole narrative.

Baricco's novel, however, allows me to take the hypothesis concerning the significance of spatiality a step further and suggest that the storyworlds instantiated by the various storylines are sometimes more than 'windows' opened on represented state of affairs.[16] In fact, they are increasingly conceived as proper spaces, simulating the reader's spatial experience not only in terms of conceptualisation of mimetic spaces but also in terms of potential for manipulation of and interaction with the surrounding (fictional) space. The occasional but crucial embodiment of the readers' cognitive operations of contextual monitoring triggers an enhanced spatial interaction with the storyworld.

An exemplary case is given by the peculiar way contextual-frame shifts are handled in the second part of the Prologue, starting from the moment when Diesel and Poomerang find the stiletto heel. Let us take a closer look at the types of verbs used to bind entities into and out of the frame: 'rimasero impastoiati', 'risucchiati', 'li spinse lontano', 'arrivarono a sedersi a tavola con lui', 'scossa feroce che li costrinse a precipitarsi indietro' (25–26 [stayed; sucked in; pushed them on; ended up sitting at the table with him; violent shake that compelled them to rush all the way back; 19]). These are all expressions that refer to actual movements of the body in space. The cognitive operations of priming and unpriming are fictionalised in terms of characters following and leaving the primed and unprimed frames, displaying a power and a freedom of movement within the storyworld that is strikingly anomalous. Or, better, if this is theoretically not much different from the ubiquity traditionally displayed by an omniscient narrator, its fictionalisation represents a far more interesting implementation that has some fascinating consequences concerning the cognitive elaboration of the narrative. At this moment of the narrative, Diesel and Poomerang are still supposed to be actual fictional characters and the reader is prompted to provide them with fictional bodies, which occupy space within the fictional world; indeed, Baricco makes sure to stress the remarkable physical features of the pair, endowing them with distinctive bodily concreteness.

In a broader sense, the employment of spatial metaphors to describe the narrative experience is not unprecedented. Richard Gerrig (1993) refers to the reading experience as 'being transported' into a fictional world; Dannenberg (2008) speaks of 'dynamics of immersion and expulsion' (22) and of plot as expressing 'the dynamic interaction of competing possible worlds' (46). M.-L. Ryan (1991: 22) properly theorises this phenomenon under the label of 'fictional recentering', although she mainly posits it with a view to exploring the modal nature of possible-worlds. Adopting quite a strong stance, Herman even observes that the core of storytelling may lie precisely in the act(s) of deictic relocation of the reader's perspective 'from the HERE and NOW of the act of narration to other space-time coordinates — namely, those defining the perspective from which the events of the story are recounted' (2002: 271).

Caracciolo, however, takes issues with Ryan's notion of recentering: he argues that it is not the reader's consciousness that is virtually relocated in the storyworld (M.-L. Ryan 1991: 104) but her virtual body, continuing with the idea that '[some] narrative texts draw on the readers' memories of bodily movements (experiential traces) as part of the process of co-constructing fictional worlds' (2014a: 160). The notion of readers' virtual bodies is developed by Caracciolo within the framework of enactivism and it is built on the principle that the structural resemblance between imagination and perception is such that they partly share the same neural resources (Kosslyn, Ganis and Thompson 2001). It follows that '[i]f perception is embodied [...], then mental imagery must be embodied too; it must be deeply rooted in our real body and in memories of our past sensorimotor interactions with the environment' (Caracciolo 2014a: 160–61). Caracciolo outlines a scalar schematisation of four degrees of fictionalisation of the virtual body, from a lower end of the scale — so called 'degree zero' — where readers are barely prompted to project their bodily-perceptual experience into the storyworld, to the highest degree of fictionalisation of readers' virtual bodies, in which the reader's bodily projection is aligned with an actual character in the narrative (2014a: 173–80).

This process of alignment taps into the readers' sensorimotor experience and can be triggered automatically, yet a critical framework foregrounding these strategies is not always necessarily the most effective one. As far as *City* is concerned, though, the embodiment of the reader's activity of contextual monitoring significantly cues the fictionalisation of her virtual body — that is, the actualisation of the reader's virtual body in the fictional storyworld. These instances are particularly relevant because the embodied nature of the focalisers is stressed in a way that I will further examine. It should not be overlooked however that this narrative mechanism does not fall into a void, and that Baricco systematically encourages the alignment (or recentering) of the readers' perspective with the perspective (if not with the fictional body) of the characters within the storyworld, thus promoting narrative engagement. The pervasive use of spatial and temporal deixis is perhaps the most effective strategy to prompt such relocation.

In the passage analysed in the Prologue, the reader's virtual body is aligned with the fictional bodies of Diesel and Poomerang. Baricco's decision to select precisely these fictional characters to cue the alignment of the reader's virtual body is not accidental and has arguably a significant impact on readers' experience of the narrative space. It has been already noted that the way Diesel and Poomerang move through different frames and fictional scenarios is entirely anomalous: they appear to be able to follow other characters with their fictional bodies but in awkwardly disembodied ways, seemingly free from the laws of physics expected to be in place in a realistic storyworld.[17] The ambiguity is to be later solved when it will become progressively clear that Diesel and Poomerang do not, in fact, have fictional actual bodies because they are Gould's imaginary friends. The reader might distance herself from these characters as they assume less realistic features, but her imagination is already involved.

Baricco makes skilful use of the possibilities of narrative: on the one hand, he exploits the engaging power of the fictionalisation of the reader's virtual body and uses it to endow the spatial dimension of the narrative structure with visibility; on the other, he does not jeopardise his credibility with the readers by unduly subverting the ontology of the storyworld and he provides a retroactive explanation of why those characters were able to move so freely and unnoticed. Furthermore, a possible risk stemming from arranging so many frame shifts is an overemphasis of the metanarrative dimension of narrative experience: if there is the chance that some readers might become more intellectually engaged by a metanarrative operation, it is also true that this could undermine the immersion into the fictional storyworld. Encouraging the reader to bring her virtual body into the narrative may, by contrast, enhance the immersion experience (Zwaan 2004), thus leaving a larger margin for metanarrative operations.

From our discussion so far an important point should be clarified. The enactivist perspective enables one to distinguish between two levels of experientiality: one that concerns the (fictional) life experience of characters, and one that concerns the reader's real narrative experience. It is at this second level that what I describe as the *space of narrative experience* emerges. The space of narrative experience is a virtual space that partly depends on story-level entities belonging to the storyworld — in other words, characters, fictional events and situations — but which also critically includes the perspective of the reader, an entity that straddles the narrative fictional storyworld and the realm of actuality.[18] Plot understanding pertains to this virtual space, as it is an emergent property of the narrative that depends on the entities belonging and modifications occurring to the fictional storyworld but is also influenced by readers' extra-storyworld knowledge. M.-L. Ryan (2016: 381) observes that 'we relate to objects in our environment not by building static mental pictures of them, but by apprehending their "affordances", that is, by mentally exploring what a virtual body can do with them': through the episode of Diesel and Poomerang, Baricco stages in the narrative itself the process of manipulation of the storyworld's configurations as it is mentally performed by readers during reading. Plot and the structure of the narrative are portrayed as a space, something that can be browsed from various perspectives and at variable degrees of detail, accessible to (some) fictional entities, potentially explorable. As an aside, it might be argued that this specific spatially-based way of conceptualising stories conveys a view of the power of narrative as resulting from the exhaustion of narrative cues and possibilities, rather than from the grasping and recounting of events in time. Let us think, for instance, of the stiletto heel that, once the contextual frames potentially stemming from it have been explored, turns into a trigger now useless: an 'occhio finito', 'senza più palpebre, senza ciglia' (28 [eye...finished; without, any longer, an eye-lid, without a brow; 21]).[19]

While I do not claim that cases of fictionalisation of the reader's virtual body always occur in narratives which are productively compatible with a spatially-oriented critical approach, in the case of Baricco there are multiple hints that converge in this interpretive direction. Reverting to the image of city as cognitive metaphor offered by the title itself, Caracciolo hypothesises that authors can tap into 'readers' familiarity with bodily and perceptual experience [...] to bring into play higher-order, socio-cultural meanings and values', thus producing a so-called 'feedback effect' (2014a: 158). More than stimulating a socio-cultural meaning, in *City* the urban landscape is called upon in a pre-eminent position to exert its feedback effect onto the higher-order cognitive practice of plot understanding. A city is something inherently spatial rather than temporal in nature. Baricco's equation of stories to neighbourhoods and characters to roads seems to imply that their exploration is not a hierarchical process and does not need to be pursued in a certain sequence; what is important is to get an idea of the overall crisscross of streets and storylines but, since they are not, strictly speaking, causally connected, the order with which this is done does not matter much.

It is worth stressing that this does not mean that time is annihilated. Mimetically, as I pointed out at the outset of the chapter, the narrative is explicitly framed in time, and temporal hallmarks are provided throughout the novel. Secondly, the way the temporal dimension is managed during the second part of the Prologue suggests its problematisation rather than its annihilation. By taking off from the detail of the heel as if it established a direct bridge with its own past, Diesel and Poomerang are able not only to reconstruct a contextual frame temporally placed in the past, but also to enter it with their actual (fictional) bodies and, from there, to move freely through other areas of the storyworld. On the other hand, however, they are not totally free from the constraints of time: while they are in the frame to which the bystander Mortensen is bound, rummaging through his drawers, the woman of the taxi has disappeared. When they finally find her again and follow her for a number of hours, it has in the meantime started raining, the crowd surrounding Diesel and Poomerang has scattered, and the light is different. It may be argued that characters — and fictional entities in general — are roads in the sense that all their punctual configurations in time can be potentially compressed into one single three-dimensional configuration that contains all its past and future unfolding. It follows that, within each series of temporally sequenced configurations related to a specific character, the reader-traveller could move potentially freely, thus turning the time attached to a fictional entity into a linearly extended space. Nevertheless, for the reader-traveller the process of exploring takes place in time or, better, the reader's experience of the storyworld exploration takes time: therefore, as soon as she leaves the exploration of a specific character or story, time has passed and more configurations have added to all the fictional entities belonging to the storyworld. The city has expanded.

Do you have it in mind?

> Un'altra bella scena era quella del menu. Dentro il saloon. [...] Dove ballava tutto un gran putiferio di cose, voci, rumori, colori, ma non dimenticare — diceva Shatzy — la puzza. Quella è importante. Devi tenere bene in mente la puzza. Sudore, alcool, cavallo, denti cariati, piscio e dopobarba. Hai in mente? Finché non giuravi di avere in mente non continuava. [63]

> [Another good scene was the menu scene. In the saloon. [...] Where a whole great confusion of things was dancing around — voices, noises, colors — but don't forget, said Shatzy, the stink. That's important. Keep in mind the stink. Sweat, alcohol, horses, rotten teeth, pee and aftershave. Got that? She wouldn't continue until you swore you had that firmly in your mind.] [57]

It should be clear by this point that virtuality enters our critical discourse from many directions. The virtual space of narrative experience, modelled on the story-level but inclusive of the reader's perspective, emerges from the embodiment of contextual-frame shifts, which encourages interpreters to move through the storylines as if they are spaces, aligning their virtual body with the fictional body of characters,

Virtuality, however, is fostered not only through strategies for contextual monitoring — that is, through how readers manage the information provided by the text; another crucial way in which Baricco relies on virtuality and, in so doing, enhances the spatially-oriented understanding of the narrative, concerns the engagement of readers' background knowledge. In its broader sense, the expression *world* or *background knowledge* refers to any kind of information not explicitly provided by the text, derived both by other texts (intertextual knowledge) or by general everyday (extra-textual) experience. In the quotation above, the text explicitly pinpoints the elements that should be born in mind in order to appreciate the narration, but in many other instances the reader is required to inhabit the mental surrounding of the story narrated in a more implicit fashion. Implicit though does not mean unguided: the core mechanism normally used to regulate the supply of narrative information is the script, and I suggest that Baricco's systematic and peculiar use of scripts fundamentally shapes the design of *City*. Indeed, although no text can be understood without drawing on some kind of prior knowledge, narratives can nonetheless variously, and purposely, exploit some of the cognitive processes at the basis of this connection, foregrounding their presence to a variable extent.

Presence is a key term here, because the complexity of Baricco's employment of scripts lies precisely in the variable extent to which he encourages and/or tricks the reader to integrate her background knowledge with the narrative, thus achieving a range of different effects. Noë's enactivist approach to perception offers some productive insights into the issue of presence in narrative, reframing it in terms of accessibility and thus outlining a much more nuanced way of understanding information as present in our mental representation of the storyworld. In what follows, I analyse Baricco's use of scripts in *City*, claiming that their activation further enhances the visibility of the spatial nature of the narrative experience by increasing the number of spaces potentially suggested to the reader. In the last section, I further support the argument of Baricco's strong penchant for spatiality by considering additional spatial conceptualisations in the novel, which resonate with the number of techniques through which Baricco taps into his readers' spatial skills.

Modes of presence

Understanding is not an input-output process. As work in cognitive psychology has amply demonstrated (Garrod and Sanford 1999; Sanford and Garrod 2009), discourse comprehension proceeds along with the intake of information, establishing immediate links between textual information and background knowledge in an admittedly shallow and partial fashion. In other words, the existence of a sort of threshold in the cognitive system has been posited, below which alternative interpretations, referential and semantic commitments keep on being monitored. Distinguishing proper propositional inferences from identifications of potential sites of reference enables a finer-grained understanding of the dynamics of narrative comprehension, and opens up to the claim that incomplete and fleeting inputs may still affect the process as a whole. In this light, it can be argued that some narratives are designed in a way such that these intermediate, liminal dynamics of discourse understanding are foregrounded. As will emerge from the remainder of the chapter and particularly from the discussion of Baricco's systematic exploitation of scripts, *City* indeed capitalises on the early phases of comprehension and builds on a cognitively rich and expanded notion of presence.

As anticipated in the introduction, the enactivist framework, which provides the background for both Noë's work on perception and Caracciolo's theories, is built on the core assumption that perception is not something that happens to us, but something we *do*. Perception is a 'skilful bodily activity' (Noë 2004: 2) that is performed not by the brain and sensory organs only, but by the animal as a whole. This theoretical position crucially endorses the hypothesis that our abstract thought evolved — both phylogenetically and ontogenetically — from prior forms of knowledge, elaborated through the sensorimotor system and from the experience of our body in space.

In his discussion of perception, Noë rejects the new-sceptic assumption that visual experience is picture-like and therefore 'sharply focused, uniformly detailed, and high-resolution' (2004: 35),[20] arguing instead that detail is present to our perception only virtually. He reformulates the issue of presence in terms of possibility to access the detail by focusing our attention on it, rather than of it being constantly and simultaneously present to our consciousness.[21] Noë distinguishes between perceptual awareness of and attended-to features in the world surrounding us: while attending to a specific feature means to move our attentional focus onto it, Noë makes the point that, even though the objects that fall outside our attentional focus cannot be distinguished in a detailed way (for example, we cannot really see the colour or exact features of objects outside our foveal region), we are still aware of their presence. Positing a continuum rather than two dichotomous categories, Noë suggests therefore that objects are not either fully present and highly-detailed or absent: perceptual presence is actually a much more nuanced activity.

A second modality of virtual presence pointed out by Noë is the amodal perception or presence in absence. This modality includes those cases when an object cannot be perceived because it is physically blocked from one's view. Consider, for instance, a cat in a neighbouring garden: even though one cannot really see it, one is aware that the cat 'continues' behind the picket fence. As Noë points out, one does not *believe* nor *think* the cat is a consistent whole: one *perceives* it as such. The example of Kanizsa's triangle (1955) is even more striking, as it demonstrates that viewers 'perceive the illusory contours of a triangle that is *not* there because the geometrical shapes arranged around it appear occluded' (Caracciolo 2014a: 169). This process takes place below the threshold of our conscious re-elaboration of perceptual inputs, and is thus deeply embedded in our cognitive functioning. To be amodally present, Noë argues, means to be 'present to perception as accessible' (2004: 63).

Although Noë's discussion concerns the phenomenology of perception, his examination bears some interesting similarities with narrative understanding. His investigation of amodal presence, for instance, actually explores the cognitive groundings of M.-L. Ryan's principle of minimal departure, by virtue of which 'readers are able to form reasonably comprehensive representations of the foreign worlds created through discourse, even though the verbal representation of these worlds is always incomplete' (1991: 52). Indeed, if incompleteness has always represented an undeniable feature of fictional storyworlds (for example, Ronen 1994), some hypotheses licensed by Noë's enactivist approach seem to suggest that, to a certain extent, this condition is not far from the way we experience the actual world. In fact, the similarities between the two processes concern the phenomenological level, thus leaving the ontological difference between the fictional and actual world unchallenged. This view prompts us to reconceptualise the problem of the presence of certain details in terms of accessibility and to foreground the question of how this presence may impinge on the understanding of the broader narrative sequence — which is the aspect I seek to illuminate with regard to Baricco's narrative technique.

Phenomenology of perception may lead to insights into narrative understanding because, according to the enactivist view, perception is also an activity irreducibly involved with sense-making and the elaboration of expectations.[22] Presence is to be understood as a matter of availability, rather than of actual representation: 'the world is within reach and is present only insofar as we know (or feel) that it is' (Noë 2004: 67). Similarly, it could be suggested that also in narrative this availability, the potential accessibility of knowledge activated through scripts, is not lost on the reader's cognizance: '*virtual* presence is a kind of presence, not a kind of non-presence or illusory presence', as Noë significantly clarifies (2004: 67), confirming the relevance of virtuality in the co-construction of storyworld and, thus, in narrative understanding.

As a general principle, it is my contention that the greater the impact of virtuality on plot understanding, the more markedly spatial is the narrative structure and its process of comprehension. The cognitive structure of plot gains in complexity when its understanding depends both on the paradigmatic interaction of narrative information with other non-actualised options and on the syntagmatic connections created by the chronological ordering of events. The management of this enhanced complexity requires navigation strategies that, in some narratives, are strongly biased in favour of specific processes. These strategies and processes could depend on the particular cognitive style of an author or on the features of the narrative, which might converge synergistically toward a particular image or cognitive domain. Bearing this in mind, let us revert to our case study and to the hypothesis of plot understanding in *City* as mapping.

How the barbarians think

Baricco's propensity to think and conceptualise in spatial terms constitutes a preferred mode that can not only be detected at the micro- and macro-levels in his novels but is also indirectly confirmed by his nonfictional writings. In a series of weekly articles that were first published in the newspaper *La Repubblica* between 12 May and 21 October 2006 and subsequently collected in the volume *I barbari* (published in 2006 and 2008), Baricco expresses his views on storytelling and on the ongoing changes in contemporary readership. Building on the features he pinpoints, it is possible to unveil interesting patterns within his own oeuvre and thus lend weight to the broader argument concerning the role of spatiality in processing narratives.

The barbarians identified by the title of his essay are those individuals who are born as readers at the beginning of the twenty-first century. According to Baricco, through the presence of these new readers in the literary system, readership is undergoing a collective mutation that involves expectations, values, and reasons for interest in approaching literature. The intellectual and academic milieu tends to look at this mutation with a sense of reproach and fear: this is the same attitude, Baricco suggests, with which established societies in the past may have looked at the arrival of hordes of barbarians at their borders. The author's core thesis is that this new generation of 'barbarian' readers distinguishes itself in two main respects: namely, a different idea of what experience is, and a different view as to where meaning lies and how it is distributed in experience. From these two tenets, Baricco derives the set of features that characterise the new readership and explores them through a number of accessible examples that range from the popularisation of wine culture to the cognitive changes brought about by the internet and digital technologies.

My intention here is not to assess the merits of Baricco's examination. In fact, similar suggestions can be found almost forty years earlier in Michel Foucault's lecture, given in 1967, on heterotopias — and it is no accident that this notion has already been mentioned in relation to *City* (Nicewicz 2009: 165; Rorato and Storchi 2004: 257). Foucault argued that

> the present epoch will perhaps be above all the epoch of space. We are in the epoch of simultaneity: we are in the epoch of juxtaposition, the epoch of the near and the far, of the side-by-side, of the dispersed. [1984/1986: 2]

Baricco's reflections are nonetheless interesting, partly because they represent a digestible folk version of ideas that were already circulating in philosophy and culture theory in relation to the postmodern (it should not be forgotten that the newspaper articles were meant to have a popular, non-specialist distribution and reception),[23] and mostly in relation to his own narrative practice.

One of the main shifts identified by Baricco is the privileged position accorded to horizontality rather than verticality, and to surface instead of depth. The barbarian, he remarks, would value experience inasmuch as it links together the largest number of experiences, not by focusing on a single aspect in a deeper way: 'La sua idea di esperienza è una traiettoria che tiene insieme tessere differenti del reale' (2008: 103 [Their idea of experience is like a trajectory that keeps reality together]). In other words, the more inclusive and multifarious the experience, the more powerful and engaging that experience will be. Closely related to this notion of experience is the conception of meaning, about which Baricco observes that to the barbarian readers '*un sistema è vivo quando il senso è presente ovunque e in maniera dinamica: se il senso è localizzato, e immobile, il sistema muore*' (56, emphasis in the original [the system is alive when meaning is everywhere and is produced dynamically: if meaning is localized and fixed, the system dies out]). Transferring this concept to the system-book, it follows that:

> La qualità di un libro, per i barbari, sta nella quantità di energia che quel libro è in grado di ricevere da altre narrazioni, e poi di riversare in altre narrazioni [...] Il libro, di per sé, non è un valore: il valore è la *sequenza*. [74]
>
> [For the barbarians, the quality of a book lies in the amount of energy that book is capable of receiving from and pouring back into other narratives [...]. The book per se has no value: its value lies in the *sequence*.]

Horizontality versus verticality, experience as trajectory, narrative as a system whose successful functioning significantly depends on the network of connections it establishes with other extra-textual sources of knowledge: spatial metaphors are used widely throughout the essay, and this should not be underestimated. Published fifteen years after Baricco's first novel *Castelli di rabbia* (1991) and seven years after *City*, *I barbari* is a useful subtext for his narrative production as it confirms that the reliance on mechanisms of narrative understanding that are ultimately rooted in sensorimotor knowledge is not casual. In fact, it reveals a consistent pattern in the cognitive strategies implemented in his narrative corpus.

This point leads to a necessary caveat. The interrelations between spatiality and contemporary culture and ideology have been a matter of extensive debate. Since the 1990s, however — that is, since computers and new media have spread massively and become commonly used — a specific strand of discussion has developed that is concerned with the implications of media upheaval within the humanities and the impact of digital technology on the way we think. Baricco himself muses on how the brains of 'barbarian' readers seem to have begun to work in a different way, to think in a different way. Although it is beyond the scope of this book, the hypothesis that digital technologies might have impacted in an evolutionarily unprecedented way on our cognitive capabilities is undoubtedly interesting, and it has been entertained by many researchers including Hadlington (2017), Hayles (2012) and M.-L. Ryan (2001) and pursued by new disciplines like Digital Humanities.

The most relevant aspect for the present work is that, irrespective of how he may frame it within broader dynamics, Baricco conceptualises this paradigmatic shift in spatial terms, by tapping into the sensorimotor knowledge of recipients (readers of his fictional and nonfictional writing alike) in order to make sense of this mutation. Indeed, both the 'old' way of thinking and the new barbarian way are explained by means of spatial metaphors: the shift is not from a time-based to a space-based way of making sense, but from a predominance of verticality to a predominance of horizontality. It is true that, according to Baricco, barbarian notions of meaning and experience emphasise spatiality over temporality because they are non-hierarchically distributed, and, for this reason, he programmatically designs his narratives to work synergistically with what he considers the preferred cognitive strategies employed by his readership. Nonetheless, this does not change the fact that the embodied nature of abstract thought is not something developed over the past decades due to the passage from the Age of Print to the Age of Digital Media (Hayles 2012), but rather something inherent in our cognition, the visibility of which might be variably foregrounded by an author's cognitive style or by his or her cultural agenda.

Scripts as means to create energy

Paraphrasing some of his observations reported above, it could be said that, for Baricco, the narrativity of a written story critically depends on the 'quantity of energy' it creates or circulates, from and to other stories. What does it mean, though, in narratological terms, to 'create energy' or to 'receive energy from other stories'? And how does this relate to the spatialisation of narrative understanding? In the remainder of this chapter, I explore the hypothesis that both issues are linked to how the narrative draws on background knowledge in order to be actualised. The working assumption is that, even if Baricco may not share the barbarians' point of view on literature thoroughly, it is likely that he follows some of these principles in order to appeal what he describes as a significant part of contemporary readership.

Since for the new readers the value of experience resides in its amount and variety, most appreciated are those books that provide the reader with multiple stimuli rather than analysing fewer in more depth (2008: 136). The energy praised by Baricco should be understood in terms of stimuli, and stimuli are in fact pieces of information, which are not provided by the text and which the narrative cues its readers to retrieve. The second asset consists in the variety of sources of such stimuli: in this regard, Baricco observes that 'i barbari tendono a leggere solo i libri le cui istruzioni per l'uso sono date in posti che NON sono libri' (2008: 69; de-italicised [barbarians tend to read only books whose 'instructions' are to be found in places OTHER THAN books]). Before considering how this information is diversified and provided in large amounts, let us turn to the bridge between 'text knowledge' and 'world knowledge' in the first place, a bridge that is built by the mechanism known as script. Below, I first sketch a preliminary theoretical description of the concept, which I then explore in greater detail through its practical applications in the novel.

In its most essential definition, a script is a 'standardized generalized episode' (Schank and Abelson 1977: 19). The notion is inherited from schema theory, a branch of cognitive sciences initiated in Gestalt psychology during the 1920s and 1930s, then revived and further expanded in the 1970s within AI research (Gavins 2005). Indeed, it is within this framework that Roger Schank and Robert Abelson carry out their studies, and in his *Dictionary of Narratology* (2003 (1987)) Gerald Prince dates the first systematic use of this notion back to them:[24]

> A script is made up of slots and requirements about what can fill those slots. The structure is an interconnected whole, and what is in one slot affects what can be in another. [...] Thus, a script is a predetermined, stereotyped sequence of actions that defines a well-known situation. Scripts allow for new references to objects within them just as if these objects had been previously mentioned. [Schank and Abelson 1977: 41]

Drawing on their research on episodic memory, Schank and Abelson posit the starting assumption that memory relies on situations (personally) experienced rather than on abstract semantic categories. It follows, the two scholars argue, that there must be 'a procedure for recognizing repeated or similar sequences' (1977: 18): the elaboration of scripts is precisely the economical measure thanks to which we are able to identify these patterns, store them in our memory, and retrieve them whenever we need to draw on them again. If we had to process everything we experience every time as if it were the first time, we would most likely not survive.

Schank and Abelson clearly state that relying on the concept of script already sets the implicit premise that world knowledge does not simply enrich or flavour the text, it enables understanding itself. Understanding — a pragmatic situation as well as a written or oral communication — does not depend only on the elements at stake, but on the recipient's background knowledge. Hence Schank and Abelson's definition of understanding as 'a process by which people match what they see and hear to pre-stored groupings of actions that they have already experienced' (1977: 67).[25] Understanding, in other words, is knowledge-based, and scripts are 'knowledge structures' that serve understanding.

Debates in literary criticism during the 1990s mark a migration of these concepts from research in artificial intelligence to the investigation of narrative (Fludernik 1996; Gerrig and Egidi 2003; Jahn 1997; M.-L. Ryan 1991; van Dijk 1979).[26] In the present discussion I mainly draw on Herman's (1997 and 2002) theorisation, which effectively integrates scripts within narratology and acknowledges their role as crucial strategies implemented by readers to negotiate narrative texts,[27] as they enable to 'build up complex (semantic) representations of stories on the basis of very few textual or linguistic cues' (2002: 97). In turn, these cues variably work as 'headers' — that is, words or concepts that, being closely involved with the action sequence of a certain script, prompt the reader to retrieve it from memory and activate it, or instantiate it (Schank and Abelson 1977: 48).

Even if all narratives ultimately rely on readers' background knowledge and on the instantiation of scripts in order to be understood, a writer's narrative style can still be typified by the use of scripts. Relying on these mechanisms is a matter of degree and extent rather than the exclusive province of a certain narrative or genre: Baricco employs scripts extensively and capitalises on the related cognitive mechanisms in a peculiar way and to pursue effects that are worth further examination. In particular, my analysis illuminates the elements within the scripts' structure on which Baricco intervenes and how these practices match with an overall foregrounding of the spatial dimension of narrative apprehension.

I mentioned earlier Scarsella's comment on the narrative in *City* as built on the alternation of styles. In fact, not only are changes in style indices of contextual-frame shifts, but in some cases styles also become associated with specific recurring contexts. Rather than a choice about rhetoric, this association is due precisely to Baricco's reliance on scripts in constructing his narrative situations. Some of the scripts more evidently exploited in *City* include the diner, the football match, the lecture, the phone call, the boxing match, the running commentary, the interview, the chase. Another set of scripts derives from Shatzy's adoption of the western genre for her story, which conventionally implies certain codified situations and roles: this is why the reference to '*the* saloon', with the definite article, does not find us lost, even though it had not been mentioned before in the text.

Indeed, a script is not simply made of sequences of actions. It also includes objects which belong to the stereotypical setting or are involved in the action, and roles played by participants. This relation between details and domain knowledge — that is, between headers and scripts — has been object of specific research. Evelyn Ferstl and Walter Kintsch (1999) carried out experiments in which participants were prompted to provide lists of words associated with a script. Their results confirmed that large parts of these lists overlapped, thus leading to the elaboration of the concept of domain knowledge as a set of concepts — objects, roles, settings — stereotypically associated with a standard script. Naturally, the reverse relationship also holds, and any word or concept belonging to a certain domain of knowledge could function as a header instantiating the script. This means that a role conventionally attached to a script — for example, a waiter in a restaurant — can be mentioned without this causing any problem to the recipient (Sanford and Garrod

2009). All these elements — codified actions, objects, and roles — can potentially be headers and they can all potentially invoke a script.[28]

Let us consider, for instance, the first of the boxing episodes in *City* (66–68 [61–64]). This narrative strand focuses on Larry 'Lawyer' Gorman, a rising star of boxing, and his coach Mondini: the two characters are imaginary figures created by Gould in his struggle against loneliness, originating from the memory of the only activity he shared with his father when they still lived together and used to listen to boxing matches on the radio. At the time the narrative is set, Gould has developed the habit of re-enacting scenes with Larry and Mondini as direct protagonists and of mimicking the running commentary of Larry's matches to entertain himself when he sits on the toilet ('E quel che si sentiva da fuori era la [...] sua voce che faceva delle voci', 66 [And what she heard from outside was [...] his voice imitating other voices, 61]). The first time the reader is presented with this embedded story, the narrative voice simply introduces Shatzy eavesdropping Gould in the bathroom, after which a dialogue ensues:

— Non siamo al tuo college del cazzo, lo sai Larry? ... Guardami, e respira ... andiamo, respira ... E VACCI PIANO CON QUELLA ROBA, CRISTO!
— Ha il sopracciglio a pezzi, Maestro. [66]

['We're not at your fucking college, Larry, you know? Look at me and breathe ... come on, breathe ... AND GO SLOW WITH THAT STUFF, CHRIST!'
'Your eyebrow's a mess, Maestro'] [61][29]

As it proceeds, an increasing number of headers (in other words, script-related cues) are offered to the reader: the vaseline on Larry's face, the bruised eyebrow and hand, the physical strain, the need to go towards someone's punches, the onomatopoeia of the boxing bell, the jargon ('sinistro al fegato e montante'; 'guardia', 67 [left to the liver and uppercut; defence, 62]). All these elements concur to fully instantiate the boxing-match script, they progressively lead the reader to deduce that the dialogue is between a boxer named Larry and his coach, and that the conversation is taking place during a break in between two rounds. Once recognised, the script also retrospectively gives meaning to the details that may have remained obscure at a first reading. Whenever references to this sport appear again over the narrative, the reader quickly realises that the narrative strand of Larry and Mondini has been taken up again and is prompted to instantiate a compatible situational script.

However, even taking into account their frequency, such uses are quite normal — if not unavoidable — and would not yet justify the hypothesis that Baricco's narratives are characterised by a distinctive implementation of scripts. Two main points are advanced to support this argument: the first one is that the systematic and peculiar way in which Baricco capitalises on standardised knowledge structures matches the theoretical principle expounded in *I barbari* according to which surpluses of narrative energy are valuable and increase the story's narrativity; secondly, I will show that scripts play a critical role in encouraging the spatial conceptualisation of *City*'s plot structure, thus fruitfully integrating with other strategies implemented at other levels.

Balancing referentiality and stereotypicality

The extensive use of scripts plays an essential role in the working of the novel and Baricco intertwines their two main functions in a nuanced and sophisticated way. Drawing on Schank and Abelson's definition quoted above, since a script is a 'predetermined, *stereotyped* sequence' that allows for 'new *references*' to objects (1977: 41 — my emphases), stereotypicality and referentiality are the key properties at stake.

The latter property, referentiality, provides the basis for the broadest and more canonical type of scripts. When the main function of a script is referentiality — which is the quality of containing references, or affordances to references — it means that its main purpose is to provide the necessary background for the narrative to unfold, as happens with the boxing match. Instantiating a script enables the narrator to refer to certain objects or roles as if they had been previously mentioned, as the saloon in the western story or adults who sit shouting on the side-lines of the soccer pitch. Once the right script is activated, no reader would fail to integrate these details correctly into the narrative.

This canonical use of script, however, gains particular visibility in *City* because of how the novel's structure is fragmented into multiple storylines, plus the abrupt shifts and relocations from one to the other, both of which require the reader constantly to re-establish new connections with different contexts with very little explicit Orientation. Baricco's systematic use of stereotypical and commonly known settings or channels (such as with instrumental scripts, like a phone call or lecture) is not accidental, because recognisability and immediacy of connections are among its target values. The series of anecdotes recounted in the Prologue, for instance, achieve coherence once they are understood as parts of a dialogue between Shatzy and Gould. However, the only way for the reader to make this inference depends on two isolated references to a hamburger (23, 29 [17, 22]) that are part of brief exchanges that have a twofold purpose: first, they lead to the identification of Shatzy and Gould as participants of the dialogue, by priming the setting of the diner to where Gould invites Shatzy during their initial telephone conversation; secondly, by referring to two subsequent moments during the meal, the two references situate the conversation in time, giving the reader a sense of chronological unfolding. Even though the overall effect might be a blurry succession of disconnected stories, the scenes are in fact anchored into a reasonable narrative structure that is recognisable only thanks to a systematic use of scripts. The immediate recognition and semantic connections ensured by scripts afford an agile and swift narration that perfectly matches with the rationale attached to the new readership illustrated in *I barbari*.

However, it is by playing with the second function of scripts — stereotypicality — that Baricco achieves the most interesting narrative effects.[30] There are two juxtaposed ways in which Baricco relies on stereotypicality: either he prompts stereotypicality only to undermine it utterly, with a defamiliarising reversal of perspective; or he fully embraces it, thus re-establishing a bond with the reader but also triggering interesting consequences as far as the spatial apprehension of the narrative is concerned.

Let us focus on the former type — that is, those cases where Baricco leverages the stereotypicality of a script, only immediately to challenge the ensuing standard horizon of expectations. Richard Gerrig and Giovanna Egidi (2003) note that scripts have the additional advantage of prompting the reader to focus on what departs from the norm, because their activation allows the writer to take for granted what is stereotypically included in a script and to report only what it unusual. Baricco, instead, forces the unusual to emerge precisely from disruptions of the stereotypical features of scripts. Rather than letting the reader down, however, these disruptions arguably achieve the opposite effect of renewing the reader's engagement praised in *I barbari* because they break the expected linearity of a message:

> Guardava una televisione. [...] Shatzy lo guardò.
> — Non aspettarti un granché, ma comunque se l'accendi migliora. [123]

> [He was watching television. [...] Shatzy looked at him.
> 'Don't expect much, but it would be an improvement if you at least turned it on.'] [123]

Here, the infraction is performed on the level of rhetoric by suddenly shifting the focus from one element of the metonymic pair, programme–television, to the other. If brief, the surprise effect is catchy.

Within the broader upsurge in research on discourse comprehension over the past thirty years, an increasing number of works have focused on the management of unexpected or inconsistent information, drawing on a range of disciplines from linguistics to psychology. Isabella Tapiero and José Otero (1999: 344) report that experiments carried out by different research teams converge on registering an improvement of memory for inconsistent items. Indeed, 'lexical items are recognized more quickly when they are unexpected, that is, preceded by a nonpredictive context, compared to a predictive context (Cairns, Cowart, and Jablon 1981; O'Brien and Myers 1985)'. The impact that these empirical findings could have on script theory is suggested by Tapiero and Otero themselves who observe that 'information that did not fit an instantiated schema [in other words, a script] received more extensive processing than conventional prototypical information' (ibid.). In other words, on the one hand, scripts enable basic discourse comprehension; on the other, when instantiated in unconventional ways they are likely to enhance the interpreter's engagement further.

The hypothesis that Baricco purposely capitalises on challenged stereotypicality gathers momentum when one considers the variety of its instantiations. The passage on the television quoted above relies on a reversal of perspective based on rhetoric, but there are cases in which the disruption of expectations affects stereotypicality at a deeper semantic level and over a prolonged narrative sequence. Chapter 14, for instance, opens with direct speech over three pages involving Shatzy, a diner clerk and Gould (106–09), and the script is immediately instantiated by a highly recognisable exchange that starts the procedure of placing an order. What follows, however, is an escalation in absurdity, in which the food-order script gets distorted by the stolid pertinacity displayed by the clerk in luring an unwilling Shatzy into a loop of bargains and special offers that would result in her having much more food than she wants, based on the fact that it is free. The action-sequence prescribed by the script is not itself undermined but, thanks to its potential for protracting the negotiation indefinitely, it rather becomes the instrumental vessel for conveying the sense of utter alienation that capitalism brings into a supposedly straightforward procedure such as ordering only the amount of food one needs. In this case, the disruption of stereotypicality is determined by the fact that the two participants playing interlocking roles regulated by the order script actually draw on two different systems of values and priorities:

— Questa settimana per ogni dessert ordinato ce n'è un altro in regalo.
— Splendido.
— Cosa prendi?
— Niente, grazie.
— Ma *devi* prenderlo, è in regalo.
— Non mi piacciono i dessert, non li voglio.
— Ma io *devo* dartelo. [107][31]

['This week, for every dessert you order you get a second one free.'
'Splendid.'
'What do you want?'
'Nothing, thanks."
'But you *have* to take it, they're giving it away.'
'I don't like desserts, I don't want it.'
'But I *have* to give it to you.'] [105]

Experimental evidence in linguistics concerning the engaging potential of unexpected information comes in support of similar hypotheses also advanced by scholars commonly referenced in narrative studies. Cognitive psychologist Bruner, for instance, lists 'breach of canonicity' among his ten features of narrative and refers specifically to Schank and Abelson's notion of script when he states that it is only when the script is 'breached, violated or deviated' (1991: 11) that one can properly speak of narrativity — that is to say that a situation becomes worth telling about (compare also Polanyi 1979).

Let us consider a second episode: Gould is interviewed by a television troupe meant to shoot a video on child prodigies (114–21 [113–20]). In a chapter mostly composed of dialogue, the disrupting element is given by the fact that Poomerang and Diesel take part in the conversation between Gould and the interviewer. At this point of the narrative, although it has not been explicitly stated, it is increasingly clear to the reader that the two friends of Gould are actually imaginary projections of Gould himself. As the interviewer proceeds to ask questions, Gould delegates his answers to Diesel and Poomerang, who offer long and articulated replies; however, from the reactions and comments of the interviewer it soon emerges that all she witnesses is a boy staring silently at her, limiting himself to awkwardly reassuring her that he feels fine and does not seem to understand her uneasiness. The result is a narrative that, after invoking the interview script, is deconstructed into a double thread: the actual one, which is a failed interview, and the virtual one, experienced from Gould's perspective and inclusive of Diesel's and Poomerang's comments, which respects the action sequences and roles prescribed by the interview script.

In addition to its subversion of the stereotypical features of the interview script, this episode is particularly interesting because it overtly foregrounds virtuality. The disruption of the script creates two overlapping mental images, one of the scene as experienced by the interviewer and one of the scene as experienced by Gould; the latter one, however, is virtual inasmuch as it is a product of Gould's imagination, artfully interacting with his perception of actuality. The reader's experience embraces them both and is enriched by the added value provided by their comparison: the narrativity of the story does not come from either of the two perspectives taken separately, but only from their joined juxtaposition. I shall consider later further reasons why virtuality plays a relevant role in the narrative experience of this novel.

In the examples just examined, scripts are evoked because of their stereotypicality which, however, is promptly subverted, thus creating the opportunity to boost the reader's attention and unexpectedly enhancing the narrativity of the situation. Conversely, a second way to exploit a script's stereotypicality stems from embracing it overtly and unambiguously. Since stereotypicality is exploited for its immediate recognisability, it might look like this type of use is similar to the first one, characterised by pre-eminence of a referential function. Although, here — in contrast to the first type — the elements invoked are not so much intended to provide utilitarian background knowledge (cf. Prince 2008: 124) as to play an engaging role.

When Diesel and Poomerang rummage through Dr Mortensen's room, they spot a selection of objects each of which is meant to convey a clear message about its owner (25–26 [19–20]): the bed mat signifies a comfortable life, arguably economically solid enough (as the bed mat is not a necessary item) without being glamorous (the implicit impression that the colour is dull); the incomplete novel is a reminder of failed aspirations to art and originality; the business card marked with lipstick alludes to a love affair, probably in the work environment; the radio-alarm which is set to Radio Nostalgia almost too overtly refers to the constant feeling of dissatisfaction and regret; on the bedside-table lies a religious-oriented leaflet that focuses on a relatively petty issue like the morality of fishing and hunting rather than revealing a troubled interior quest for spirituality. Far from aiming at realism here, objects almost become symbols. In fact, each object is mentioned to work as a header and to create a direct link with a whole context, a whole situation codified by narrative clichés or folk psychology. Technically speaking, these potential digressions should be gathered under the rubric of 'fleeting-scripts', coined by Schank and Abelson (1977: 47) — namely, scripts whose headers are called up but which are not properly instantiated, as the narrative does not provide any inputs connecting with events prescribed by the standard episode.

Another instance of scripts used to emphasise their stereotypicality can be identified in the narrator's description of Gould's house, which ends with the following summarising sentence:

> L'impressione generale era quella di una casa signorile dove l'FBI era passata a cercare un microfilm con le scopate del Presidente in un bordello del Nevada. [32]

[The general impression was of a house belonging to rich people where the FBI had gone to look for a microfilm of the president screwing in a Las Vegas brothel.] [24]

Clearly, the referents are not to be taken literally, as Gould surely has nothing to do with the FBI or any presidential affair. The only plausible reason for such a choice, I suggest, is the vivid stereotypicality of the image: thanks to its topic and its visual effectiveness, the image establishes a link in the first place with the cinematic medium. By using it, Baricco cues the reader to activate a pointer to a script — unnecessary to the unfolding of the current narrative — which immediately multiplies the narrative experience by creating connections not only with another medium, but also with a whole other genre, that of the crime or political scandal scenario. The specificity of the references (a microfilm rather than some photos; the determinate article in referring to *the* President; the geographical location of the brothel) stimulates the outlining of a digression in the form of a basic story, despite being obviously unrelated to the narrative that the reader is currently engaged with. The effect is quite close to that achieved in the previous example, where the selected objects almost create a tacit parallel story of Dr Mortensen. In both cases, the non-instantiated reference to highly stereotyped scenarios enriches the narrative by means of its virtual presence within the cognitive horizon of the reader.

Taking a step back and looking at the taxonomy of scripts' uses outlined so far, scripts can be instantiated by foregrounding their referential function or their stereotypical function. The first case encompasses more canonical uses of scripts, which are invoked in order to provide an immediate and recognisable referential background to the narrative; their use represents a distinctive strategy for Baricco because he systematically relies on them to maintain the intelligibility of a fragmented and multilinear narrative. The second way focuses on stereotypicality, which, in turn, can be invoked either to be challenged or complied with. The two strategies prompt two different types of narrative experience as they trigger different modifications of the narrative structure as it is understood by readers. A reversal of perspective like that operated on the metonymic pair programme/television — that is, in cases of subverted stereotypicality — amounts to a paradigmatic branching of the narrative into two counterfactual unfoldings, the one originally expected and the one actually instantiated.[32] As remarked also in relation to the episode of the interview, the reader holds both forking paths activated in mind and the additional information stems precisely from contrasting and comparing the two options (Riddle Harding 2007 and 2011) — hence, the enhanced engagement. By contrast, when stereotypicality is complied with, the result is that the narrative hints at diverging unexplored narrations, rather than at counterfactual scenarios. If the previous use aims at foregrounding the discrepancy between counterfactual expectations and fictional actuality, here we have a syntagmatic extension of the narrative structure and the partial activation of a completely new and seemingly 'unnecessary' surplus of narrative inputs which remain liminal to the actual narrative.

Before concluding this section of the discussion, I shall briefly comment on the close relation between *City* and Baricco's nonfictional work *I barbari*, as indeed many of the strategies implemented in this novel align with ideas that will be later elaborated in terms of 'creation of new energy'. The values of swiftness and connectivity are pursued through a narration that shifts from contextual frame to contextual frame as smoothly as possible. The decision of frequently moving between storylines does not follow from the need to keep track of quickly changing scenarios, but rather from a specific storytelling style that privileges short and dense scenes juxtaposed over prolonged narrative passages. In *I barbari*, Baricco seeks to identify the principle that keeps a narrative machinery going for the barbarian reader. To say it with the terminology employed in this book, he seeks for a generalised principle of narrativity that might fit a contemporary readership, writing that,

> Il propellente di quel movimento è fornito, anche, dai punti in cui passa: che non consumano energia, [...] ma la forniscono. In pratica il barbaro ha delle chances di costruire vere sequenze di esperienza solo se a ogni stazione del suo viaggio riceve una spinta ulteriore: non sono stazioni, sono sistemi passanti che generano accelerazione. [2008: 136]

> [The fuel for that movement is also provided by the stations it passes through, which do not consume energy [...] but rather provide it. In other words, barbarians have the opportunity to build meaningful sequences only if at each station of its journey they are pushed further on: more than stations, they are a system that creates continuous acceleration.]

In this light, a fragmented narrative that divides the reading experience into several smaller chunks better suits the barbarian notion of maximised experience. Subversion of the stereotypicality of scripts — be they rhetorical, semantic or discursive — thus succeeds in transmitting that 'acceleration' through the swift reversal of expectations. Straightforward exploitations of stereotypicality, finally, inject additional stimuli into the narrative, building the impression of a network expanding beyond the boundaries of one specific story. Baricco systematically employs scripts to purposely surround *City*'s storylines of a halo of potential narrative material, virtually present and yet left unexplored.

Further spatial conceptualisations in City

To make sense of a narrative according to a spatial-oriented paradigm is not an all-or-nothing affair. Although I would call for a general rethinking of the definition of plot according to more flexible criteria that do not unavoidably assume chronology as the main organising principle, I do not argue that this paradigm has to always be confined to spatiality. Throughout this chapter, however, I have sought to introduce the theoretical groundings for a spatial-oriented understanding of plot comprehension and, at the same time, to show how *City* represents a productive example of narrative that stimulates readers to adopt spatial-oriented strategies for plot understanding. Among the elements endorsing such a hypothesis I have so far pinpointed the image of the urban space as cognitive metaphor to make sense of the fragmented narrative; the embodiment of the process of contextual monitoring and the engagement of readers' virtual body; the impression, enhanced by means of a skilful use of scripts, of the narrative structure as a space to be explored, a space potentially larger than the one defined by the storyworld actually co-constructed by the text of *City*.

The spatial metaphor of urban space proposed in the blurb of the novel, where Baricco writes that his novel is built like a city, is also further elaborated in the narrative through the words of Shatzy. The alignment between cues in the paratext and at thematic level corroborates the idea of the text as designed to prompt a certain spatial-oriented mode of understanding in its readers:

> Tutte quelle storie sulla tua strada. Trovare la tua strada. Andare per la tua strada. Magari invece [...] sono gli altri le strade, io sono una piazza, non porto in nessun posto, io *sono* un posto. [186]
>
> [All that nonsense about your road. Finding your road. Taking your own road. Maybe [...] others are roads, I am a plaza, I lead nowhere, I *am* a place.] [189]

Operating once again a reversal of perspective and deconstructing the common saying of 'finding one's way', Baricco advocates for his characters the possibility of being places themselves, rather than entities that have to go to places. It is worth remarking that this shift does not exclude potential existential development: the juxtaposition of being a place vs. going somewhere does not amount to static vs. dynamic, nor to flat vs. round characters. What is undermined, instead, is the established cognitive metaphor equating 'change' with 'movement forward'. If characters can be places, then they may appeal to readers inasmuch as they can be explored.

On the other hand, the metaphor of 'life as a journey' (Dannenberg 2008: 67–85; Turner 1996: 88–90), after being apparently rejected, returns in the description of Gould's life as a river to be navigated (219–21 [221–23]). The oscillations in the use of this metaphor suggest that the author is less interested in the search for a metaphor that uniquely captures a truthful view of life, and more in dismantling conventional metaphors and exploring multiple ways of cognizing experience and reality by building on the ensuing estrangement. In fact, the image of life as a river is used to contest, not the direction forward, but the linearity of movement as desirable condition: like meanders, apparently meaningless digressions and diversions might be regarded not as unwanted distractions but as the best or the only way to proceed. Baricco casts doubt on linearity as an absolutely positive value, subverting the assumption that everything should be assessed on the basis of its distance from unshaken straightforwardness. Projecting this idea onto narrative, we could interpret it as the endorsement of a notion of plot that is not inherently linear and whose organising principle cannot be chronology or causality only but has to admit for more complex dynamics.

Although they prompt interesting observations, 'characters as places' and 'stories as roads' are fairly linear metaphors, as they both involve analogical relationships between basic-level concepts.[33] As it describes the spatial configuration of a thought, the following example is more complex:

> *Sto vedendo un pensiero*, pensò Gould.
> I pensieri quando pensano nella forma dell'interrogazione. Rimbalzano deambulando per raccogliere intorno tutti i cocci della domanda, secondo un

> percorso che sembra casuale e fine a se stesso. Quando hanno ricomposto la domanda si fermano. Occhi al canestro. Silenzio. Stacco da terra, l'intuizione carica tutta la forza necessaria a ricucire la lontananza da una possibile risposta. Tiro. Fantasia e ragione. Nell'aria sfila la parabola logico-deduttiva di un pensiero che ruota su se stesso sotto l'effetto di una frustata di polso impressagli dall'immaginazione. Canestro. La pronuncia della risposta: come una specie di respiro. Pronunciarla è perderla. Scivola via ed è già cocci rimbalzanti della prossima domanda. Da capo. [189–90]
>
> > [*I am seeing a thought*, Gould thought.
> > Thoughts when they take the form of a question. They bounce, strolling around to pick up all the fragments of the question, following a course that seems random, an end in itself. When they have reconstructed the question they stop. Eyes on the basket. Silence. Lifted off the ground, intuition gives it all the strength necessary to sew up the distance to a possible response. Shoot. Fantasy and reason. In the air unrolls the logically deduced parabola of a thought sent spinning by a flick of the wrist initiated by the imagination. Basket. The statement of the response: a sort of breath. To state it is to lose it. It slips away and already it is the bouncing pieces of the next question. From the beginning.] [192]

In this case, an action-pattern is mapped onto the cognitive activity that underpins the elaboration of a thought, which Gould identifies in terms of starting point, trajectory, and target. This action-pattern, integrating space and time, stands out as strongly embodied. Its organising principle is deeply rooted in sensorimotor knowledge because narrativity is conveyed through the shared experience of a pattern of sequenced movements of the body in space. Another passage confirms this typifying trend of Baricco's cognitive style:

> il tiepido lampo, che gli arroventa la coscienza e si abbatte sulla recinzione della sua narcosi da uomo stancamente sposato, con gran rumore di lamiere e lamenti. [25]
>
> [the warm flash [...] burning his consciousness and breaking on the defences of his stupor — the stupor of a wearily married man — with a loud crash of metal and lament.] [19]

The adjective 'married' indexes the state of affairs of 'being married', which entails a history, a sequence of previous necessary actions defined by a script — meeting, engagement, marriage — but conceptualises them in terms of a space around which a boundary has been built, and connotes it negatively by describing it as a narcotic state. The glimpse of the beautiful woman in the taxi is described in terms of something immaterial (a flash) that hits something material (the boundary) and nonetheless exerts a very material effect on it, provoking a loud metallic noise that is associated, in our world knowledge, with something solid, like iron, crashing.

All these examples display the same cognitive strategy underpinning narrativity: Baricco starts from a nucleus, a state of affairs or an event, and then unfolds it, turning it into a space to explore and conceptualising the transformations it undergoes in terms of steps to retrace or parts to describe. My further suggestion is that the same strategy is applied to the novel as a whole: *City* portrays the existential impasse of the main character, Gould, and explores it as if it were a urban space. By offering the image of the city in the title, Baricco designs a text that encourages readers to assume that the spatial relations holding between the various narrative strands composing *City* are more important, in order to achieve an understanding of the narrative as a whole, than the temporal relations of cause-and-effect. As a city can be known only piecemeal by means of individual practice and exploration, so this narrative is to be understood by comparing and contrasting its characters and their stories. As I have sought to illustrate in this chapter, this cognitive metaphor does not stand alone: it is backed up by additional strategies that emphasise the embodiment of narrative understanding as an exploration practice and therefore work synergistically with the image of the city to be walked through.

Although some narrative strands do not even interact with each other, they are all variously related to the same centre, the protagonist Gould. Particularly significant are the embedded storylines created by Gould's own imagination. They capture and dramatise his reactions to the world around him, at a stage where he is not ready yet to act on them in reality. Larry's training before the final boxing match with Poreda, which would mark Larry's definitive entrance to the world of professional boxing, is recounted exactly when Gould is uncertain about whether to accept the place offered by the prestigious university of Couverney, which would mean to embrace his destiny as child prodigy (180–83 [182–85]): in a three-page stream of consciousness, Larry's thoughts exhibit a mix of pride, ambition, childlike desire for approval, and fear of failure, which correspond exactly to Gould's feelings about his own future. Along the same lines, Larry seems to finally win when Gould is on a train running toward an unknown destination, away from Couverney (240 [243]). The fact that Gould is consciously modelling Larry's story dampens the metanarrative effect of *mise en abyme* and rather looks like a psychological strategy implemented by the boy to cope with reality.[34]

To some extent, a similar analysis could be applied to Shatzy and her story. Motives and stylistic details of the Western stem directly from small triggers and events in her everyday life: the syntactic rhythm characterising the beginning of the chapter on the prostitute of Closingtown comes from an old song she once learnt (85, 93 [82, 89]); the story of Fanny and Pat Cobhan issues from the mere desire to design a story that could be suitably concluded with a verse of a poem Shatzy liked, 'Muoiono nello stesso respiro, gli amanti' (92 [89]); the twin sisters Dolphin copycat the twin sisters at the Ideal House Exhibition of her childhood (43 [36]). Unlike those of Gould, Shatzy's stories seem to come from a desire to imagine dramatized versions of her life rather than from her inability to deal with it. At any rate, both her and Gould's imaginary productions result in a re-assertion of the power of imagination and storytelling.

Yet, a careful look reveals that *City*'s design is made more complex by the fact that the relationship between storylines is not always straightforward. The stories imagined by Gould do not serve to understand Gould only, just as the Western invented by Shatzy illuminates her character and even more Gould and his mother Ruth. The embedded Western narrative tells the story of Closingtown, a windswept town on the edge of the desert, none of whose inhabitants can die because their destinies are stuck and Time has stopped. The city's destiny is closely associated with that of a giant clock — the Old Man — which was built by the city founders but no longer works; however, as the watchmaker Phil Wittacher discovers, the clock is not broken but has, rather, stopped. In the final part of the novel, the reader finds out that the narrative voice of Shatzy's Western is actually Gould's mother, Ruth, hospitalised in a mental healthcare institution where Shatzy has worked for a few years as a nurse after Gould's disappearance. During one of the breaks from storytelling, Ruth admits a certain parallelism between Closingtown and her own mental situation:

> Lo stesso prof. Parmentier, una volta, mi disse che, se questo mi aiutava, potevo immaginare quello che mi succedeva in testa come qualcosa di non molto diverso da Closingtown. Succede che qualcosa strappa il Tempo, [...] Diceva che questa era la mia malattia, volendo. Julie Dolphin la chiamava: smarrire il proprio destino. Ma quello era il West: si potevano ancora dire, certe cose. [260]

> [Prof. Parmentier himself, once, told me that, if it was helpful, I could think of what was happening in my head as something not very different from Closingtown. Something tears Time, [...] He said that that was my illness, if you like. Julie Dolphin called it: losing your own destiny. But that was the West: certain things could still be said.] [265]

Embedded narratives and parallel storylines are used to provide alternative contexts that allow to frame in a clearer way issues that are too complex or painful to be directly looked at in the (fictional) actual storyworld — or, simply, to frame them from a different perspective: in a world governed by science, a doctor could never describe a disease in terms of 'losing one's destiny', as is possible in a Western story.

Closingtown, as the epitome of a state of existential impasse, can be related to both Ruth and to her son Gould. Baricco stresses the difference between being broken and stopped, and his emphasis encourages to extend the validity of the consideration beyond its local reference to the clock. Gould's existential struggle is also rephrased in the narrative strand involving him and Prof. Taltomar, where it is summed up by the formula: 'O guardi o giochi' (120 [Either you watch or you play, 120]). And indeed, the moment that marks Gould's resolution to embrace life and its uncertainties instead of remaining on the path traced for him as child prodigy, is depicted as a mechanism getting suddenly unjammed: for the first time, looking at a ball bouncing towards him, he abandons the usual stillness, takes the ball, and kicks it back into the park. In other words, he ceases to be unresponsive and responds to the external world's inputs.

As soon as Gould's impasse is overcome, the narrative ends: the storyworld develops into uncharted territory. The map traced by the plot so far would no longer be the same as it was revolving around the mapping process of Gould's state of mind and his emotional state prior to his decision to break with his destiny as child prodigy.

★ ★ ★ ★ ★

In this chapter I have built on an examination of Baricco's novel *City* to outline a first type of plot the organising principle of which is rooted in spatiality. This type is epitomised by the image of the map because it potentially includes narratives that aim at portraying a dynamic equilibrium, the point of which is less to follow the narrative development of the states of affairs characterising a storyworld than to explore its premises or conditions. Understanding this type of plot involves strategies that can be associated with spatiality because comprehension critically depends on the mutual interrelations between parts rather than on their causal or chronological unfolding. As a provisional generalisation, it could be hypothesised that fragmented narratives are more likely to rely on spatially-oriented strategies than those which are not, because their disjointed structure already disrupts linearity. However, this is neither a necessary nor a sufficient condition for a plot to be deemed as spatial: in fact, in the next chapter I consider how the understanding of crime fiction plots may be regarded as spatially-based even though fragmentation does not enter the picture.

By contrast, virtuality stands out as an undeniably relevant factor of spatial plots. In *City*, virtuality is called for by the over-instantiation of scripts, which augments the domain of referents present to the reader's consciousness despite not being fully actualised in the storyworld, and by the embodiment of processes of narrative comprehension — in other words, contextual monitoring. In the next chapter, I continue the exploration of potential conditions for plot understanding to be deemed as spatial, arguing that virtuality can be emphasised also by other means than through the instantiation of scripts. Similarly, the fictionalisation of the reader's body and/or cognitive activities will be reasserted as a practice that impacts on the spatially-oriented understanding of narrative.

Notes to Chapter 1

1. Among the scholars who acknowledge Baricco's narrative skills, see Casadei (2007) and La Porta (1999). Nicewicz (2011) offers an overview of the broader debate referring, among others, to Berardinelli et al. (2006), Berselli (2006), Ferroni (2005, 2006a, 2006b), Jansen (2002).
2. Five weeks after the publication of Baricco's novel, the newspaper *La Stampa* released a sales ranking chart reporting it in second position after Camilleri's *La mossa del cavallo* (Rizzoli). Another novel by Camilleri, belonging to the Montalbano series (*Un mese con Montalbano*, Mondadori), held the sixth position: http://www.archiviolastampa.it/component/option,com_lastampa/task,search/mod,avanzata/action,viewer/Itemid,3/page,8/articleid,0496_04_1999_1165_0008_11630175/ (accessed 1 March 2021). See also Di Bari (2008).
3. Pezzin (2001) offers an intentionally general and descriptive introduction to Baricco's oeuvre; Giannetto's (2002) and Zangirolami's (2008) monographs take into account the whole production of the author with a particular focus on the fascination for storytelling and the theme of destiny, respectively.
4. As to the ambiguity of Baricco's underlying criticism, however, consider Shatzy's attitude toward the same scene at the diner (or toward the Ideal Home Exhibition), which seems to prompt a negative interpretation first and then instead is surprisingly praised by the character: 'io guardai tutto quello ed è chiaro che c'era solamente da pensare *che vomito, ragazzi*, una cosa da vomitare tanto era triste, e invece quello che mi successe fu che [...] io pensai *Dio che bello*' (14, emphases in the original [I looked at all that and it was clear that the only thing you could think

was *How disgusting, folks*, something so sad it would make you puke, and instead what happened was that [...] I thought *Lord, how lovely*, 8]).

5. In Beltrami 2019 I argue that Foucault's (1984/1986) notion of heterotopia would better describe the type of places conjured up in *City*. In fact, Nicewicz does refer to heterotopias in her article, but she does not offer any further indication as to how to understand the similarities and dissimilarities with Augé's non-places and appears to use the two concepts interchangeably. By contrast, I suggest that Augé's and Foucault's notions capture different features of places, and that privileging their interpretation as heterotopias also illuminates the broader interpretive shift I argue for, from city as a theme to city as cognitive metaphor.
6. See also Fauconnier and Turner (2008) and Gallese and Lakoff (2005: 469–70).
7. A quick but effective example from Lakoff and Johnson (1999): at the first step of the process that connects our sensorimotor experience with our capability to elaborate abstract thought, there are primary metaphors, such as *Affection is Warmth*. Affection is a subjective experience that we make sense of by drawing on our sensorimotor experience of warmth, which is something understood by and through the body. However, Lakoff and Johnson themselves remark that the affiliation of an individual to a specific culture is crucial and its impact on the way certain concepts are elaborated should not be underestimated.
8. The expression has some affinities with the concept of epistemological metaphor, advanced by Eco in relation to his concept of open work (1962: 23).
9. Remarking the importance of change in narrative — and, thus, the fact that narrative requires a progression of some sort and therefore a movement through time — reasserts once again the undiminished significance of time.
10. In her discussion of linguistic theories of reference, Emmott (1997) distinguishes between 'referent in the text' models and 'referent in the mind' models, opting for the latter type. Such distinction and the predilection for the 'referent in the mind' model was firstly posited and explicitly argued for by Brown and Yule (1983).
11. Although contextual monitoring — including both binding and priming — concerns episodic relationships, Emmott stresses that when readers process a text they have to remain aware of non-episodic relationships too, which remain true beyond specific contexts.
12. Young's notion of 'taleworld' corresponds to what, along with Herman, I define here 'storyworld', whereas 'storyrealm' is 'the narrative discourse that reports the story' (2005: 186).
13. It should be noted that the American translation has not reproduced these variations in the use of diacritic markers.
14. Here the difference between *priming* and *binding* emerges quite clearly: when the woman is *bound out* of the frame, it means that she fictionally leaves the frame, disengaging her whereabouts from the topological coordinates of the frame under consideration. If, instead, she were *unprimed*, it would have meant that she is not into focus anymore but she is still bound in to the frame, that is fictionally still present on the scene, unless otherwise indicated.
15. Despite the competition of concepts such as that of embedded or framed narrative, contextual frame theory remains a productive framework. First, because it is more broadly applicable and accounts for other types of relations in addition to embeddedness; secondly, because it does not simply describe a relation between narrative levels, but rather explains how readers elaborate and manage such relation.
16. The term 'window' was employed by Marcel Just and Patricia Carpenter (1985), who 'noted that it is difficult to imagine a whole map in detail, and the way we cope with this is to create a "window" on the area in which we are interested. They suggested that the cognitive map contains embedded systems, and that processing involves moving up and down through this hierarchical system depending on situational demands (Kitchin and Blades 2002: 71).
17. This according to M.-L. Ryan's (1991) principle of minimal departure, which posits that a fictional storyworld tends to correspond to the actual world unless otherwise stated. As to the fact that Diesel and Poomerang can seemingly escape the laws of physics in *City*'s storyworld, I will show later that they are subject to the irreversibility of time.
18. My definition is irreducibly connected to the theoretical and methodological framework adopted: it relies on concepts such as storyworld and mental model, on a focus on plot, and on a critical position that takes into account the reader's perspective and narrative reception.

19. I further explore this idea in Chapter 3, with regard to Calvino's interest in combinatorics.
20. This view is known as 'snapshot ideology' and is variably endorsed by scholars such as Blackmore et al. (1995), Dennett (1991), and O'Regan (1992).
21. Also Dannenberg (2008: 62) speaks in terms of accessibility of background knowledge of real history in order to understand counterfactuals, and M.-L. Ryan (1991) discusses accessibility relations (see also Chapter 3).
22. For a discussion of the relation between understanding and elaboration of expectations, see Noë (2004: 63), Schank and Abelson (1977: 146 ff.)
23. In addition to Foucault and Augé already cited, see Hutcheon (1988) and Jameson (1991), among others.
24. Prince also further distinguishes script ('stereotypical plan') from schema and plan, defining the former as a generic 'serially ordered, temporally bound frame' and the latter a 'goal-directed schema' (2003 (1987): 86). Schank (1986) later introduces the notion of explanation pattern to describe adaptable scripts. See also Mercadal (1990), Minsky (1975) for frame, Rumelhart (1976) for schemata. In linguistics, Gutt (1991) and relevance theory (Sperber and Wilson 1986) examine this type of inferences as part of 'linguistic predictability'.
25. Along the same lines, memory can be understood in terms of 'organization of prior experience into patterns of expectations for current experiences' (Herman 2002: 97; cf. Bartlett 1932: 201–14).
26. Cf. Hogan (2004) for a discussion of exempla versus schemas and prototypes. See Herman (2002: 85–113) for a broader review of classical and structuralist accounts of narrative sequences, and their relations with the script-based approach.
27. Herman actually distinguishes between scripts and frames, as characterised by a dynamic and a static nature respectively. In the present work, however, I will refer to scripts only in order not to create confusion with the notion of frame in Emmott's sense.
28. By this point, it should be clear that the non-propositional view of thought is critical to the approach advocated in this book. It is only by relying on mental models that are not necessarily stored in verbal form that one can ensure an adequate flexibility and automaticity in recognising the semantic connection between a known context and an element traditionally attached to it which however has not yet been referred to in a certain text.
29. There might be a translation misunderstanding here, as the bruised eyebrow is Larry's, not Mondini's.
30. Scripts are always invoked in the light of both their referentiality and stereotypicality. By distinguishing uses of scripts according to their function, I am relying on a scalar differentiation that points at what function is pre-eminent in each case.
31. The episode of the Chinese restaurant (136–38 [136–39]) displays a similar purpose, pursued through an analogous technique: the breaking down of the standard sequence of the script, focused here on the use of chopsticks, allows the author to point out the absurdity or negativity of some common interactions, thus advancing a criticism of everyday social and human dynamics.
32. Counterfactuality will be thoroughly explored in Chapter 2, in relation to the crime fiction genre. For the moment, suffice it to say that counterfactuals are events or situations that are impossible because they missed their chance to be actualised in the fictional storyworld.
33. Lakoff and Johnson (1999: 26–30) distinguish a basic-level from higher- and lower-level categories (e.g. 'car' vs. 'vehicle' vs. 'sport car'). Regarded as the cornerstone of embodied realism, basic-level concepts are characterised by four conditions: (1) they are the highest-level concepts whose mental images can stand for the entire category and (2) have similarly perceived overall shapes; (3) a person would use similar motor activities for interacting with category members; (4) they are fundamentally body-based, which means that they are mediated by the body and they represent the level at which most of our human-scaled knowledge is organised.
34. According to Prince's definition, a *mise en abyme* is 'a textual part reduplicating, reflecting, or mirroring (one or more than one aspect of) the textual whole' (2003 (1987): 53). I shall consider this narrative device further in Chapter 3.

CHAPTER 2

❖

Plot as Trajectory: Navigating Counterfactuals in Andrea Camilleri and the Crime Fiction Genre

At first glance, crime narratives might stand out as the triumph of chronology or causality-driven plots. Yet what a cognitive approach helps highlight are the mental operations arguably performed by readers while reading crime fiction. In this regard, my suggestion is that, in order to reconstruct a chronologically sound sequence of events, one is encouraged to employ comprehension strategies that are spatial in nature because they require readers to navigate a cognitively complex virtual scenario. Virtuality, therefore, is once again in the spotlight.

This chapter, however, marks a change in method. While for the first plot type I started from a specific novel, deducing certain features that typify a hypothetical set of narratives, the second case study — Andrea Camilleri's *Montalbano* series — is already explicitly associated with a set of narratives, grouped under their affiliation to the genre of crime fiction. The pre-eminence of virtuality will be investigated as the criterion arguably contributing to a spatial understanding of plot, the role of which becomes critical in narratives that capitalise on the modal structure of the fictional universe.

In fact, crime fiction narratives represent the perfect case study to examine the systematic exploitation of modally structured storyworlds and, consequently, virtuality. As anticipated in the Introduction, to bring modality into the picture primarily means to account for the various modes of existence of the entities belonging to the storyworld, including virtual modes such as possibility and impossibility. The investigation process, which is conventionally the central feature of crime narratives, consists precisely in the assessment of characters' intentions (conceptualised, as I will explain, in terms of their private mental worlds; M.-L. Ryan 1991) and in the evaluation of counterfactual sequences of events leading to the crime, with the purpose of identifying the actual one. Private worlds of characters and counterfactual speculations are not static and are, as plot itself, rather subjected to constant re-assessments and revision. My contention is that crime narratives, due to their strongly teleological nature, are conventionally read by readers in the constant attempt to guess and anticipate the outcome of the competition among the various virtual worlds. The resulting pattern stemming from these negotiations is the plot. Crime fiction plots can be conceptualised in terms of trajectory because this image schema well captures the forward-oriented tension that guides readers through the process of navigation through alternative scenarios — rather than merely following its linear unfolding.

My objective is to describe the cognitive processes underlying the comprehension of stories approached as crime narratives. From a genre studies perspective, the hypothesis proposed here may serve to shed some light on the mechanisms conventionally exploited by this type of narrative. More specifically, I then suggest that Camilleri's novels particularly capitalise on the modally-articulated structure of the storyworld, enriching it with secondary yet centripetal storylines that can be regarded among the main typifying features of his narrative style.

By building my argument on the conventional features of crime fiction I do not intend to impose any norm on the genre: rather, I suggest that those narratives which do exhibit the conventional features of the crime genre — in other words, a teleological character and the centrality of the investigation process — can be regarded as a relatively homogeneous set inasmuch as their plots are likely to be structured in a way that invites a spatially-oriented interpretive approach. More importantly, my point is that, as far as the reading of a specific narrative continues to comply with certain conventional traits, the reader will continue to apply certain conventional expectations to understand the story. When the reader approaches Carlo Emilio Gadda's *Quer pasticciaccio brutto de via Merulana* (1957) — to mention just one example of atypical, non-teleological crime story — she soon realises that the novel systematically disobeys the conventions of the genre, and she will probably re-assess her understanding strategies accordingly.[1] If any, the effectiveness of deviations from these conventional features reveals precisely how these conventions are deeply rooted in the first place, to the point that breaking them is likely to impact strongly on the reader. As a matter of fact, it could be also argued that relying on conventionality does not seem out of place with regard to a genre that traditionally reveals a penchant for self-regulations, epitomised by S. S. Van Dine's 'Twenty Rules for Writing Detective Stories' (1992 (1928)) and Ronald Knox's 'Decalogue' (1992 (1929)). However, the aim of this book is to identify plot types on the basis of the cognitive strategies and patterns prompted in their reception, not to impose a grid of rules that must be respected in order rightfully to belong to a genre.

The spatial-oriented approach to plot understanding adds a fresh perspective to the study of the crime-fiction genre. By foregrounding the modal structure of the storyworld and re-describing the investigation as the process of negotiation between alternate possible worlds, this chapter advances an alternative way of describing the peculiarity of crime stories. The proposed hypothesis illustrates that spatiality in its broader sense could be regarded as a *fil rouge* diachronically connecting phases and trends across the crime fiction genre. In this light, the development from classic instantiations to more recent subgenres of crime narratives could be rather interpreted as a scalar shift of focus from spatiality as operating at the level of the abstract and geometric principles of order behind the orchestration of the crime and its resolution (Todorov 1971/1977: 45) to spatiality as impacting on the crime story in terms of socio-historical concerns related to its mimetic setting.

Within this broader picture, Camilleri's (1925–2019) crime series featuring Inspector Salvo Montalbano represents a highly interesting case study because it simultaneously manages to adhere fully to the traditional constraints imposed by the genre and to use these very features to build up its own specificity. With the first novel published in 1994, the series includes twenty-eight novels and three collections of short stories (and two more featuring young Montalbano) and revolves around the character of Salvo Montalbano, chief inspector at the police station of Vigàta, the fictional counterpart of the real town of Porto Empedocle (Agrigento). Although Camilleri's first creative efforts date back to the late 1940s, it was not until 1978 that he published his first novel which he had completed ten years earlier. *Il corso delle cose* is a historical novel, a narrative genre dear to Camilleri and one which he continued to explore in other four novels up to 1994 and, then, in parallel with the *Montalbano* stories. Often set in a more or less imaginary Sicily, these novels are characterised by sharp irony and a strong civic criticism. However, it is Camilleri's fortunate crime series that elevates him and his oeuvre to a 'caso letterario', attracting growing critical attention (Capecchi 2000: 9).

The scholarship so far has mostly focused on the peculiar linguistic *pastiche* employed by Camilleri (La Fauci 2001; Novelli 2002; Santulli 2010; Vizmuller-Zocco 2001 and 2010) and on thematic elements including the figure of the Inspector, the Sicilian setting, and the affiliation to the detective genre (Bonina 2007; Borsellino 2002; Buttitta 2004; Demontis 2001; Eckert 2008; Ferlita and Nifosi 2004; Marrone 2003; Pistelli 2003; Rinaldi 2012; Vitale 2001).[2] Fewer contributions (see C. Bertoni 1998) consider the *Montalbano* series from the perspective of narrative studies, which is instead the approach adopted in this book. The narrative structures of the *Montalbano* stories are worth exploring because they exhibit an interesting synthesis between the centripetal drive that traditionally characterises crime fiction and centrifugal forces of digression and epistemological impossibility that characterise the twentieth- and twenty-first-century developments of the genre and more general experimentations in narrative. On the one hand, Camilleri fully embraces the traditional stance, ensuring a final closure which, if it does not fully restore justice, at least satisfies the reader's curiosity and resolves the suspense. On the other, the increased structural complexity displayed by his stories demonstrates an attempt to reconcile the new possibilities pushed to the extreme by unconventional crime stories and the traditional readerly pleasures expected from the genre (Di Grado 2001; Farrell 2011).

In the light of its prototypical quality within the *Montalbano* series, I will specifically focus on *Il ladro di merendine* (1996), exploring how it benefits from this innovative perspective. Acknowledging the importance of the domain of virtuality draws attention to a holistic approach to narrative comprehension as opposed to a rigidly teleological one, and leads us to recognise the crucial role played in Montalbano's investigations by secondary narrative instances including literary references, theatre-like *mises en abyme*, dreams, and minor cases. The presence of this multifarious corollary strongly typifies Camilleri's crime novels, as it resonates as much as and perhaps more than the main detection line, often contributing to the resolution of the crime on Montalbano's part and to the global meaning of the narrative in the reader's eyes.

In the first section of this chapter, I will outline the main articulations of the scholarship focusing on space and crime fiction. While I do not intend to provide an exhaustive discussion of the latter, I will sketch its main lines in order to prepare the ground for the topic I intend to examine in the main part of the chapter: here my focus will move from space as an object of representation to spatiality as an organising principle — or logic — operating behind the process of narrative understanding. This overview draws on scholarship on the crime-fiction genre and its subgenres precisely with the objective of making a case for the existence of a set of expected and typical features. My subsequent discussion relies on these conventional features to select the apt theoretical frameworks and tools to work on them (in other words, possible-worlds theory), and to advance the hypothesis that, in fact, spatiality has always played a more or less evident role in crime-fiction plots.

In the following section, I shall refer to examples taken from Camilleri's novels — in particular, *Il ladro* — to show why possible-worlds theory is a particularly profitable framework for analysing how readers make sense of plots in crime fiction and how it consequently endows the storyworld with a vigorously spatial dimension. Later on, I shall look more closely at the dynamic dimension of plot understanding and at how it takes place during reading, thus foregrounding the role of the reader. Here I will also consider the strategies that typify plot comprehension of the *Montalbano* series and how these strategies further enhance the spatially-oriented features of crime fiction narratives. The attention on spatiality will allow me to make a point of how way-finding techniques may intervene in the active management of the modal changes implemented in the storyworld throughout the narrative. The image schema of trajectory will be used to capture the way in which readers make sense of their negotiation through multiple epistemological possibilities, which makes of virtuality a three-dimensional space where readers orient themselves. I will suggest that, within the storyworld, characters are read as trajectories in the first place, for the detective seeks to understand their intentions and goals in order to shed light on their potential involvement in the crime and foresee their future actions. Understanding the plot as a trajectory emerges from the reader's perception of the multiple characters' actions as trajectories and from the integration of the detective's understanding of the storyworld with the reader's awareness of the narrative as an artefact expectedly complying with certain conventions.

Despite the fact that it epitomises the second plot type, the concept of trajectory will necessarily be further complemented at the end of the chapter, after all the elements have been examined. In fact, this confirms how these image schemata — map, trajectory and fractal — are meant to epitomise the distinctiveness of each type, as distinguished from other modes of spatially-oriented narrative experiences. These selected images are the result of my examinations rather than their starting points.

Spatiality cornered

At the convergence of geography and literature: the privileged position of crime fiction

During the last few decades, the relation between the crime-fiction genre and space has attracted an upsurge of attention and produced an increasing number of critical works. The ground for such convergence of interests has been prepared by a larger synergy between literature and geography, with the latter usually looking at the former along the lines of Armand Frémont's (1976) encouragement to see literature as one of the new instruments of geographical inquiry.[3] While I refer to Fabio Lando (1996) for a reasoned overview of the interdisciplinary branches straddling geography and literature from a geographer's perspective, it might be said that the fortunes of literature in this field started in the 1970s with the rise of cultural geography, as narrative was deemed particularly well-positioned to explore and convey the pivotal concept of 'sense of a place'[4] — that is, 'the result of the amalgamation between reality and culture and between visual and symbolic reality' (Pezzotti 2012: 3 n. 1). In the majority of cases, crime fiction was individuated as a privileged literary genre for looking at representations of environments and of social dynamics in space, for it manages to successfully integrate the objectivity of geographical reality with the subjectivity of individual and collective perspectives. Even for Leonard Lutwack (1984), who evaluates the role of space in literature from the quite different lens of ecology, the identification of the Gothic genre as a forerunner of crime fiction takes place on the grounds that it was the first literary tradition to establish 'a peculiarly intense relationship between the characters and their immediate environments' (Allen 1954: 100), soon followed by Balzac and the realistic novel of the late eighteenth century.[5] Works such as those by Philip Howell (1998) and Lisa Kadonaga (1998) focus on crime fiction and display an excellent acquaintance with the bibliography on literature and on this genre specifically, yet they still belong to a research strand that privileges the geographer's interest.

The opposite perspective — namely, literature drawing on geography to approach traditional issues with fresh eyes — is closer to the scope of the present discussion and has been embraced by a number of works flourishing mainly since the 2000s. Starting from the publishing context, these studies reveal a shift of emphasis onto literature and aim to investigate the ways in which crime fiction problematises issues related to space, place and identity. Due to the nature of these matters, the research focus is usually narrowed down to specific cultures, languages or regions; for the present discussion, I will therefore concentrate on the Italian case.

In literary studies there was a certain delay in critical attention with respect to the Italian *giallo*, unlike what happened in the United States, United Kingdom and France in the post-war period.[6] This is mostly due to the difficulties affecting the genre on its way to being accepted as a fully-fledged and worthy literary production, a stigma that remained hard to ignore until the 1980s. Still today, the fact that some critics feel the need to object that it is 'reductive' to regard Camilleri's works as *gialli* reveals the long-term effects of this derogatory view (Dorfles 2004). It is not accidental that when credited authors such as Gadda, Leonardo Sciascia or Antonio Tabucchi approached the crime genre, scholars tended to underscore how they subvert and deconstruct the genre's traditional structure, in particular its teleological nature. Pieri (2011) reports that Eco's *Il nome della rosa* (1980) marked a significant critical turning point toward the final collapsing of the barrier between 'high' and 'low' literature, confirmed by the translation and publication in the same year of a collection of theoretical essays on crime fiction by Renzo Cremante and Loris Rambelli (1980).

Notwithstanding the initial critical scepticism, Italian crime fiction has since followed the international trend of the genre in proving to be a highly effective ground for questioning social reality and exploring its interrelation with geographical and cultural context. Especially from the 1990s, the presence of Italian and foreign crime stories on the literary scene was so vast that critical interest ultimately had to ensue, even though particularly earlier works were much stronger in historical approaches rather than analysis (Pieri 2011). Studies that took the analysis of specific authors as their standpoint progressively attempted to reach out toward wider considerations on the genre as a whole, drawing on international scholarship elaborated by, to name but a few, Stephen Knight (1980 and 2004), Glenn Most (2006), Martin Priestman (1998 and 2003), John Scaggs (2005), and Peter Thoms (1998). In line with what was registered by English, North American and French researchers, Italian critics also did not fail to stress space-related features: Luca Somigli (2005) claims that the crime-fiction genre has become increasingly popular in Italy because of its attempt to grasp the contradictions of reality, while Margherita Marras (2005) advances the enticing proposal of Sciascia as initiator of the tradition of the 'giallo nazional-regionale'.

Until the turn of the century, however, with the exception of the pioneering work by Massimo Carloni (1994) that for the first time examines the crime-fiction genre through the lens of geography, this connection, so rich in potential, has been mostly been explored in articles and essays which are necessarily limited in their scope. It was only in 2011 that Giuliana Pieri edited the first collected work in English on Italian crime fiction, in which attention is proportionately distributed between representations of space, gender and *impegno* (that is, social and political commitment).[7] The following year, Barbara Pezzotti (2012) publishes a study unprecedented in slant and scope that programmatically foregrounds the representation of place in contemporary Italian crime fiction and offers an overview of the genre on the basis of its geographical setting.[8] The innovative contribution added by Pezzotti's monograph resides in the fact that she does not simply acknowledge the geographical setting, but rather aims to build on it to analyse the perception of ongoing changes in the social and physical landscape, thus drawing critical connections between a certain setting and the specific features of Italian crime series. Space intended as mimetic setting, therefore, has indeed been the focus of a strong interest by researchers variously interested in crime fiction; this chapter seeks to take a step further, and asks whether spatiality may be involved in this genre also at the cognitive level.

Spatiality, a metamorphic interest

Cultural geography has undoubtedly triggered new attention to be paid to the issue of space in crime fiction and yet, looking back at previous historical phases and subgenres of crime fiction, my discussion aims to make the case that spatiality has always loomed large in the genre, variously disguised and operating at different levels. When in classic detection stories plot was 'elevated above all considerations (often including credibility), and [...] realistic character development takes a back seat to the construction of the puzzle' (Scaggs 2005: 35), spatiality stands out through the crucial role of topological settings and the geometries of the deduction process. If it is true that the most successful detection stories owe their popularity to distinctive characters such as Sherlock Holmes or Hercule Poirot (or Montalbano himself, although he is more of a rounded character than the classic ones), these characters are often praised for and typified by the way they think and manage virtuality throughout the investigation, rather than for their existential or emotional background. Then, when with the hardboiled genre the impeccability of plots starts swaying and characters assume more detailed and human traits, spatiality still finds its way through the socio-historical impact of the environment.

Although Scaggs (2005) accounts for a number of influences and forerunners that contributed to the protean richness of the genre — from Old Testament stories[9] to Elizabethan revenge tragedies, from cautionary tales to the Gothic novel (Bell 2003) — the official birth of crime fiction is traditionally set by scholarship with the publication of Edgar Allan Poe's 'The Murders of Rue Morgue' in 1841. Poe's tales of ratiocination epitomise the classic phase of crime fiction, usually addressed as detective or mystery fiction, whose main features remain fundamentally unchanged across the subsequent so-called Golden Age, the period in-between the two world wars that was characterised by the achievement of a wide popularity of the genre among readers. Authors such as Poe, Arthur Conan Doyle or Agatha Christie selected their favoured settings mainly aiming for stylistic effects (for example, the incongruity of murder in a pastoral setting) or for the possibilities they offered to the formal operation of the mystery. In this sense, the concept of setting is used with a specialised meaning that stresses its 'being formed by a set of fictional spaces which are the *topological focus* of the story' (Ronen 1986: 423). This latter function even produced sub-genres, such as the locked-room mystery, the country-house or snowbound mystery, or the murder afloat (Scaggs 2005).

The interest in the sociological complexity of the setting can be traced back to the hardboiled tradition started in the United States in the late 1920s, with the narratives of Dashiell Hammett and Raymond Chandler. The hardboiled genre programmatically moves its crimes from the circumscribed middle-bourgeois and aristocratic settings of classic detective and mystery fiction to a typically hostile urban environment, whose toughness forges a new type of detective, usually a private eye, as rough as the context he lives in. The type of crimes changes, too: from the cleverly planned designs of classic fiction to the illegal activities of organised crime or the misdeeds of serial killers. In both these latter instances, elucidating the social background is pivotal to the resolution of the case. It could be almost suggested that the metropolis itself is the ultimate source of criminality, which makes the struggle of the solitary hero a never-ending battle. This shift does not originate in a vacuum: from a literary perspective, this trend develops from pulp magazines and dime novels based on sensational stories that were common in the United States since the Civil War (Pykett 2003; Porter 2003), whose English counterparts are to be found in the 'penny dreadful' and 'shilling shockers' (Scaggs 2005); culturally, the genre is intrinsically linked to the phenomenon of urbanisation, whose exponential growth since the eighteenth century raised problematic issues related to social order. For instance, Pezzotti's enticing integration of the two perspectives fostered by classic detection and hardboiled fiction stands out as an example of the never-ending process of retrieval and renovation of techniques and *topoi* within a genre: in her analysis of Sicilian and Sardinian crime fiction, Pezzotti projects the fascination with the circumscribed location onto the confined space of the island, suggesting that this 'amplified version of the locked room of classic detective fiction' is used here to 'magnify the issue of a still-elusive common identity' (2012: 163).

To the new problems posed by a changing social environment brought about by the Industrial Revolution, Poe's stories — followed by the British tradition of Wilkie Collins, G. K. Chesterton and Arthur Conan Doyle, and by Emile Gaboriau, Maurice Leblanc and, later, Georges Simenon in France — replied by giving voice to an exquisitely Victorian faith in rationality and scientific methods of thinking, which are mirrored in and impose their logic on the narrative structure. As Knight aptly puts it, order 'is the overt method and the covert purpose' (1980: 110) of these narratives, which always revolve around its disruption and restoration, and therefore around one main question: who did it? And *whodunit*, indeed, becomes the label that defines the whole genre between the first and second world wars. The need to answer this initial and ultimate question works as overarching thematic and plot constraint (Porter 1981). Praised in the classic and Golden Age fiction, order irremediably loses its purity in the hardboiled and following subgenres, which in turn abdicate their reassuring function. Here, even the brightest scenario, one in which justice partly succeeds and the murderer is punished, always retains some degree of disorder that tacitly reasserts the intrinsic criminal nature of society and of the individual. Reverting our attention to topographical space, it is no accident that it is Christie, the queen of the Golden Age, who most frequently used to attach proper maps of their closed settings to her novels: as Ricardo Padrón (2007: 256) remarks, maps need 'visibility, stasis, hierarchy, and control', and as such they bear witness of the authorial stern belief in an objectified sense of place and time (Scaggs 2005: 51; cf. Knight 1980: 120) that reasserts the very possibility for order and control.

Another way to rephrase the transition from classic detective and mystery stories to the following forms of crime fiction has been proposed by Julian Symons (1972), who sees a viable interpretive key in the passage from the main questions of *who* and *how* to the question *why*. In other words, while in earlier phases the point was the formal design of the crime, later it became the investigation of the reasons and causes behind it, thus justifying the increasing importance and problematisation of the social background. To be sure, a crime 'always occurs and it is solved [...] in a specific location and in certain milieus and social strata' (Porter 1981: 73), and it is the mounting foregrounding of this latter aspect that has prompted the convergence between geography and crime fiction in the first place. From an initial concern over urban space, subsequently extended to its articulations (city, postmodern metropolis, sprawl), interest has spread to society as a whole.

What I have sought to demonstrate so far is that spatiality has been a continuous presence in crime fiction, cross-cutting its various sub-genres. By way of explanatory simplification, it could be suggested that spatial practices undergird crime narratives in three main ways: in terms of setting, order, and social background. By referring to setting I am thinking about classic detective and Golden Age mystery fiction, where a self-contained, enclosed and manageable space includes all the elements that have led to the crime and all those that are necessary to its solution. This kind of space easily lends itself to visual mapping, is regarded as objective and knowable, which is mirrored in the structuring formal features of the investigation. Detection is often conceived of as a puzzle: order is the main concern of and at the same time dominates these narratives, where each piece has (or will be returned to) its rightful place. In the hardboiled subgenre, conversely, the highly formalised unfolding of vicissitudes engages with the complexity of the social background, thus becoming increasingly blurred. No longer individuated by neat deductive practices, spatiality transforms and re-adjusts its own role, emerging as a wider environment to be questioned and critically explored.

Camilleri had an in-depth knowledge of crime fiction. This is not only thanks to his personal history as passionate reader of the novels of Simenon and Manuel Vàzquez Montalbàn, but also because of his career as production manager in RAI following his studies in directing at the Accademia Nazionale d'Arte Drammatica. Here, during the 1960s, Camilleri sponsored and was involved in the production of three crime series: *Le avventure di Laura Storm*, the series of detective Sheridan, and *Le inchieste del commissario Maigret*, based on Simenon's novels. Camilleri not only did put himself to the test with crime fiction as a writer but also transferred his own reading passions to the character of Salvo Montalbano, who is portrayed as a keen reader of Sciascia, Simenon, and Vàzquez Montalbàn (*La forma dell'acqua*, 158; *Il cane di terracotta*, 41–42; *La gita a Tindari*, 70).

There are, however, specific technical reasons that led Camilleri to privilege this genre for his writing. In an interview with Marcello Sorgi in 2000, when asked why he chose the crime-fiction formula, Camilleri explained that he needed this genre as a cage that could impose order onto his imagination. He said that it was Sciascia, the sharp critic of the twentieth-century socio-political milieu and personal friend, who encouraged him to approach the detective genre in this way. To be sure, these are not the only ones relating crime genre to some kind of operating constraints, to be either complied with or challenged. Bruno Ventavoli observes that 'the *giallo* is a genre with both strict rules and the freedom to represent reality'. Carlo Lucarelli avers that the goals of tension and surprise prevent the genre from having rules, but at the same time he admits that it nonetheless has a *grammar*. Similarly, by arguing that a *giallo* is such only when it completely betrays the rules of the genre, Marcello Fois is actually confirming their silent (in other words, virtual) role (reported in Pezzotti 2012: 173 and 186). In her article on Camilleri and the revived pleasure of 'reading for the plot', Clotilde Bertoni (1998) reports that, according to the author, 'lo schema del giallo in un certo modo imbriglia il recupero dell'intreccio, garantisce al racconto la tensione salda, avvincente del *suspense*' [the patterns of the *giallo* somehow lead to retrieve plot, they provide the story with robust tension and the engagement of suspense]. These words suggest that by 'reading for the plot' Bertoni primarily means the pleasure of a final closure, a teleological structure satisfactorily centripetal. They also show that, despite the number of narratives that variously challenge this trend, Bertoni feels that the teleological aspect is still a conventional and typifying element of the *giallo*.

Following the same tendency toward abstract and ordering simplification, in one of the first critical works that sought to assess the detection genre without dismissing it, Tzvetan Todorov (1971/1977) marks the presence of two stories as its dominant feature: the story of the crime and the story of the investigation. It should be noted that although this conceptualisation shall result productive in some respects (in other words, elaboration of expectations), it also immediately cues the adoption of a structuralist view based on the distinction of fabula and sjuzet. And yet, to reduce each storyline to a single-world version would strongly limit the critic's analytic possibilities. The double-story structure is the premise of a crime narrative, not what it capitalises on.

I do not reject Todorov's description, as I do not contest Peter Brooks' (1984) claim that the structure of detective fiction mirrors the structure of all stories since it is a construction made by the detective and the reader. Rather, this chapter has a different focus. It does not concern itself with how the crime-fiction genre captures structural aspects that belong to all narratives, but rather seeks to identify features or strategies that are distinctive of crime fiction and, more specifically, distinctive of the way readers understand crime-fiction stories as they read them. Arguably, one of these typifying processes is the investigation. Since the investigation requires a negotiation of potential alternate scenarios, it follows that crime fiction as a genre capitalises on the exploration of virtuality. This does not exclude that there can easily be crime narratives that disrupt this principle: however, I suggest that it is on this generalised model that readers' expectations are commonly modelled and it is against this blueprint that their understanding strategies are triggered. In fact, conventions or expectations can only be disrupted when they are part of the readers' world knowledge in the first place.

Possible worlds: a modally articulated narrative structure

Crime fiction as epistemological genre

Due to the historical genesis of the genre and its long-standing engagement with the representation of social dynamics, spatiality is deeply ingrained in crime fiction. While it is beyond the scope of this book to analyse the close interconnections of crime fiction (or even just of Camilleri's novels) with spatiality as mimetic space, I do intend to make a point about the meaningful position occupied by the setting in this genre. Semantic reference to spaces, indeed, represents one of the parameters pinpointed at the beginning of this book that contribute to making it more likely and easy for readers to tap into their sensorimotor and spatial knowledge. This phenomenon has been described by Caracciolo (2014b: 61) as 'spill-over effect', which describes how elements at the story-level can influence the way readers interact with discursive structures — such as plot itself. It follows that thematising spatiality might modulate readers' response and possibly make them more prone to engage in spatially-oriented comprehension strategies.

Let us revert to the order-imposing schema typical of the *giallo* that attracted Camilleri, and let us try to reformulate it in different terms. Brian McHale (1987: 9), for instance, describes the detective fiction genre not in terms of structures of constraints operating on the narrative, as Todorov suggested, but as the epistemological genre par excellence. All crime stories, in other words, revolve around knowledge issues, fundamentally summarised by a few primary questions: *Who committed the crime? How? Why? How does the detective get to know this?* As Scaggs muses, this means that narratives belonging to this genre are programmatically 'organised "in terms of an epistemological dominant" whose structure and devices raise issues concerning the accessibility, transmission, and reliability and unreliability of "knowledge about the world"' (2005: 124). Most importantly, these epistemological issues involve both the reader and the system of characters internal to the narrative world. McHale highlights that in crime fiction narrativity is ensured not just by the story of the crime (in other words, its inherent tellability), but above all by the way it becomes known: who knows what and, ultimately, what the reader knows and how. In the case of Camilleri's novels, the perspective of the narrative voice is linked to Montalbano's focalisation, hence the general dependence of the reader's knowledge on the Inspector's knowledge. This dependence is surely arbitrary, and indeed there is a certain variability across the spectrum of crime fiction stories (for example, in the Sherlock Holmes stories the perspective is Dr Watson's). However, irrespective of whether the focalisation is or is not the detective's, it has to be aligned with that of a (set of) character(s) belonging to the storyworld; it has to reach the reader through textually encoded entities.

Possible-worlds theory: reality vs. fiction

Building on the assumption that, conventionally, narrativity of crime fiction resides precisely in the ways in which contradictory and conflicting knowledge(s) interact with each other, and in how the privileged figure of the detective manages to make sense of their reciprocal relationships, we should bear in mind that knowledge is not a matter of all-or-nothing. In order to conceptualise the modifications and updates of the epistemological statuses undergone by the various characters throughout the narrative, a more complex system of reference is needed. This is provided by M.-L. Ryan's possible-worlds theory, supplemented by Dannenberg's work on counterfactuality.

When Ryan introduces possible-worlds theory, she acknowledges that the notion of 'world' was already in use in a loosely metaphoric way among literary critics, but also observes that it enters the field of textual semiotics significantly enriched and analytically sharpened by logicians:[10]

> The theory of possible worlds is a formal model developed by logicians for the purpose of defining the semantics of modal operators [...]. The theory has two concepts to propose to textual semiotics: the metaphor of 'world' to describe the semantic domain projected by the text; and the concept of modality to describe and classify the various ways of existing of the objects, states, and events that make up the semantic domain. [M.-L. Ryan 1991: 3]

I have considered the profitability of the concept of storyworld in the Introduction, but as soon as modality enters the picture the situation becomes more complex, with interesting consequences for crime fiction. The concept of modality, indeed, enables us to formalise the variations within the multifarious epistemological landscape sketched above, which represents the major source of narrativity of this specific narrative genre.

The theory of possible-worlds entertains the hypothesis that there is not just one world. Even if we disregard the doubling of actual and fictional world, the point is that they are both systems of reality. Each system is endowed with a modal structure that comprises a central world, where the subject can potentially recentre, and a set of alternate modal possibilities surrounding it, each defining a world on its own — alternative possible worlds (APW). Due to the multiplicity of worlds it comprises, a system of reality is usually referred to as 'universe'. Absolutely speaking, there is only one actual world (AW) and that is the reality we live in. However, the concepts of modal logic can be applied recursively, which means that a fictional world conjured up by a narrative can be in turn designated as the actual centre of a universe of its own. A 'textual universe' thus ensues, 'the image of a system of reality projected by a text' at whose centre there is a textual actual world (TAW) surrounded by the other modally diversified worlds of the system (M.-L. Ryan 1991: 109–23).

Projecting these observations onto Camilleri's novels, it may be posited that the fictional world of Montalbano is the actual world of the textual universe projected by the fictional text. Incidentally, Ryan's framework can also help clarify the potentially problematic issue of seriality. In my analysis, I freely move from one novel to another and refer to Montalbano's Sicily as if it were always the same sociological and geographical background. These intuitive critical moves gain theoretical validity if one suggests that the *Montalbano* series as a whole should be understood as one single textual universe, progressively expanding. Indeed, it may be argued that when it comes to narrative series — irrespective of the medium — a conventional agreement between authors and their readership is in place. According to this tacit pact, textual worlds conjured up by subsequent instalments (in other words, novels) maintain the same textual referential world — that is, the world that (fictionally) exists independently of the textual actual world (M.-L. Ryan 1991: 25). The textual worlds construed by different novels are linked to each other through accessibility relations that hold unvarying, with the exception of chronological compatibility. In other words, perfect accessibility is ensured only if we posit that any textual actual world, starting from that conjured in the second novel (*Il cane di terracotta*, 1996), is accessed by a subject relocated in a textual actual world displaying the properties set at the end of the novel published immediately before. The *Montalbano* series respects chronological linearity, and its textual referential world (TRW) registers any change affecting its properties: a character that is introduced in one novel may reappear in a subsequent one, and it will be approached as if the characters (and the reader) already know it. Ingrid Sjostrom, for instance, firstly appears in Montalbano's world in *La forma dell'acqua* (1994), and the relationship between her and the inspector linearly develops in time; the same holds for Montalbano's girlfriend, Livia, who already belongs to the initial TRW of the first novel. Similarly, when Montalbano's father dies in *Il ladro*, he remains dead in the following novels, leaving Montalbano to deal with the ensuing emotional trauma.

Ryan's modal structuring of the narrative universe may also aid in formalising the relationship between the fictional Sicily, emerging from the textual actual world of the *Montalbano* novels, and the real Sicily, belonging to the actual world.[11] Camilleri, in fact, changes the names of the main settings, turning Agrigento in Montelusa and Porto Empedocle into Vigàta.[12] However, this is done less to disguise than to transfer episodes and settings of Camilleri's biographical experience onto a level of imagination such that human and social dynamics are still reliably in place and yet they lose their specific real referent, thus operating a conflation of particularised localism and generalised universalism (Calabrò 2004). In his texts, Camilleri transfers the properties that in the actual word are attached to 'Porto Empedocle' to the fictional 'Vigàta', and those attached to 'Agrigento' to 'Montelusa'. Nevertheless, the social and geographical background remains ultimately semantically accessible, because the reader can easily infer that names are the only property that changes against a whole set of untouched essential properties that define specific places in the actual world.

Articulating virtuality: the private worlds of characters

Until now, the notion of a possible world has served to define the ontological status of Montalbano's fictional storyworld as opposed to the actual — in other words, nonfictional — world of reality, and to clarify the reciprocal relations between the textual universes described by different novels belonging to the same series. Within their own systems of reality, however, all the worlds outlined so far pertain to the factual domain, which means that they encompass 'what exists absolutely in the semantic universe of the text' (M.-L. Ryan 1991: 112).

Outside of the factual domain, the domain of the virtual — in other words, nonfactual — spreads out, encompassing what exists in the mind of characters and which may or may not be actualised eventually.

> These constructs include not only the dreams, fictions, and fantasies conceived or told by characters, but any kind of representation concerning past or future states and events: plans, passive projections, desires, beliefs concerning the history of TAW, and beliefs concerning the private representations of other characters. [M.-L. Ryan 1991: 156]

'Insofar as they owe their existence to an act of the mind, the entities found exclusively in possible worlds differ in ontological status from the objects of the actual world', argues Ryan while she weighs up various approaches within possible-worlds theory, seeking the most adequate one to the formulation of a theory of fiction (1991: 20). In its original context, this consideration is meant to corroborate the ontological difference between fictional constructions (in other words, literary characters) and actual entities. However, playing on the principle of recursivity of modal logic, the whole system could be recentred onto the fictional world to distinguish also here factual from virtual, so that one could draw on it to explore how the world is made sense of by fictional characters.

Sensing its importance, although classic narratology rejected a systematic employment of modal logic, some structuralists attempted not to let virtuality go unnoticed. Maybe it is no accident that the name occurring once again is that of Todorov (1969). In his attempt to formalise the plots of *The Decameron*, he realised that 'events considered possible by characters, but never enacted, had as much impact on the development of the plot as events presented as facts' (M.-L. Ryan 1991: 3–4).[13] Modal logic allows Ryan to refine her view of the narrative structure even further, not only distinguishing between factual and virtual but also formalising the various modes of existence within virtuality, according to different systems of modality. Drawing on Lubomir Doležel (1976) and Thomas Pavel (1975), Ryan proposes three main systems that relate the private worlds of characters (APW) to the textual actual universe by means of sets of operators: permission, prohibition, and obligation for the *deontic* system; goodness, badness, and indifference for the *axiological* system; knowledge, ignorance, and belief for the *epistemic* system.[14] These operators function as common denominators of sets of propositions that describe similarly modalised mental constructions of a character, each of which constitutes a specific possible world. Ryan's reference to propositions acts as a reminder of the fact that readers' understanding of the private mental worlds of characters are always textually encoded, if they are to be included in the designed co-construction of the narrative storyworld. It is the text that may or may not be designed to tap into a certain world knowledge — which, in turn, is not necessarily propositional.

It will be possible, therefore, to speak of Montalbano as a character endowed with an obligation-world, which describes the system of commitments and prohibitions that depend on rules established by society or values privately held by the individual; a wish-world, modelled according to what Montalbano perceives as good or bad — and anything within the continuum in-between; and a knowledge-world, which can be correct/incorrect, complete/incomplete, total/partial, depending on the extent to which what Montalbano knows to be objectively true in the fictional actual world (M.-L. Ryan 1991: 114 ff.).

It is particularly the knowledge-world that plays a crucial role in the understanding of crime fiction plots. To rephrase McHale's description in the terms of Ryan's modally articulated narrative structure, it may be argued that crime fiction programmatically capitalises on the richness and variety of epistemological worlds. Their virtuality enables these possible worlds to be fluid, in their content and reciprocal relations: produced by the mental constructions of characters, they can change as easily and quickly as people change their mind. A knowledge-world is said to be in agreement with the textual actual world when what the character holds to be true, is true also in the textual actual world; contrariwise, it is in disagreement or conflict when the character holds to be true something that is irrevocably false in the textual actual world.

More blurred is the intermediate condition of indeterminacy. According to Ryan, indeterminacy may stem from either nonconsideration or noncommitment to a truth value:

> An incomplete K-world fits on its reference world like a cover with some holes in the middle; the location of the holes is determined, and the character knows where his or her knowledge is defective. A partial K-world is like a cover that is too small, the regions beyond the cover remaining unsurveyed. [1991: 115]

Interestingly, the issue of characters' private worlds meets counterfactuality when it comes to false beliefs (Goldman 2006). False beliefs occur when the K-world of a character is in disagreement with fictional reality. However, they can be crucially exploited by either the detective or criminal subjects to deceive the opposite faction: until they are held as true, false beliefs can provoke the same effects of real beliefs. In *Il ladro* Montalbano attempts to secretly record his meeting with a shady secret services officer in order to blackmail him. His technological inaptitude makes him fail but he still manages to convince the officer that a video has been recorded:

> [Montalbano] ragionò che in fondo non era tanto grave non aver registrato niente, l'importante era che il colonnello l'avesse creduto e continuasse a crederlo. [LM 226]

As anticipated, Todorov's view of crime stories as characterised by the double story of the crime and its reconstruction represents a prerequisite for the understanding of crime fiction narratives because it significantly affects the reader's expectations. Confirming my underlying argument that sees the epistemological world as crucial to the design of detection, Ryan posits the situation of the enigma as a form of conflict stemming from 'an incomplete K-world with well-defined areas of indeterminacy' (M.-L. Ryan 1991: 121). In this respect, the figures of the detective and of the reader are truly alike (Hühn 1987) because, in order to proceed, they both have to circumscribe those areas of the storyworld about which their knowledge is indeterminate. For the detective, this process is triggered by being assigned a case. For the reader, it is prompted by the conventions of the genre: these conventions design a specific system of expectations such that the reader knows that some crime is going to be committed and that epistemologically grey areas are going to be cued by the text as favourite sites to be unveiled to identify the solution.

Incidentally, it is worth remarking how this case serves to stress the crucial pragmatic value of genre conventions that, far from being normative, rather scaffold the process of understanding. For the same reason, I tend to resist an uncontrolled application of the parallelism between detection and reading process, pre-eminently suggested by Roland Barthes (1966/1975; see also Hühn 1987; Marcus 2003; Pyrhönen 1999; Scaggs 2005; Thoms 1998).[15] However appealing the metaphor may be, I believe it is important not to dismiss the role of expectations attached to the genre affiliation, as would be done if one assumes that comprehension strategies associated with detection are activated even when the narrative does not prompt them in any way, textually or paratextually encoded. Finally, Barthes' analysis is based on a prior and more fundamental metaphor, that of reality or world as text, which is deeply connected to a propositional view of thought, an approach from which my work preliminarily distanced itself.

The dynamics of the investigation

Some may object that conflicting knowledge-worlds are actually common in any kind of narrative. All stories concern human actions, which are understood as the mirror of complex systems of intentions underlying them and projecting one onto the other; these blends of wishes, plans, knowledge and obligations are indeed conveyed by private possible worlds.

Nonetheless, crime fiction poses quite a particular scenario. Interpreting the detection frame in terms of conflicts stemming from incomplete epistemological worlds is an appealing cognitive reformulation, but it would be ultimately pointless if it stops at being simply this, a rephrasing. Drawing on the third novel of the *Montalbano* series, *Il ladro*, I intend to explore some of the consequences of this rephrasing, underscoring how crime fiction capitalises on a more or less complex orchestration of virtuality.

In *Il ladro*, Montalbano's investigation begins with the finding of the lifeless body of Aurelio Lapecora in the lift of the building where he lived together with his wife. The indeterminate epistemic area — what events and intentions led to the murder of Mr Lapecora — is quite clearly defined. If this were not a crime novel and an equivalent gap in knowledge was pinpointed, readers could reasonably guess that the gap would eventually be filled but they would have no specific expectations about how this will happen. Conversely, in crime fiction, the reader's expectations are fairly clear, a clarity that is mirrored in the customary investigation procedure. First, the detective has to gather as many clues as possible in order to reduce the width of the areas of indeterminacy. On this basis, the second phase consists in winnowing down all the hypothetical accounts of events, until the actual one is outlined. These two phases, often intertwined, represent the main part of the narrative, both quantitatively and qualitatively: not only does the investigation itself cover the greatest number of pages, but it is in its convolutions that the reader takes the utmost pleasure. In other words, the expectations stemming from the affiliation to the crime fiction genre concern the subject of the narration as much as they impact on the operative cognitive strategies expectedly cued in the reader.

Reverting to Todorov's insight, one can see that a far more complex situation is envisaged: a crime story is made not only of the story of the criminal and that of the chaser, but also of the more or less thick forest of hypodiegetic virtual stories. From this initial situation, alternate possibilities are progressively pruned, as they turn out to be incompatible with what emerges as the fictional true story behind the crime. Understanding the plot of a crime narrative, indeed, does not simply mean reconstructing the account which is ultimately true, but to be able to follow this process of negotiation among virtual narrative private worlds and action-sequences.

Counterfactuality

Once clues are gathered, Montalbano can start examining various options, sifting through different possible explanatory scenarios. Clues are the posts delimiting the space wherein virtuality can start unfolding. It has been said that the virtual, or nonfactual, comprises all that is not an objective fact in the textual actual world. Knowledge-worlds, obligation-worlds and wish-worlds represent sets of beliefs, values and desires of characters that basically exist in the present, even though they usually stem from past causes or states of affairs and they cast their potential effects onto the future. In addition to these possible worlds, Ryan argues that the virtual can be articulated in a twofold way according to temporal accessibility: the virtual in the future, which comprises still actualisable plans and expectations, modelled on the private worlds of a character; and the virtual in the past, which consists in counterfactual events that are 'impossible, since they missed the chance to be actualized' (1991: 114).[16]

Although crime fiction presents the reader also with alternative hypotheses concerning the future — for instance, plans on how to catch the murderer or prevent from committing another — the investigation process strictly understood falls under the latter category of counterfactuality. Through the figure of the detective, an array of different potential stories is overtly offered to the reader for assessment. Montalbano is strategically positioned at the centre of a network of relationships with colleagues, friends, and people involved in the case that are designed to prompt the enunciation of multiple conjectures. These may be spelled out to another character or remain solitary speculations reported by the narrator; sometimes they are merely hinted at and remain unknown to the reader until they are implemented and determine actual effects in the fictional universe. Unlike Dannenberg's liminal plotting, which individuates the reader's 'semiconscious mental images' (2008: 38), these conjectures are mental constructions of Montalbano's extended mind (Clark and Chalmers 1998; Menary 2010) but they are also explicitly proposed by the text. In Ryan's terminology, they constitute textual alternative possible worlds (TAPW), in the sense that they are not simply inferred by readers, but are textually encoded. Here resides one of the major distinctive features of crime fiction, for it appears blatant that possible-worlds created by characters do not simply enrich the narrative matter but constitute its substantial core.[17]

And yet these hypotheses are endowed with an ambiguous epistemological status, which can be productively explored by integrating Ryan's account with further observations advanced by Dannenberg (2008).[18] By proposing a loose classification of plots into two macro-categories defined by either convergence (in other words, coincidence) or divergence (in other words, counterfactuality), Dannenberg broadens the applicability of the concept of counterfactuality, describing it as opposed to the actuality of AW but introducing the possibility that it may in fact be actual in TAW. She accounts for counterfactuals not only as feedback devices on the actual, but, more generally, as means able to problematise the issue of truth itself (2008: 137–38). In the present discussion, I shall emphasise counterfactuality as not merely an isolated device seldom employed, but as a fundamental thought pattern that we employ in our everyday life. Scientific evidence indeed suggests that the capability to consider alternate outcomes is pivotal in developing an understanding of causality in children (Calabrese 2013). Concerned with the issues of plausibility and possibility, counterfactual thinking is a basic mechanism that serves to test the significance of events that happen around us.

This thought pattern can be reasonably regarded as a distinctive feature of crime fiction because it practically constitutes the investigation process, which is the quantitative and qualitative core of crime stories (irrespective of its success). When Montalbano calculates, weighs and considers alternative possibilities, he is employing counterfactual thinking. I revert now to my previous warning about the ambiguous epistemological status of Montalbano's speculations to point out that, if counterfactual thinking relies on a clear contrastive relationship between various hypotheses, such comparison is carried out — fairly enough — against no actual course of events. The actual course of events, the true story of the crime, is what should be mentally reconstructed through counterfactual thinking. The status of Montalbano's conjectures is ambiguous because necessarily suspended: in order to get to the solution, Montalbano must keep the possible scenarios simultaneously activated and indeterminate; realistic and detailed enough to be able to speculate on their features, flaws and points of strength, but uncommitted enough not to overshadow other potential, less immediate hypotheses. Technically speaking, all of these narratives but one will ultimately result in being counterfactuals. Yet it is important to the success of the detection that they are all processed as if they were actual accounts of events, in order to test their coherence with the factual elements (in other words, clues) at the Inspector's fingertips.

> «Escluso che l'intento di Ahmed fosse quello di farsi ammazzare mitragliato al largo del suo paese natale, non riesco a pensare che due ipotesi. La prima è quella di farsi sbarcare nottetempo in un posto isolato della costa per rientrare clandestinamente nella sua terra. La seconda è quella di un incontro in alto mare, un abboccamento, che doveva assolutamente essere fatto di persona».
> «Mi persuade di più quest'ultima».
> «Macari a mia. E poi è capitato qualcosa di imprevisto».
> «L'intercettazione».
> «Giusto. E qui c'è un bel travaglio d'ipotesi. [...]» [LM 137]
>
> ["Unless Ahmed's intention was to get killed off the shores of his native land, I can come up with only two hypotheses. The first is that he wanted to be put ashore at night, at an isolated spot along the coast, so he could steal back into his country undercover. The second is that he'd arranged some sort of meeting at sea, some secret conversation, which he absolutely had to attend in person."
> "The second seems more convincing to me."
> "Me too. And then something unexpected happened."
> "They were intercepted."
> "Right. But here that hypothesis becomes more of a stretch. [...]"] [155]

To shed light on the difference between the use of counterfactuals in crime fiction and the use of virtuality as explained in relation to *City* and its half-instantiation of scripts, I shall refer to the concept of semantic domain discussed by M.-L. Ryan (1991: 112) in association with the concept of narrative universe:

> While the narrative universe consists of a collection of facts established for the various worlds of the system, the semantic domain accepts any kind of meanings: statements of fact, generalizations, symbolic interpretations, subjective judgments expressed by the narrator, or formed by the reader.

The narrative universe, therefore, is described as opposed to the larger totality of the semantic domain, of which it represents a sub-domain. Virtuality as evoked in *City* of course relies on textual cues, but it encourages the reader to engage with the semantic domain and to expand it, even including vague impressions loosely prompted by the text. Montalbano's manipulation of counterfactuals, instead, involves virtual private worlds but strictly pertains to the narrative universe, as the whole investigation is a quest for knowledge about the textual actual world. Knowledge-worlds propose images of the textual actual world, and they are assessed according to the degree of coherence and consistency they display against the textual actual world. Counterfactuals hypotheses are used by Montalbano to make a point about his actual world, while *City* prompts the proliferation of uninstantiated scripts, which are not actualised nor are likely to affect the fictional actual world, but only the reader's understanding of it.

The 'disnarrated'

In this light, one can hardly overestimate the extent to which crime fiction relies on the ongoing update and comparison of different (discordant and concordant) embedded narratives as maintained by various characters, the detective and the reader. Fully aware of the centrality of this delicate interplay, in the *Montalbano* series Camilleri exploits the whole spectrum of virtuality. In the previous section, I focused on counterfactuality as a narrative strategy employed to explore the past, that is the investigation process proper. However, crime narratives — and investigation practices broadly meant — often involve explorations of the future too, which is still virtual inasmuch as it actualisable but not actualised yet: it is something which may or may not happen. Montalbano may need to look ahead either in order to interject the culprit, or to prevent them from operating again, or, as a mid-stage, for prompting determinate reactions in some characters in a way such that they favour Montalbano's goals, as I will show later on. Before continuing, I would like to focus my attention onto a particular sub-type of counterfactual called the disnarrated. In fact, the disnarrated constitutes the strictest version of counterfactual, but the fact that I shall consider it in its own right endorses my claim that investigative speculations may have a different status.

Although attention to the issue is not unprecedented (Labov 1972; Shklovsky 1965), as far as literary studies are concerned the category of disnarrated was singled out by Prince (1988) as opposed to those of unnarratable and unnarrated. While these two categories comprise events that actually happen but cannot be narrated or are not worth narrating — because either they transgress some limit or fall below the threshold of narratability — the disnarrated, conversely, pertains to the virtual because it individuates events that *do not* happen and yet are recounted in the narrative. It is worth specifying that Prince counts as disnarrated only events that are referred to in a negative or hypothetical mode: this means that the set of cases designated by his disnarrated is smaller than that defined by Dannenberg's notion of counterfactual. Prince would include hypothetical counterfactuals but not alternate histories, which are recounted in the indicative mode and construct autonomous counterfactual worlds.

To distinguish the two categories also serves to make sense of the different narrative properties exhibited by counterfactuals and disnarrated, which in fact produce different effects. As a matter of fact, Prince mentions the detective genre and categorises the possible and false solutions the reader encounters in these narratives as disnarrated: however, I contest such conclusion and argue that the hypotheses considered by the detective emerge as definitively *nonactual* only retrospectively, as until the solution is unveiled they do not clearly pertain to the realm of the impossible. In other words, the disnarrated is attributed to the heterodiegetic narrator, not to a character. Following Dannenberg's terminology, Montalbano's conjectures are *externally focused* counterfactuals, because they analyse events that are external to his own life (this goes irrespective of the first- or third-person narration):

> Era chiaro che Karima e il giovane possedevano la chiave dello scagno, sia che l'avessero avuta da Lapecora sia che ne avessero fatto fare un duplicato. Ed era pure chiaro, macari se non c'erano testimoni in preda all'insonnia, che Karima, la notte prima che Lapecora venisse ammazzato, aveva passato qualche ora in casa della vittima, il profumo di «Volupté» stava a dimostrarlo. *Possedeva anche le chiavi di casa o era stato lo stesso Lapecora a farla entrare*, approfittando del fatto che la moglie aveva pigliato una dose abbondante di sonnifero? Ad ogni modo, la cosa pareva non avere senso. Perché rischiare di farsi sorprendere dalla signora Antonietta quando potevano comodamente incontrarsi nello scagno? *Per un capriccio? Per condire col brivido del pericolo un rapporto altrimenti prevedibile?*
>
> E poi c'era la facenna delle tre lettere anonime, indubbiamente confezionate nello scagno. Perché Karima e il picciotto bruno l'avevano fatto? *Per mettere in una posizione critica Lapecora?* Non tornava. Niente avevano da guadagnarci. Anzi, rischiavano che il loro recapito telefonico, o quello che era diventata la ditta, non potesse più essere utilizzato. [LM 77; my emphasis]
>
> [It was clear that Karima and the young man had keys to the office, whether they had been given them by Lapècora ro had copies made themselves. It was also clear, even though there were no insomniac witnesses, that the night before Lapècora was murdered, Karima had spent a few hours in the victim's home. This was proved by the scent of Voluptè. *Did she also own a set of keys to the flat, or had Lapècora himself let her in*, taking advantage of the fact that his wife has taken a generous dose of sleeping pills? In any case, the whole thing seemed not to make sense. Why risk being caught in the act by Mrs Lapècora when they could easily have met at the office? *For the hell of it? Just to season an otherwise predictable relationship with the shrill of danger?*
>
> And then there was the matter of the three anonymous letters, unquestionably

pieced together in that office. Why had Karima and the dark young man done it? *To put Lapècora in a difficult bind?* It didn't tally. They had nothing to gain by it. On the contrary, they risked jeopardising the availability of their telephone number and whatever it was the company had become.] [83]

The emphases in italics mark the counterfactual hypotheses entertained by Montalbano. Even when the enunciation is ascribed to the narrative voice, these counterfactuals are still clearly depending on Montalbano's focalisation — they are his own mental constructions. The following example, instead, which I propose should be classified as disnarrated, displays a verbal status that is completely different from that of the counterfactual sampled above. I suggest that the scope of the disnarrated should be limited to counterfactual statements or accounts that are to be understood as independent from the detective's perspective.[19] As such, they have a stronger metanarrative character and may still exert an interesting influence on the reader's sense-making process:

> Lo spettacolo si sarebbe diviso in due parti.
> Parte prima: la signora Palmisano, scesa dalla corriera da Fiacca, quella delle sette e venticinque, sarebbe apparsa dall'inizio della strata cinque minuti dopo, offrendo alla vista di tutti la sua solita, scostante compostezza, senza che le passasse per la mente che da lì a poco una bomba le sarebbe scoppiata sulla testa. Questa prima parte era indispensabile per godersi meglio la seconda (con rapido spostamento degli spettatori da finestre e balconi a pianerottoli): al sentire dall'agente di guardia la ragione per la quale non poteva trasìre nel suo appartamento, l'ormai vedova Lapecora avrebbe principiato a fare come una maria, strappandosi i capelli, facendo le voci, dandosi manate sul petto, invano trattenuta da condolenti prontamente accorsi.
> Lo spettacolo non ebbe luogo. [LM 38–39]

> [The show was going to be in two parts.
> Part one: Signora Antonietta, stepping off the bus from Fiacca, the seven twenty-five, would appear at the top of the street five minutes later, with her usual unsociability and self-possession in full view, and with no idea whatsoever that a bomb was about to explode over her head. This first part was indispensable to a full appreciation of the second (for which the spectators would move quickly away from balconies and windows and onto landings and stairwells): upon hearing from the officer on duty why she shouldn't enter her apartment, the widow, now apprised of her widowhood, would begin behaving like the Virgin Mary, tearing out her hair, crying out, beating her breast while being ineffectually restrained by fellow mourners who in the meantime would have promptly come to her aid.
> The show never took place.] [37]

At first, the use of future perfect leads the reader to assume she is being told something that is going to happen: it is only at the end of the passage that the sequence of events is retrospectively transferred into the realm of the unactualised. Although, as I noted before, what has been narrated cannot be unnarrated: irreversibly, every piece of narrative contributes to the way the matter is progressively and finally cognized. And here, Camilleri cleverly tricks the reader. By ascribing to the disnarrated category the expected reaction of a woman just informed about the death of the beloved husband, the author tacitly puts a doubtful alethic flag on it. The dramatic scene does not actually take place, and Camilleri dutifully provides a reasonable justification for the 'missed show' (the widow is soberly welcomed directly at the bus stop by a thoughtful neighbour, precisely in order to spare her the public humiliation).

However, the ambiguity remains: would the widow's reaction have matched the narrator's prevision? Through this narrative device, Camilleri diverts the reader's attention and postpones the moment when concrete suspicions will suddenly point toward the widow, the actual murderer of Aurelio Lapecora. The delay in detecting the strongly suspicious attitude of the widow comes out as crucial to the story's narrativity: the false belief that Mr Lapecora was assassinated by someone external to his family prompts Montalbano to broaden the focus of his investigations and to discover the illegal network controlled by two dangerous criminals whose plans had been inadvertently crossed by the jealous wife's intentions. By deceitfully attaching the disnarrated scene to Antonietta Palmisano, Camilleri simultaneously attracts the reader's attention — by foregrounding the artificiality of the act of narration — and distracts it from the narrated matter — namely, the awkward demeanour of the widow.

In line with Heta Pyrhönen's (2005) emphasis on the metanarrative spin of detective fiction, the disnarrated draws the reader's attention to the possibility itself of manipulating and handling hypothetical worlds, something that Montalbano constantly does.[20] It might be tentatively argued that, because of its metanarrative function, in Camilleri's narrative the disnarrated includes counterfactuals that cast their effect on the reader only, and not on Montalbano: in other words, this label could be adopted to pinpoint those counterfactuals that are employed as discourse strategies, rather than to express a semantic dimension inherent to the plot (M.-L. Ryan 1991: 169).

Detection as way-finding

In the previous sections, I sought to demonstrate why the investigation process can be said to crucially depend on counterfactual thinking. But how does its dynamic work? How can Montalbano extricate himself from the bundle of possible courses of events that his mind unravels in front of him to arrive at the solution?

I referred earlier to the analogy between the detective's investigation and the reading activity as sign-interpretation and meaning-formation. I specified that I would privilege an alternative way of cognizing the mystery — or the story of the crime, to say it with Todorov — as a space to be explored rather than as a text resisting interpretation; this is in the attempt to take a step away from the deconstructionist view of everything as text which would still imply language as main pilot-notion. That being said, I agree that the past course of events leading to the crime can be understood as something to be reconstructed, and Peter Hühn's (1987) article well captures two main aspects of this process. First of all, the role of reader's expectations, stemming from the genre affiliation: the assumption of a course of events to be reconstructed — Hühn's 'text' — has the effect of transforming the textual actual world 'into a conglomeration of potential signs' to be made sense of in a coherent way (1987: 454). Clues function indeed as hallmarks to be borne in mind when the plausibility of counterfactuals is assessed. Similarly, the emphasis on expectations allows to stress the fruitfulness also of Todorov's identification of the two stories as distinctive of the crime genre, which is no longer just a descriptive feature but rather actively operates in addition as a pointer in the sense-making process. The second aspect underscored by Hühn that still holds, even if we interpret the story to be reconstructed as a space rather than as a text, is the process of trial and error that regulates detection.

To conceive the unknown past as a space to be explored calls for a powerful analogy between narrative understanding and way-finding. Following this argument, I retrieve the notion of cognitive mapping, briefly introduced in Chapter 1. It should be remembered that, according to Downs and Stea (1977: 6), cognitive mapping is 'an abstraction covering those cognitive or mental abilities that enable us to collect, organize, store, recall, and manipulate information about the spatial environment', irrespective of this space being real or fictional. My claim is that, by extension, the same concepts could be applied to the sense-making of spatial relations concerning any kind of entity or information: when it comes to questions such as how the subject relates to the various parts of an entity (say, an unknown course of events) or how its parts relate to each other (in other words, the various counterfactual hypotheses), we are always relying on some sort of cognitive mapping ability. Downs and Stea take into account this possibility themselves, remarking that:

> The ways in which cognitive mapping touches upon ongoing life are many and varied. We solve abstract problems using spatial representations that we can mentally rotate and manipulate. We use spatial mnemonics to recall a sequence of important ideas. We make use of spatial imagery and metaphors in verbal and written communication. [1977: 27]

My suggestion is that the concepts of cognitive mapping and way-finding as understanding could be applied both to the mimetic space and to virtuality. In other words, the detective is expected to navigate the setting of the crime to reconstruct the criminal's movements and potential alibis, as well as to navigate the virtual space of characters' private worlds and the virtual space emerging from the interaction of counterfactual hypotheses.[21] Consequently, as I shall illustrate later in the chapter, the reader can be said to employ the same way-finding strategies to make sense of the plot through the space of narrative experience.

As to the space of the setting, 'solving a mystery frequently involves reconstructing the complex movements of individuals through space and time, akin to problems faced by spatial scientists' (Kadonaga 1998: 414). Similarly, in her entry on 'Detective Fiction' for the *Routledge Encyclopedia of Narrative Theory*, Pyrhönen (2005) defines it a quest, with an image that accentuates the spatial nature of the cognitive process required of the reader: solved or not solved, the crime novel always stages a chase, of a criminal or of his/her motives. Ultimately, it is a quest for knowledge, as Antonio Tabucchi once described it.[22] It is indeed beyond doubt that a crucial part of the investigation consists in the reconstruction of the physical movements of the criminal.

Montalbano's visits to the crime scenes and to various places where victims, potential criminals and witnesses have been, are essential to the process of detection. Nonetheless, these movements would mean nothing were they not associated with some underlying intention (Palmer 2003 and 2004; Zunshine 2006 and 2008): hence the implication that movements in the setting and the space of private worlds of characters are irreducibly interconnected. Montalbano attempts to follow traces that are not only positions in the topographical space, but also intentional paths: the cognitive advantage of retracing past trajectories is overtly displayed in *Il ladro*, where Montalbano asks Antonietta Palmisano to re-enact for him the exact movements she made on the morning of the murder. When she starts recounting, he specifies: 'No, signora, forse non mi sono spiegato bene. Lei non me lo deve dire quello che fece, me lo deve far vedere. Andiamo di là' (LM 85 [No, signora, perhaps I didn't make myself clear enough. I don't want you to *tell* me what you did, I want you to show me. Let's go in the other room, 92]). Perplexed, the widow physically retraces her steps through bedroom, bathroom and kitchen, followed by the Inspector. The renewed performance of her past actions confirms to Montalbano a crucial detail without him having to ask directly, thus retaining an advantage over the widow: she has not entered her husband's studio, where Montalbano believes Karima, the victim's lover, was hidden on the day of the murder.

At some other times, however, walking the crime scene is not enough to achieve a better understanding of the case and Montalbano has to perform some purely mental work by going through various counterfactual hypotheses. But how does this examination, and the consequent selection, work? In my analysis, I do not focus specifically on the content of each hypothesis, limiting myself to point out that simulation abilities together with a rich knowledge of human types are definitely useful qualities for a good detective. Each counterfactual outlines a possible course of events and, therefore, a different possible world: as he mentally co-constructs it, the detective should employ his cognitive mapping abilities in order to integrate the counterfactual parts with the factual data at his disposal; as already noted, traces and clues function as fixed signposts in an otherwise changeable chart.

Manipulation of counterfactuals: points of divergence

The reference to changeability marks a crucial issue: Montalbano must be able not only to outline different counterfactual scenarios but also to mentally manipulate them, as posited by Downs and Stea (1977) in the quotation above and in line with the enactivist view of perception as action, in order to test their plausibility or to supplement them with additional clues as the investigation proceeds. In particular, a successful problem-solving activity depends on the detective's capability to keep track of counterfactuals as points of divergence.

The notion of point of divergence is a key concept in Kathleen Singles' (2012) theorisation of alternate history, and it indicates the event that sets the deviation from the actual past into a counterfactual course. In this case, since I am not referring to the relationship between history and its narration, with point of divergence I mean the point that sets the difference between one course of events and any other alternate one. It follows that in order to select among his hypotheses the one which is *not* a counterfactual and that coincides with the fictional truth, Montalbano has to remain aware of the various events that represent points of divergence, and out from which divergent paths potentially branch. In *Il ladro*, Montalbano sifts through a series of hypotheses with his colleague Valente in order to solve the unclear death of a Tunisian fisherman: a turning point is reached when they suddenly realise that an element that they had so far given for granted — the fact that the boat from which the shooting had started was a Tunisian guard ship, as reported — may have actually been a private ship. 'Siamo sicuri che fosse una motovedetta militare tunisina?' (LM 138 [Are we sure the patrol boat was Tunisian?, 157]): a simple question turns the identity of the ship into a point of divergence whose modification has profound consequences on the whole reconstructed narrative.

Reasoning about points of divergence draws the attention to another aspect, also remarked on by Singles. If points of divergence are events or details that determine a divergence in the subsequent development of events, there are yet other events that despite being included in different counterfactual hypotheses may not hold the same value in all accounts. Indeed, Singles (2012: 99) argues that 'shared' events — that is, events that belong to both the real and the counterfactual string of events (in this case, to different counterfactual reconstructions) — 'are not to be considered the same events' because 'each event gains meaning depending on its position in a given plot'.

Singles' observation endorses the principle that the counterfactual hypotheses outlined throughout an investigation constitute different possible worlds, each endowed with autonomous ontological status and in search of their own internal coherence. I noted earlier that a particularity of counterfactual accounts in crime fiction is that they do not have an actual account against which to assess their truth value; in fact, reconstructing the actual course of events is precisely the reason for their production. Nevertheless, counterfactuals do have at least one yardstick against which one should attempt any provisional assessments and on which the detective can build to start winnowing down his options: that yardstick is coherence. To remain a viable hypothesis, an account has to be internally coherent and, at the same time, it has to include all the factual elements Montalbano is aware of. Clues apparently unrelated have to be connected together in a non-contradictory way, while a psychological profile of the criminal has to be traced to provide a coherent set of intentions that matches with the physical actions.

In this light, one can fully appreciate how it is not accidental that the image of the jigsaw puzzle has been often employed in relation to detection since its early phases.[23] Puzzles involve reconstructing the right spatial combination of pieces precisely, such that it ultimately reveals the coherent picture it is supposed to. Moreover, marking another striking analogy with the investigation process, puzzles work on the basis of a process of trial and error, possibly preceded by a selection of the plausible pieces likely to fit in a specific area. In other words, to make a puzzle one usually assembles small parts and then proceeds by trying out different pieces until the scattered, disjointed portions are finally put together, thus obtaining a complete, coherent picture. Analogously, when Montalbano starts investigating, he provisionally construes a counterfactual account, mentally runs it, identifies its weak or incoherent parts, and then proceeds to manipulate and substitute the incoherent parts with other hypotheses, sometimes testing out the consequences that potentially stem from different points of divergence.

In *Il ladro*, Camilleri puts the image of the puzzle to a very good use. The excerpt below features Livia while she is telling Montalbano of a conversation she had with François, the orphan kid whose mother has been murdered and whom Montalbano has temporarily taken under his wing:

> «François sostiene che i puzzle sono noiosi perché sono obbligati. Ogni pezzettino, dice, è tagliato in modo che s'incastri con un altro. E invece sarebbe bello un puzzle che contemplasse più soluzioni! [...] Sarebbe bello, disse, se il giocatore potesse essere messo in condizioni di creare un suo puzzle alternativo pur con gli stessi pezzi» [...] Quando niscì dal bagno, già pronto per andare in ufficio, vide che François aveva smontato il puzzle e, con una forbice, rifilava diversamente i pezzi. Tentava, ingenuamente, di non seguire il disegno obbligato. E tutt'a un tratto Montalbano cimiò, come colpito da una scarica elettrica. [LM 153, 156]

> ["François also thinks puzzles are boring, because they have fixed rules. Every little piece, he says, is cut so that it will fit with another. Whereas it would be more fun if there were a puzzle with many different solutions! [...] It would be fun, he said, if the player could actually create his own alternative puzzle with the same pieces." [...] When he emerged from the bathroom, all ready to go to work, he saw that François had taken the puzzle apart and was cutting the pieces into different shapes with a pair of scissors. He was trying, in his naïve way, to avoid following the set pattern. All of a sudden Montalbano staggered, as if struck by an electrical charge.] [174–75, 178]

Camilleri flirts with the classic image of detection as puzzle only to play with it, defying the idea that this art of putting pieces together should be possibly complex but ultimately unproblematic and neatly objective. In fact, in the 'snack thief' case things are intentionally arranged by the criminals in a way that is meant less to muddle the waters and more to cue a completely coherent — but false — interpretation of the situation. In order to reconstruct the truth, Montalbano has to 'trim the pieces differently' like François does — namely, to think of intentions and goals that are not the immediately expected ones.

Indeed, the metaphor of the puzzle returns in the novel, once again with a destabilising effect:

> Il primo puzzle era risolto, perfettamente, dentro lo schema determinato. Fahrid, Ahmed, la stessa Aisha erano rimasti fuori. Con loro, usandoli bene, il disegno del puzzle sarebbe risultato ben diverso. [...]
> Non parlò né di Fahrid né di Moussa, vale a dire del puzzle più grande. [...] E fino a qui gli era andata bene, non aveva dovuto dire farfanterie al Questore, aveva solo fatto delle omissioni, contato la mezza verità. [LM 193, 199]

[The first puzzle had been solved, perfectly, within its specific outline. Fahrid, Ahmed, and even Aisha had been left out of it. With them in it, had they been properly used, the puzzle's design would have been entirely different. [...]
He made no mention of either Fahrid or Moussa — of the larger puzzle [...]. And up to this point it had gone well for him; he hadn't had to pull any wool over the commissioner's eyes. He'd only left a few things out, told a few half-truths.] [224, 232]

In the first passage, Montalbano has just released an interview for local television in which he outlines the case of the murder of Lapecora as a crime of passion with ensuing blackmail; this account corresponds to what the criminals want Montalbano to believe and, by publicly pretending to adhere to it, the Inspector is actually sending a clear message to those really responsible who are affiliated to the Italian secret service. Referring to the different version of the story that he gave to the police commissioner, Montalbano demonstrates full awareness of the fact that the configuration of events can totally change depending on what pieces are included in the picture. The murder of Lapecora is indeed a crime based on financial interest disguised as a crime of passion, but by ignoring some crucial details Montalbano could have easily disregarded the broader picture, in which the petty interests of Antonietta Palmisano are reduced to just a risible portion of the whole and appear even more trivial as opposed to the deeply corrupted network and the criminal organisation that are involved in the bigger puzzle.

By offering to different officers mismatching versions of the case — and especially by using an iconic image of unquestionable order belonging to the classic crime fiction tradition to describe this action — Montalbano strongly debases the reader's faith in justice and the idea that any breached order could be actually restored, thereby reasserting the topicality of a theme that has widely dominated the genre since hardboiled fiction.[24] Moreover, the very idea of truth is epistemologically undermined inasmuch as in the private worlds of different characters the private actual world — that is, what really happened — will include different elements and different configurations of events. Actual accounts are multiplied, but this multiplication will remain at the level of the virtual, since the two principal minds, that of the detective and that of the reader, are aligned with one another and with the axis of the fictional actual.[25]

The multiple spaces of narrative understanding

Spatialising time

Although crime fiction might be easily seen as crucially dependent on the temporal succession of events, I suggest that, whenever Montalbano reconstructs the timing of a murder, what is at stake is a spatialisation of time. Along similar lines, also Dannenberg (2008: 65) claims that '[t]he bodily experience of negotiating and perceiving space underlies many sense-making operations, including the comprehension of time'. Not only am I inclined to agree with her statement in its broadest sense, but I also think that it shows the aptness of this conceptualisation in relation to crime fiction in particular. If humans tend to make sense of time by drawing on their sensorimotor knowledge, from a literary critical perspective there are undoubtedly narratives which focus on the complexity of the experience of time. By contrast, conventional crime fiction is arguably one of the genres whose readers most readily assume the objectivity of the timeline. Crime narratives, in other words, rarely engage the subjective dimension of experienced time.

As the detection proceeds, milestones and points of reference in time are established as if time is a space to be acquired, processed and mapped. Chronology, in crime fiction, is conceived as a sequence of slots to be filled in coherently. Montalbano's investigation in the building where Lapecora is murdered (LM 20–31 [15–28]; see also *La gita a Tindari*, 33–42) represents an almost archetypal crime situation, as it recalls classic detective fiction and its circumscribed environments (Borsellino 2002). The building provides a closed setting, neatly structured in floors and apartments inhabited by families each of which has a different relationship with the victim and moves between floors using the lift; the mobility of the lift, where the corpse has been found, contributes to multiply the possibilities for actions occurred in each time slot. Following Gilles Fauconnier and Mark Turner (2008: 54), the lift works as timepiece — namely, a device that by anchoring time to a space promotes a spatial conceptual mapping of time itself. Montalbano orderly proceeds floor-by-floor, gathering testimonies and accounts of everyone's movements between 7am and 8am, the time-span individuated by the coroner Dr Pasquano for the possible time of death.

Temporal gaps are assessed in relation to spatial movements performed by the characters. When Montalbano questions one of the residents on the movements of the lift and, therefore, of Lapecora and his murderer, the man answers: 'Per il tempo che ci mise ad arrivare, per me era fermo al quinto piano. Credo d'aver fatto il calcolo giusto' (LM 21 [Based on the amount of time it took to arrive, I'd say it was on the fifth floor. I think I calculated right, 16]). Clues work as signposts to be placed into a pattern, and in (temporal) relation with one another. The same function of the building in *Il ladro* is potentially performed by other devices, such diaries or journals (for example, *La voce del violino*, 53), which not only imply a series of spatial movements but also offer a spatially-based structure to conceptualised chronology: in the diary, for instance, each day is represented by a specific space on the page. The spatialising function of clues would remain predominant even if one was not to consider the physical movements implied by each appointment: it works as a mental grid to be filled in, in order to populate the past storyworld with a complete and reliable narrative of the characters' actions.

Mark Johnson (1987) explores how the cognitive schemata of 'path' and 'link' scaffold our understanding of time, endowing it with a linear spatialisation, and describe them as the most common cognitive framework adopted to make sense of temporality. Yet, when Dr Pasquano sets the limits of the temporal territory to be mapped, in order to reconstruct the actual events Montalbano has not only to put the pieces in the right order, but also to compare incompatible sets of events, to weigh them and to sort out which ones are false. Time runs linearly, but at each moment along the timeline an entirely different storyworld is potentially attached, and such time mapping is made more complex by multiple interrelated variables.

It might be suggested therefore that one more schema should be added to those of 'path' and 'link' in Dannenberg's discussion of spatial mappings of time (2008: 65–73): the schema of the container as three-dimensional space, in which multiple narrative lines can potentially unfold. Indeed, a conceptualisation of time in three-dimensional rather than linear terms — namely, a full spatialisation of time — is called for by the more elaborated view of counterfactual storyworlds. In fact, during the detective's speculative activity consisting in the cognitive elaboration of counterfactuals (examined in the next section), the timeline remains one. This is because the point is not the proliferation of equivalent alternate hypotheses as it might happen in science-fiction stories, but the individuation of potential ways to illuminate those delimited areas of indeterminacy that still affect the account of the crime. Or, better, if hypotheses may proliferate, and if every clue potentially works as a 'fork' in the sense that it sets the event or detail that make potential reconstructions diverge, these hypotheses do not expand indefinitely, moving away from each other: the present time — in other words, the here-and-now in which the detective is situated and from which he operates his reconstruction — represents the resulting fork into which all counterfactual accounts must converge. The known conditions of the here-and-now have to be met by all the hypothetical reconstructions in order for them to be deemed as plausible.

Dreams, literature, 'tiatro', and minor investigations

The large part of what has been noted so far is hypothetically applicable to a broad selection of crime fiction narratives. Building on features that are conventionally ascribed to the genre, I argued that spatiality programmatically scaffolds the understanding of detective fiction because of the crucial role played by virtuality. In particular, I suggested that navigation through counterfactuals and private worlds of characters is what constitutes the investigation process, which usually represents the most relevant part, quantitatively and qualitatively, of crime narratives. In this section, however, I focus on strategies that specifically characterise Camilleri's crime narrative in his *Montalbano* series, and which further endorse the spatiality of the process of plot understanding. I should like to momentarily divert my attention from counterfactuality, as it typifies crime fiction in general, and consider instead Camilleri's habit of interweaving Montalbano's main cases with a number of secondary narrative inputs of various kinds.

From generic denominations (link, parallelism, juxtaposition) to strategies established in the literary tradition (*mise en abyme*, intertextual reference, dream), these labels all entail modes of comprehension that do not primarily depend on causality nor chronology. The structure of sense-making prompted by these narrative devices is, instead, pre-eminently spatial (Dannenberg 2008: 66–67). This is because, for the reader, meaning stems from the configurations of events and their reciprocal relationships rather than from their temporal unfolding. As anticipated at the outset of the chapter, under discussion is not the causality underlying the unfolding of the crime, but the process of comprehension of a narrative that takes as its own focus the reconstruction of this crime, of this causality. That being said, it is meaningful that Montalbano rarely arrives to the solution of the case in a straightforward manner and following a neat application of rational logic only, as classic and Golden Age detectives could have done. According to Nino Borsellino (2002: xlii), in this respect Montalbano is similar to Gadda's detective Ciccio Ingravallo 'nel rifiuto della logica più lineare, di causa-effetto' [refusing linear, cause-and-effect logic]. The understanding of crucial nodes — both for Montalbano and, consequently, for the reader — often comes from analogical, and therefore inherently spatial, associations. To look at the strategies implemented in the *Montalbano* series through a spatial-oriented framework highlights how they are not isolated instances, thus suggesting that Camilleri further exploits some inherent possibilities of the genre to personalise his narratives and adapt them to his specific poetics and view of reality.

The articulation of the crime narrative into digressions or even dead-ends — articulation that sometimes threatens to turn into dissolution of the narrative — is not new to the genre. Scholars concur that, starting with the hardboiled and noir sub-genres in the 1920s, twentieth-century crime fiction is characterised by an increase in entropy that mirrors the fading trust in the possibility to re-establish the disrupted order (Pezzotti 2012). Alongside with Gadda, another illustrious example in the Italian tradition and in Camilleri's background is Sciascia, with his unresolved crime narratives denouncing the utter powerlessness of those who pursue justice and his challenge to the teleological nature of crime fiction (Borsellino 2004).

Also in the *Montalbano* series, the Inspector's and the reader's attention are frequently diverted toward secondary or parallel lines of investigation. Sometimes, Montalbano finds these more interesting than the main case and ends up irrationally devoting most of his attention and investigative efforts to them.

> «Sa, m'è capitato di seguire una sua inchiesta, quella che venne detta del 'cane di terracotta'. In quell'occasione, lei abbandonò l'indagine su di un traffico d'armi per buttarsi a corpo morto appresso a un delitto avvenuto cinquant'anni prima e la cui soluzione non avrebbe avuto effetti pratici. Lo sa perché l'ha fatto?».
> «Per curiosità?» azzardò Montalbano.
> «No, carissimo. Il suo è stato un modo finissimo e intelligente di continuare a fare il suo non piacevole mestiere scappando però dalla realtà di tutti i giorni. Evidentemente questa realtà quotidiana a un certo momento le pesa troppo. E lei se ne scappa». [LM 233]
>
> ["You know, I happen to have followed an investigation of yours, the one about the 'terra-cotta dog'. In that instance, you abandoned an investigation into some weapons trafficking to throw yourself heart and soul into tracking a crime from fifty years ago, even though solving it wasn't going to yield any practical results. Do you know why you did it?"
> "Out of curiosity?" Montalbano guessed.
> "No, my friend. It was a very shrewd, intelligent way for you to keep practicing your unpleasant profession, but by escaping from everyday reality.

Apparently this everyday reality sometimes becomes too much for you to bear. And so you escape".] [274–75]

In *Il ladro*, too, Montalbano follows two cases which turn out to be irreducibly — if casually — intertwined. Camilleri arguably inherited from Sciascia the penchant for staging frequent interactions with contingent storylines, described by C. Bertoni (1998) as 'itinerari sghembi' [askew itineraries].

However, I suggest that Camilleri uses contingency and diversions in a quite different way from Sciascia or Gadda. It is not the purpose of my discussion to assess the impact of chance in Camilleri against the conventions of the genre. Yet I argue that (seemingly) contingent storylines do not much make the case for the determinant role of chance and chaos in life, either with disruptive or resolving effects (Polacco 1999). Unlike the works of Sciascia and Gadda, in which digressions and a proliferating model of causality hinder and hijack the investigation, in the *Montalbano* series they often play a critical role in solving the main case and therefore substantially contribute to convey the meaning of the narrative as a whole. In other words, parallel narratives participate in the understanding of the story, rather than undercutting it. Both Camilleri's peculiar use of parallel investigation and the use of counterfactuality, which I suggest aligns with the genre conventions, endorse the view that meaning is likely to emerge from the negotiation of parallel options, rather than from the linear following of a sequence of events.

It is not only the interaction between multiple investigation strands that characterises the *Montalbano* series. Notably, Camilleri also shows a passion — almost an obsession, according to Pezzotti (2012: 127) — for weaving a network of intertextual references to his favourite authors into his stories. These links do not simply enrich the cultural background; they can play a more active cognitive role. For instance, the comparison with the configuration of elements and intentions as arranged in John Le Carrè's (1961) *Call for the Dead* helps Montalbano realise what happened in his own case (Capecchi 2000: 78):

> Seguendo la logica di Smiley [Le Carrè's detective], era dunque possibile che Lapecora avesse lui stesso scritto le lettere anonime contro di sé. Ma se ne era l'autore, perché, macari con qualche altro pretesto, non si era rivolto alla polizia o ai carabinieri?
> Aveva appena formulato la domanda, che gli venne da sorridere per la sua ingenuità. [...] Grazie a Smiley, tutto quatrava. Tornò a dòrmiri. [LM 81, 82]

Literature constitutes indeed a repository of patterns and situations that Montalbano can paradigmatically access and employ to make sense of his (fictional) reality.

If literature works as privileged background knowledge for Montalbano, it tends to remain a passive one. An analogous role, similar to some extent to the *mise en abyme*, is also played by Montalbano's dreams which, often placed at the outset of the story (*Il cane di terracotta*, 129–30; *La pista di sabbia*, 10–12; *La gita a Tindari*, 205–06; *Una lama di luce*, 9–18), are usually pre-figurations of the investigation to come, or of some aspects of it.[26] By contrast, references to theatre and Montalbano's engagement in deceiving put-ons represent instances of a more active kind. Both Camilleri himself and Montalbano are aware of their nature as 'tragediaturi', as dramatists. In *Il gioco della mosca* (1995: 83), Camilleri writes that the 'tragediaturi' is 'chi organizza beffe e burle, spesso pesanti, a rischio di ritorsioni ancora più grevi' [someone who sets up jokes and pranks, often heavy and at risk of even heavier retaliations]: the role definitely entails deep connections with the issue of humour — which I am not going to explore here (Borsellino 2002: xvi) — but above all links to a strong dramaturgic talent and to a preference for staging scenarios to involve other characters and lure them into acting as the 'tragediaturi' wants them to, instead of violently coercing them.

The theatrical pretence is sometimes a way for Montalbano to bend the situation to his will, such as with the capture of Tano u' grecu in *Il cane di terracotta* (here, see also the set-up arranged by Rizzitano with the corpses of the two murdered lovers in the cave). Or, in *Il ladro*, Montalbano sends a fax to the Driver and Vehicles Licensing Agency in Rome and deliberately conveys a certain (false) impression in order to make the other characters react in a way that is advantageous to him (185 [215]). These put-ons could be regarded in some sense as forced instantiation of counterfactuals — counterfeited events, in fact: interpolations of reality orchestrated by Montalbano, who reveals to be such a deep connoisseur of the human mind to be able to play with others' expectations and intentions to unmask their criminal deeds. This strategy is employed at times when Montalbano sets up a fake scenario that lets the suspect indulge in the false belief that Montalbano has been misled, and therefore makes them fall in some contradiction (for example, *Il ladro*, 'Il gatto e il cardellino' in *Gli arancini di Montalbano*, *La voce del violino*).

More commonly, the dramaturgic drive reveals itself in Montalbano's taste for whimsically putting on various fake attitudes, almost mask-like, when he liaises with the superiors he despises. Pointing at the recurrence of these narrative practices emphasises how consistently Camilleri refracts his narrative into a number of sub-narratives which variably mirror and interact with the main case. Far from suggesting digressions or a centrifugal dissolution, however, these patterns always converge back toward one another, reciprocally illuminating hidden aspects and perhaps offering alternative perspectives, but always retaining a strong network of internal connections that holds the narrative together as a whole. In fact, it is this ultimate centripetal drive that distinguishes Camilleri's novels from more experimental works like those of Gadda. Again, to rely on this type of relations among the parts of the narrative distinctively endorses the spatial nature to the process of plot understanding.

The theatre framework, though, also stands out as a technique to put reality in perspective and at distance, in order to be able to look at it and assess it, paradoxically, in a more objective way. In *La forma dell'acqua*, Pino transcribes the conversation he had with his boss after finding the corpse of the boss' friend and political ally: when Montalbano finds the transcript, Pino admits that 'quella telefonata l'ho scritta perché me la volevo studiare, non mi suonava, parlandone da omu di teatro [...] è tutta sbagliata come commedia, il pubblico si metterebbe a ridere, non funziona' (70 [I wrote down that conversation because I wanted to study it. Something didn't sound right to me — speaking as a man of the theatre, that is [...] as drama it's all wrong. The audience would just laugh. It doesn't work,

93–94]). If this effect could also be interpreted as a consequence of the distancing, it is perhaps not out of place to ascribe it to Camilleri's own decennial experience as theatre director, which arguably made him more instinctively sensitive to the effectiveness of the dramatic representation rather than to cold, reasoned assessment of a state of affairs. Similarly, in *La gita a Tindari*, Nenè Sanfilippo re-elaborates in a science-fiction novel the horrors of the trafficking of children connected to illegal organ trade in which he finds himself involved, and it is by reading this novel that Montalbano realises what happened.

Finally, to this theatrically-informed view of reality also belongs the taste for reversals. This is primarily epitomised by the trope of the 'scangiu', meaning 'swap' but also 'misunderstanding' (Borsellino 2002: xviii). Already a central motif in Pirandello, whose Mattia Pascal swaps his identity with that of Adriano Meis and back, the 'scangiu' is extensively adopted by Camilleri in his narrative.[27] In *La voce del violino*, an inestimable violin is swapped with a cheap one and a shoe is swapped with a grenade; the whole novel *La giostra degli scambi* (2015) revolves around subsequent swaps. The similar theme of the mirror recurs throughout the stories of the collected volume *La paura di Montalbano* (2002) and in *Il gioco degli specchi* (2010). The mode of the 'scangiu' is also intimately related to that of falsification, which assumes quite an ambiguous connotation; in fact, as emerges also in *Il ladro*, falsifications are constantly staged both by criminals to protect their traces and by Montalbano himself, either to trick his suspects or even to deliberately circumvent law protocols whenever they collide with his personal view of justice. Looking at these elements, a prevalence of binary oppositions might be noticed. Juxtaposed or simply placed parallel to each other, twofold options often structure the narrative, contributing to convey the impression of meaning as always stemming from the negotiation of at least two possibilities. Particularly telling is the episode of the olive tree (the 'ulivo saraceno', inheritance of Pirandello's *I giganti della montagna*) in *La gita a Tindari*, where Montalbano intuits how to solve a case by looking at the branches of the tree and realising that, although seemingly independent, they actually stemmed from the same point. This observation makes him realise that the two cases he is following are actually interconnected, although he does not dare to reveal so to his vice (*La gita a Tindari*, 217).

The examples I have considered in this section reverberate particularly through crime narratives also because this genre is traditionally regarded as 'an inherently self-reflexive form, which exposes simultaneously the constructedness of its narratives and the motives underlying their creation. [...] the "case" becomes a story about making a story' (Thoms 1998: 1; cf. Hühn 1987, Scaggs 2005, Sweeney 1990, Pyrhönen 2005). As first highlighted by Todorov, crime narratives stage a double understanding process — of the mystery and of the narrative. In the next chapter on Calvino I shall further consider how self-reflexivity is another quality that may impact on the fruitfulness of a spatially-oriented approach to a certain narrative.

Three spaces

Camilleri's stories — partly because of the peculiarities of the author's writing, partly because of the affiliation with the crime genre — seem to be the site of a number of spaces that encourage one to navigate them rather than regarding them as inert bi-dimensional backgrounds (Schneider 2001).

The first space is that of the setting, understood in the traditional narratological sense. The complexity of the setting space is endorsed in two main ways. The first way consists in the long-standing attention to the social dimension of the environment, which contributes to problematise the setting and to endow it with socio-historical depth. It pertains to the genre as a whole and has been discussed in the first part of the chapter. Moreover, in this specific case it is likely that the fictional setting's proximity to the real landscape of Sicily may contribute to its cognitive perception as a verisimilar navigable topographical space.

Secondly, Camilleri's narrative style contributes to enrich the sense of setting as a space to be lived in and navigated. In this regard, Katherine Hayles' (2012: 183) exhortation to conceive space as 'an emergent property constructed through interrelations and containing diverse simultaneous trajectories' rather than as an inert container may be aptly in place. Hayles borrows from geographer Doreen Massey (2005) the idea that a place is not a fixed site with stable boundaries (as suggested by a Cartesian view of space, infinitely extendable, with seamless transitions from one scale to the other, infinitely sub-divisible and homogeneous),[28] but rather a 'lively' space, a 'dynamic set of interrelations in constant interaction' (Hayles 2012: 185).

The ample and regular use of phone calls plays precisely this role in the *Montalbano* series. Camilleri's decennial experience as screenwriter and director for theatre and television led him to master dialogue as a narrative device, on which he heavily relies in his novels (Capecchi 2000: 26). The phone call is a particularly suitable technique because it combines the mimesis of the dialogue with the possibility to streamline the narration, cutting down temporal gaps and diegetic parts needed to frame a new scene. Both isolated phone calls and longer telephonic threads during which the narrative voice remains silenced abound in the *Montalbano* narratives (for example, LM 122–24). For the purposes of the current argument, my point is that the selection of telephony as favourite semiotic resource (Brown 2015) does contribute to convey a certain sense of the environment. By means of phone calls, the space primed by the narrative (Emmott 1997) becomes much larger than that defined by the sole setting where Montalbano is located. Montalbano remains at the centre, but his world reaches out to different characters whose activities contribute to his investigation, coordinating and keeping track of them. That the same narrative strategy can have entirely different purposes can be appreciated by comparing the use of telephony made in crime narratives and in *City*. In the latter case, phone calls are mostly used to comply with the value of swiftness and to rhetorically engage in conversational narrative; in *Il ladro*, instead, they serve to create a network between people and locations. Reverting to Hayles' words, phone calls activate distant spaces and make them present at the same time, thereby conveying that simultaneity and that dynamism of interrelation from which a more complex sense of fictional space shall emerge.

The second space taking shape during the reading process is that of virtuality, made visible thanks to possible-worlds theory and the introduction of modal logic. This determines a fundamental shift in the way the storyworld is cognized, as the single-storyworld is multiplied into a system of private worlds mentally constructed by characters. This new perspective foregrounds how characters' factual actions stem from underlying systems of private beliefs, values, and wishes, only ultimately distilled into action. By doing so, it foregrounds the mind behind the action. Ryan's perspective encourages to consider each character as a potential hub for recentering and, at the same time, as a mind pursuing its own goals. The virtual dimension construed in the *Montalbano* stories turns into a three-dimensional space because its paradigmatic structure is constantly brought to the fore, in addition to its syntagmatic structure. When Singles posits that each counterfactual sets a deviation that constitutes an entirely separate world, she also reflects on how one should 'reason about the "distance" between worlds' (2012: 101). In the case of crime fiction, counterfactuals do not set an irreversible path; on the contrary, they are created by the detective as potential courses of events to flexibly test the plausibility of different reconstructions of the crime. This means the ensuing narrative structure is not a rigid one. The investigation consists precisely in the detective/reader's contemplation and assessment of the 'dynamic "space" between multiple continuations' (Singles 2012: 121), that is between various possible configurations of events that may or may not coincide with the (fictionally) real past in the narrative. It is at this level — or in this space — that the notion of trajectory can be first fruitfully applied.

The view of characters as responding to private systems of priorities, with subsequent projections and plans to be pursued in a (provisionally) coherent way, attributes a sort of 'intentional directionality' to them. This suggestion is surely not unprecedented. Fauconnier and Turner (2002; Fauconnier 1997) devote much attention to the way intentions and life-paths are almost invariably cognized in spatial terms, while Dannenberg (2008) refers to characters as trajectories and vectors from the very first page of her introduction, as if appealing to common intuitions. In physics, trajectory is the virtual line that a moving object follows through space. To replace 'objects' with 'characters' in the new semantic system means to include agency and intentionality into the picture. To argue that readers understand characters as trajectories means that while they read they strive to assess the type of force exerted on them — that is to say, their K-worlds and W-worlds, their knowledge and plans — in order to foresee what they are going to do next, how they will interact with the detective and the investigation. Although the mathematical description of a trajectory, not including speed, cannot be used to predict the position of the object in space, its very definition theoretically implies the existence of a space. To understand the unfolding actions of characters as tracing trajectories fosters a perception of the storyworld along Hayles' lines, as an interactive space and not simply an inert setting for the narrated events.

Seemingly analogous concepts have been contemplated as epitomes of the present discussion and discarded in favour of that of trajectory: 'path' is undoubtedly related to movement and connects points in space but exists independently from its use by any agent, while 'route' is rather semantically focused on the frequency with which a path is used. Trajectory, instead, is supposed to be traced while the movement is performed — therefore retaining the connection with the idea of something in progress — and at the same time it includes a projection forward that mirrors the pivotal role of expectations. As such, it aptly accounts for an emerging three-dimensional virtual space prompted by the interactions among the private worlds of characters and related actual movements through the mimetic space. After outlining the third virtual space of the storyworld, in the following section I shall consider the shift from conceiving characters as trajectories to describing the plot as trajectory.

The third space I pinpoint is, once again, the space of the narrative experience, which is the virtual space defined by the arrangement and modifications of possible worlds (the virtual space just described) as made sense of from the perspective of the reader. Plot pertains to this space precisely because the notion of plot inherently implies the presence of a reader, someone equally able to totally immerse herself in the storyworld and to remain aware that it is a fictional world created through a reading experience. Positing an additional space inclusive of but expanding beyond the virtual space of the storyworld is made necessary by the shift in perspective: as Edwin Abbott admirably suggests in *Flatland* (1884), taking a step out of a world entails the acquisition of an extra dimension. The inclusion of the reader marks a fundamental difference from the virtual space of private worlds, and somehow captures the difference between M.-L. Ryan's (1991) theorisation and that of Dannenberg (2008): although Ryan does not reject the reader, her examination closely focuses on the formal structure of the narrative world; Dannenberg's work, instead, considers the dynamics of plot from the perspective of their reception and the way they are made sense of, during reading and retrospectively.

The space of virtuality and the space of narrative experience are obviously connected in the tightest way. It might be suggested that, although this is true for any narrative, in crime fiction this link is even more accentuated by the conventionally strong alignment between the detective (centre of the system of private worlds of characters) and the reader (centre of the system that includes plot understanding) (Hühn 1987; Marcus 2003; Pyrhönen 1999; Scaggs 2005; Thoms 1998). The two figures, detective and reader, work as connected pivots of two ontologically separate systems: as in a transmission gearbox, they function as gearwheels connected to different parts that move independently but affect each other as parts of the same mechanisms. Due to this interdependence, in the analysis of the management of counterfactual hypotheses these two spaces may sometimes overlap, following the overlapping of detective and reader. It should be borne in mind, though, that they pertain to two (theoretically) different spaces.

Plot as trajectory

How do we shift from conceiving characters as trajectories to conceiving plots as trajectories? It goes without saying that the latter would not be possible, nor reasonable, without the former. Plot is a macrodesign (Herman 2002) that emerges from microdesigns such as characters, events and situations, but also crucially depends on the cognitive activity of the reader who is uniquely able to look at the storyworld from both an internal and external perspective.

Naturally, story-level elements (microdesigns) do inform the discursive structures (macrodesign) that emerge from them, according to the aforementioned spill-over effect. An understanding of characters as trajectories, modelled by the competing underlying influences of knowledge-worlds, obligation-worlds and wish-worlds, is achieved in the first place by the detective him- or herself — that is, by an entity belonging to the storyworld. The detective, in other words, seeks to interpret the people revolving around the crime in order to understand their intentions and thoughts in the same way the reader does. However, it is only the reader who holds expectations that come from knowing that the narrative is an artefact: for instance, it is only the reader who can assume that a seemingly random character might be significantly involved in the case, and it is only the reader who can guess that the closer they get to the ending of the book the more likely it is that the solution of the crime is approaching.

It follows that the process of plot understanding should not rely on completely different strategies, but critically entails one step higher in abstraction. It is marked by the inclusion of the reader's perspective and therefore by the entrance to the space of narrative experience. Assuming that understanding primarily means making meaningful connections, in the space of the storyworld the reader understands characters' actions by relating them to their private mental worlds and to fictional circumstances and context, thus outlining individual trajectories. At the same time, with an operation of recentering on to their own perspective as readers and by recursively applying the principles of modal logic, readers have to navigate through different counterfactual configurations of characters' trajectories endowed with their own directionality: from the competition among potential characters' trajectories, the general trajectory of the plot progressively emerges. The trajectory of the plot is a macro-trajectory or, as Dannenberg suggests, the 'dynamic sum of the alternate possible worlds generated by the text' (2008: 63). Another viable variation is proposed by M.-L. Ryan, who describes plot as 'the trace left by the movements of these worlds within the textual universe' (1991: 119).

Precisely by virtue of her ability to keep one foot inside and the other outside of the storyworld, the reader is able to carry out this simultaneous understanding along two axes: on the one hand, focusing on the micromovements of individual entities of the storyworld; on the other, assessing how these micromovements may entail modifications of the space of narrative experience. The attempt to look for a consistent pattern that can impose unity on a set of scattered and seemingly unrelated or incompatible events and narratives is precisely the cognitive task that is required by crime fiction and that constitutes the main pleasure for the reader. The reduction represented by the image schema of trajectory is the clean solution sought by the detective and by the reader. To put the same concept another way, it could be suggested that the plot trajectory accounts for the temporal unfolding during reading of consecutive spatial configurations of possible worlds in the view of an expected final resolution.

It is important to specify that what matters in the process of plot understanding is not a final resolution in itself but rather the reader's expectation of it. This shift of focus from narrative comprehension achieved retrospectively to the process of comprehension itself marks an important step away from a rigidly structuralist framework and accounts instead for the dynamic nature of narrative understanding. As noted also by Dannenberg (2008; cf. Brooks 1984 and Kermode 1967), final closure is a specific convention of a strongly teleological genre. Readers expect characters' trajectories to converge towards it as soon as they approach the end: the concept of trajectory aptly accounts for this tension. Again, it should be remarked that this does not exclude that some narratives may intentionally break these conventions and expectations: this, however, reinforces rather than undercuts their influence on readers while they are immersed in the process of understanding the story. The reader approaches crime fiction narratives with a pre-determined set of expectations which makes plot understanding strongly directional, as much as characters' trajectories have a directionality expressing their personal goals and intentions. The concept of trajectory well captures the directionality typical of this narrative genre. My suggestion is that plot is not simply compared to a trajectory: building on the dynamics illustrated in this chapter, readers understand plot unfolding as a trajectory across the space of the narrative experience. This means that the image schema of trajectory works as a procedural strategy that guides readers' process of sense-making of the narrative as it proceeds.

★ ★ ★ ★ ★

In this chapter, I have built on the parameters identified in Chapter 1 to elaborate a second spatially-oriented plot type. This plot type arguably encourages a spatial understanding of the narrative, but it does so by stressing different cognitive strategies and therefore achieves an overall different narrative experience. The two image schemata of map and trajectory point to such dissimilarity. The first plot type, epitomised by the map, refers to narratives which could be regarded as static and whose point is primarily to understand the dynamic equilibrium behind a state of affairs or a situation. The second plot type is epitomised by the trajectory and includes narratives that are strongly teleological in nature, characterised by strong readerly expectations guiding the plot's unfolding.

Crime fiction narratives represent a category of stories — in this case, a genre — that conventionally fits this reception profile. M.-L. Ryan often remarks that narrativity depends not only on narrative content or aesthetic considerations but also and crucially on the degree of conceptual and logical complexity of the storyworld (1986: 326). This is the case with the structure of the virtual dimension usually exhibited in crime fiction, as the conventions related to this genre demand a system of strongly competing private worlds and for the management of a paradigmatic system of counterfactual possibilities. In order to understand them, readers ought to rely on sense-making strategies that are closer to spatial orientation practices rather than being based on the understanding of chronological causality only. Camilleri particularly exploits this conventional spatial quality of crime fiction understanding and further enhances it in his *Montalbano* novels by designing cases that can be solved thanks to the combined integration of multiple inputs. In addition to the primary detection strand, narrativity in Camilleri's stories is typically ensured through parallel investigations that enrich the main one by analogy or juxtaposition (but hardly by direct cause effects), and through small narratives in the form of dreams or theatre-like put-ons.

This chapter makes the case for an engaged virtual dimension as a potentially core criterion for prompting a spatially-oriented understanding of narrative. By adopting the crime fiction genre as broader case study, Chapter 2 stresses the importance of expectations and conventions when it comes to any theorisation about reception, thus reasserting the pragmatic rather than ontological nature of narrativity. Similarly, it is suggested that a spatial approach to plot understanding should be cued in readers by multiple interacting criteria: in this case, a strong pointer toward spatiality is represented by the central role it traditionally plays in crime fiction also at other levels — from the importance of setting in socio-historical terms to abstract geometric principles of order operating in conceptualising plots. Among others, one of the contributions this study hopes to make is precisely the re-evaluation of spatiality as potential *fil rouge* of crime fiction, a privileged interest that, taking various shapes and emerging at different levels throughout the history of the genre, is described here also in its impact on the narrative structure and on the strategies designed for its comprehension.

Notes to Chapter 2

1. On the unconventional nature of Gadda's masterpiece as a detective story, see G. Guglielmi (2002/2017).
2. A significant part of the secondary bibliography on Camilleri is characterised by a rather descriptive approach and, interestingly, by a keen attention to the relationship with the extra-textual domain.
3. Lando (1996) individuates five major directions of research: a) 'the geographical fact in literary works'; b) 'sense of place'; c) 'cultural rooting'; d) the 'inscape'; e) 'culture and ethno-territorial consciousness'.
4. For a discussion of the implications of the complex term 'place', see Entrikin (1991), Frémont (1976), Relph (1976) and, in particular, Tuan (1975 and 1977).
5. Lutwack argues that place may get into literature in two ways: as idea — that is, 'as attitudes about places and classes of places that the writer picks up from his social and intellectual milieu and from his personal experiences' — and as form — that is, as 'materials for the forms he uses to render events, characters, and themes' (1984: 12).
6. The term *giallo* to indicate the genre in Italian stems from the colour of the cover of a series of crime fiction books launched in 1929 by Mondadori; the label is now recognised and widely accepted by scholars.
7. See Rinaldi (2011) for an extensive bibliography on Italian crime fiction.
8. See this work for a vast bibliography on Italian crime fiction and the importance of place in literature and in this genre specifically. Among later book-length studies combining Italian crime fiction and space, see Paoli (2016) and Pezzotti (2016).
9. Interestingly enough, both Camilleri (*La voce del violino*, 48) and Scaggs (2005) identify the story of Edipo as precursory detective story.
10. For an in-depth discussion of the transition of the concept of possible world from philosophy to literary theory, see Ronen (1994).

11. I touch this issue only marginally here as it would require a much larger discussion and a whole set of different questions and theoretical frameworks. In fact, an exhaustive analysis would require not only an investigation of the relationship between fictional and real Sicily but also an examination of the film adaptation and the complex semiotic transformations undergone by the fictional characters in this process (cf. Clausi et al. 2007; Marrone 2006). The television series starring Luca Zingaretti in the role of Inspector Montalbano, directed by Alberto Sironi and produced by Palomar for RAI, first aired in 1999; it counts fifteen seasons to date, each composed of four or two episodes which, although mostly based on one novel, usually integrate the main plot with other short stories featuring Montalbano. In 2008, BBC Four purchased the transmission rights and broadcasted the series, subtitled, in the United Kingdom. The large success led to the production of a prequel series in 2012, *Il giovane Montalbano*. The influence not only on the audience/readership but also on the author himself has been so deep that Camilleri admits that 'Ora mi succede che quando scrivo un nuovo *Montalbano* rischi di influenzarmi non tanto il personaggio televisivo di Montalbano, quanto piuttosto il paesaggio' (Scarpetti and Strano 2004: 129). In fact, the scenographer Luciano Ricceri shot most of the scenes in the eastern part of Sicily instead of the western part where Agrigento and Porto Empedocle — fictional counterparts of Montelusa and Vigàta — are situated.
12. Already in *Un filo di fumo* (1980), a peculiar historical novel that precedes the *Montalbano* series, Vigàta appears as the fictional counterpart of the real town of Porto Empedocle, birthplace of Camilleri himself and of Luigi Pirandello. And probably as a homage to Pirandello should be intended the other fictitious name, invented by the Sicilian playwright to indicate Agrigento in the short story 'Le tonache di Montelusa' (now in *Novelle per un anno*, 2015).
13. Todorov proposes four modal operators to provide a classification of nonfactual propositions: *obligatory* mode, *optative* mode, *conditional* mode, and *predictive* mode. A few years later, Claude Bremond (1973) suggests a distinction between descriptive (actual) and modalised statements, which 'anticipate the hypothesis of a future event, or a virtual action' (86; English translation from M.-L. Ryan 1991: 110).
14. Ryan also mentions the alethic system, which relates AW to TAW, relying on the operators of possibility, impossibility, and necessity. Since I am not concerned with the relationship between real and fictional, here, I shall leave this categorisation aside.
15. Nicolson (1946) and Porter (1981) argue instead for an analogy between the detective and the professor or the scientist.
16. Substantial work has been done recently on counterfactuality, in the field of cognitive science (Fauconnier and Turner 1998 and 2002; Turner 1996) and psychology (Kahneman and Miller 1986; Roese and Olsen 1995).
17. The reading of crime fiction narratives as characterised by a negotiation of possible worlds and counterfactual hypotheses arguably holds even in those uncommon instances where the perspective is that of the criminal instead of the detective's: there is simply a reversal, with the criminal seeking to figure out the detection process on the police's part (Hühn 1987: 462–63).
18. I believe that Dannenberg represents a reasonable middle ground between Ryan's strict definition — which admittedly provides the most flawless examination and application of the concept — and implementations such as that of Fauconnier and Turner (2002: 217–47), who sketch a much broader definition of counterfactuals, arguing that it is not an absolute property but rather a space that may also depend on the point of view one takes. This latter elaboration, although fascinating and thought provoking, may be indeed too loose.
19. Alternatively, the passage may be regarded as a mental construction of the community, which would function as focaliser.
20. By contrast, interpretations of the genre as governed by the parallelism between the detective and the reader (Hühn 1987) would argue that the main activity performed by the detective is the interpretation of signs, rather than the manipulation of hypothetical scenarios.
21. The disnarrated acts in this process as a virtual space that is created and subsequently removed; as such, it impacts on the cognitive map of the interpreter in the same way counterfactuals do, but with an additional tag that flags it as positively removed and poses an interrogation mark over the reasons of its design.

22. '[Q]uel motivo di ricerca e interrogazione che è caratteristico della letteratura poliziesca' (Tabucchi et al. 1995: 20).
23. Spatiality is pre-eminent also in another game dear to the classic detective tradition: chess. The game of chess is close to a classic view of detection as a system of moves and countermoves.
24. Camilleri is not new to this type of conclusions: also in *La forma dell'acqua* and *Il cane di terracotta* we have the same multiplication of 'truths'.
25. Cf. M.-L. Ryan (1991: 166 ff.) for an example (John Fowles' *The French Lieutenant's Woman*, 1969) where, by imagining several possible outcomes, the omniscient narrator 'refuses to select one path in the realm of the possible and call it the history of the one and only actual world'.
26. They become more frequent in the later novels of the series, perhaps to mark an increasing anxiety towards ageing on the part of Montalbano and therefore towards his own capability for relying on rational thought in his profession.
27. That the trope of 'scangiu' owes much to Pirandello clearly emerges from the title of Camilleri's (2000a) biographical fiction of the Sicilian playwright.
28. A view endorsed by current digital technologies such as GPS or Google Maps.

CHAPTER 3

❖

Plot as Fractal: Calvino's *Se una notte d'inverno un viaggiatore*. A Vertigo of Variation and Repetition

To choose a single guiding image to represent plot understanding seems almost counterproductive when facing an author like Italo Calvino (1923–1985), who was always diffident of final definitions. Yet, Calvino's passion for exactitude, geometric figures, and formal design is such that, once the constraints and features of the text have been isolated, it has not been impossible to justify their inner workings (SI 686). In a bid to find the balance between the temptation of a perfect image, able to fully epitomise a complex narrative such as *Se una notte d'inverno un viaggiatore* (1979), and the awareness that there will always be other images that could better explain specific details or features of this work, I analyse *Se una notte* through the image schema of the fractal.[1] The core of this chapter discusses the hypothesis that the process of plot understanding in *Se una notte* is spatial in nature and, more specifically, functions according to the same principles of fractality which is characterised by the repetition of a certain pattern at different scales. The storyworld construed in *Se una notte*, in fact, is complex and articulated enough to provide clear levels at which recurring elements are recombined from time to time, in a pattern of variation within repetition that bears close affinities with fractality. Fractality not only captures the principle regulating the relationship between the narrative as a whole and its parts — chapters and intercalated novels — but it also describes the process of understanding arguably implemented by readers during reading.

Furthermore, Calvino's oeuvre exhibits features that preliminarily position it within the scope of my research. These include signals of a wide-spread influence of spatiality on Calvino's cognitive style; a keen metanarrative attitude, carried out through an exploration of virtuality in all its articulations, from counterfactuality (what cannot happen) and potentiality (what might happen) to absence (what does not happen); and Calvino's deep interest in the dynamics of reception and in the role of the reader,[2] which gain strong pre-eminence in *Se una notte* through the display of textual cues that positively prompt the engagement of the readers' virtual body. *Se una notte* is usually associated with the so-called semiotic period of his career, which includes works characterised by the ongoing metanarrative reflection on literature as a means of representation and knowledge (Bonsaver 1995: 55).[3] The metanarrative and self-reflective element is indeed a crucial reason why I selected *Se una notte* and Calvino because, by including the interpreter's perspective in the narrative representation, narrative levels are multiplied and the storyworld(s) gains in ontological complexity. As Patricia Waugh (1984: 23) argues, musing on Frank's (1945) study, 'self-reflexiveness [...] generates "spatial form"', hence the assumption that any narration that reflects on itself acquires a spatial dimension.

To approach Calvino critically today is not an easy task. Quantitatively, the amount of critical work already published and the number of perspectives adopted are virtually impossible to process in their entirety, as scholars already began to acknowledge in the 1990s. Qualitatively, the degree of artistic self-awareness and self-reflection that has been demonstrated by Calvino himself — either explicitly expressed in his essayistic production or implicitly emerging from his fictional works — is such as to induce in the critic an acute sense of humility. Not to mention the protean and prolific nature of Calvino's imagination and experimentation in the first place. It is no accident that Claudio Milanini (1990) chose the essay-form for one of the first monographic works on Calvino, significantly entitled *L'utopia discontinua*.

Attempting to resist such a centrifugal approach, Guido Bonsaver (1995) designed a study that examines the heterogeneity of Calvino's art and interests and yet provides a global reading of his oeuvre, arranging his volume around three perspectives — historic-literary, stylistic and structural, and deconstructionist — and grounding them in robust textual analysis. Along similar lines is Martin McLaughlin's 1998 monograph, prompted by the publication of letters and pieces of both fiction and non-fiction in the Meridiani Mondadori series that gave access to new material and provided unprecedented insight into the diachronic development of Calvino's production.

The specific perspective adopted in the present work owes much to the argument developed by Kathryn Hume (1992). Unlike Bonsaver and McLaughlin, who attempt to combine a chronological discussion of Calvino's works with their critical interpretation, Hume offers a precise hypothesis concerning Calvino's metaphysics and explores it synchronically through relevant texts. She maintains that, despite the multifarious nature of Calvino's production, an unchanging core can be identified at the heart of his fictional and non-fictional writing, an underlying quest which could be formulated in terms of a dialogue 'between an active consciousness [a Cartesian cogito] and a complicated, particulate cosmos', a 'confrontation between mind and matter' (1992: 16, 33). Hume models a remarkable overview of Calvino's poetics and his attitude towards the relationship between the whole and its parts, arguing that Calvino elaborated a perception of reality as undifferentiated mass threatening the cogito, which is represented by the individual's mind and rationality (41). In doing so, she posits quite a polarised view, wherein Calvino supposedly oscillates between the two opposite principles of chaos and order: the former exemplified by the magma, flux and paste, and the latter epitomised by the crystal and, overall, a particulate vision of the world. Following Hume in her philosophical and interdisciplinary perspective is Kerstin Pilz (2005), who investigates Calvino's oeuvre in its interrelations with science and explores the critical and methodological consequences of the inclusion of the notion of system in Calvino scholarship.

Equally fruitful to my project is the dialogue with Olivia Santovetti's (2007) work on digression, where she links Calvino's propensity for modelling and form to plot specifically, rather than to narrative structure generically. With a move that closely reminds what I seek to do in this book, Santovetti speaks of 'making plots as making models' (2007: 195). Drawing on views of 'model' advanced in *Palomar* (1983),[4] she reads *Se una notte* as an example of 'imperfect model' because it displays 'a plot that is able to contain, in spite of many interruptions and multiple interpolations, the centrifugal and disbanding element. This is a nonlinear plot which finds its meaning and vitality in the subversion and metamorphosis of its own structure' (2007: 193–94). Santovetti interprets digression as a strategy that, although disruptive in some sense, does not hinder the understanding of *Se una notte* but rather enriches it as it manages to instantiate multiplicity within the narrative. My own argument intends to refine and further explore the patterns that readers may sense beneath this 'subversion and metamorphosis'.

My only concern with Santovetti's theoretical argument might be that, by way of premise, she posits digression and plot as complementary yet juxtaposed elements, where digression is understood as a centrifugal force that brings variety and disorder into the linearity and order established by the plot (18). By contrast, I would suggest that digression can impart a different pace on certain plots, but that the notion of plot ought to be revised to become a more inclusive and flexible concept itself, able to potentially include digressive movements. In fact, Santovetti herself seems sometimes to go back on her own premises, blurring the definition of plot as counterpart of digression, and speaking instead of 'linear plot' and 'digressive plot' (194). Most importantly, I prioritise the fact that she strives for an explanation that accounts for the continuity and the unity of the text, which she finds in the notion of imperfect model, flexible and metamorphosing. In other words, even though *Se una notte* is a composite work made of ten different incipits technically linked by the frame only, Santovetti refuses to overlook the fact that, provided that *Se una notte* is presented to the reader as a novel, the mechanism that keeps its parts together must be one single, flexible mechanism, and not a series of different models — as, for instance, suggested by Franco Ricci (1982: 96).

While it stands out as a fascinating case study to advance my overall hypothesis that narrative understanding may be spatial in nature, the innovative reading offered in this chapter provides an additional angle for looking at *Se una notte*. French poet and mathematician Jacques Roubaud, also member of the Oulipo,[5] observed that with the semiotic trilogy Calvino moves from narratives based on a axiological principle — like the *Cosmicomiche*, where short stories are built around a scientific principle or anecdote about the history of the universe — to narratives based on a geometrical model. A grid-like structure had been recognised in *Il castello dei destini incrociati* (1969, 1973)[6] and equally famous is the diamond-shaped arrangement imposed by the table of contents in *Le città invisibili* (1972).[7] However, an equally convincing explanation of the structural constraints operating in *Se una notte* was lacking to date: to acknowledge the fractal-like organisation of the novel fills in this gap and opens new avenues of research on the relevance of spatiality in Calvino's cognitive style more broadly.[8]

Patterns of order and disorder

While it is not my purpose to offer an in-depth analysis of Calvino's ideas on order, it is relevant to our discussion to outline the varied and long-standing nature of his reflections on this subject. In particular, I shall advance some observations as to how the notion of fractality interestingly positions itself in the wake of the progressive transformation undergone over the years by the mutual interrelation of order and disorder, and how this meditation not only intersects Calvino's views on spatiality and genres but also impacts on his use of specific narrative strategies such as the frame or visual representations associated to stories.

Despite it being almost impossible to trace an irreversible trajectory, a significant turning point in Calvino's views on order can be reasonably identified between the late 1960s and early 1970s. While at an early stage order is mostly intended as something juxtaposed to disorder (Guj 1988; Varsava 1986), already in the cosmicomical stories order and disorder are increasingly presented as a complementary binomial pair: the unresolved tension is a recurrent subject of debate between Qfwfq and Vug ('I cristalli') as well as at the heart of Qfwfq's dilemmatic choice between Xha and Wha, equally fascinating to him for different reasons ('I meteoriti'). Pilz identifies in Calvino's 1973 re-examination of the concept of utopia (which he had discussed before in relation to Fourier's utopian society project, grounded on fine-grained classifications and orderings) an important demonstration of his change of views with respect to pristine order and its advisability, as it proves that 'for him it is no longer the perfection of the model that counts, but its flaws and what remains hidden' (2005: 136). In Calvino's maturity, therefore, while the crystalline idea of order becomes irreducibly nuanced with symptoms of disorder, disorder ceases to be mere shapelessness and acquires properties (or it becomes carrier) of a different type of order (Capozzi 1988; Hayles 1991; Piacentini 2002). When in 'Molteplicità' Calvino praises the missing sixty-sixth chapter in *Le Vie mode d'emploi* (1978), a deliberate error in the otherwise geometrically perfect work of Georges Perec, he clearly sees it not as a defect but as something that, on the contrary, enhances the overall order (Pilz 2005: 139). By the early 1980s, it appears that order and disorder are so irreducibly intertwined that their co-existence even becomes a desirable condition.

The operation of writing itself, which can be seen sometimes as an attempt 'to put order into the disorder of experience' (Guj 1987: 866), is an ordering practice that however should not deny the protean and disordered nature of reality. Calvino is well aware of this double-faced feature when he uses the image of the flame to complement that of the crystal: while the latter epitomises clarity and formal order, the former represents an 'immagine di costanza d'una forma globale esteriore, malgrado l'incessante agitazione interna' (SI 688–89 [constancy of external forms in spite of relentless internal agitation, *Six Memos*]). The underlying disorder and sense of the changeable nature of reality will never cease to wield its powerful fascination on Calvino, and it has been subsequently conceptually elaborated by scholarship in terms of complexity (Pilz 2005), chaos (Hume 1992), shapelessness (Guj 1988), or multiplicity.

Restating a connection already advanced in Chapter 2 between order and spatiality, in the short autobiographical piece 'Dall'opaco' (RRIII 89–101) Calvino establishes an explicit link between the Ligurian landscape and the type of relations he learnt to individuate when it comes to make sense of his own experience, be it individually elaborated (in the form of his own thoughts) or interactively so (in the type of relations he may isolate in the world around him). Interestingly enough, in the description of plausible mental operations outlined in 'Dall'opaco' (see below) we can already find essential properties of fractality: discontinuity within continuity, slanting yet unavoidable relations between levels of (fictional) reality, all projected against the horizon of an overarching epistemological frame that embraces an irreducible heterogeneity. If we compare 'Dall'opaco' with a passage from *Se una notte*, we would soon realise how the pattern of vertical and horizontal relations, further typified by internal irregularities, deeply influenced the kind of order Calvino tends to impart to his narratives:

> le case anche loro che tagliano verticalmente la linea dei dislivelli, poggiate mezzo sul gradino di sotto e mezzo su quello di sopra, con due pianterreni uno sotto uno sopra, e così anche adesso che ordinariamente le case sono più alte di qualsiasi palma, e tracciano linee verticali ascendenti più lunghe in mezzo alle linee spezzate e oblique del livello del suolo [RRIII 90]

> [houses likewise cutting vertically across the line of the shifts of height, standing half on the level below and half on the level above, with two grounds floors one below and one above, and likewise even now that houses are usually higher than any palm tree, and trace longer vertical ascending lines amid the oblique and broken lines of the ground levels] [131]

> Tutte queste linee oblique incrociandosi dovrebbero delimitare lo spazio dove ci muoviamo io e Valeriano e Irina, dove la nostra storia possa affiorare dal nulla, trovare un punto di partenza, una direzione, un disegno. [79]

> [All these oblique lines, intersecting, should define the space where we moved, I and Valerian and Irina, where our story can emerge from nothingness, find a point of departure, a direction, a plot.] [77]

While it is impossible to determine whether one thing directly caused the other, it is significant that Calvino himself senses a connection between his early exposure to this specific topographical space and his predilection for geometry as viable ordering system. It was Pietro Citati who described this tendency of Calvino in terms of *esprit géométrique*, drawing on Blaise Pascal's stark juxtaposition between an analytical versus discursive (*esprit de finesse*) way to cognise the world (1959: 233). Yet also in this respect it would be better to avoid any dualism, and it may be suggested that Calvino rather combines the two modes into a spirit of geometric finesse, aiming at ordering reality without denying its complexity (Bonsaver 1995: 165).

To further enrich our mental map of issues that bring together order and spatiality we must mention Calvino's interest in folk tales, as it represents the literary analogous and direct implementation of his passion for geometric patterns and correspondences. Calvino's in-depth work on the Italian folktale, culminated in the editing of the *Fiabe italiane* in 1956, played a critical role in the elaboration of his idea of narrative, especially as far as its spatial features are concerned: indeed, he admits that his interest in folktales was mainly sparked by his desire to stress the artificiality and rationality of storytelling, together with its elements of order and geometry (Bonsaver 1995: 53). As I shall explore later on, the formalist understanding of the folktale in terms of functions and limited sets of constants upon which certain variations can be operated will be particularly relevant to Calvino's conceptualisation of narrative (see SII 1541–43, 1611–28). Through the folktale, Calvino enucleates the lesson that the system of internal relationships among elements might be more meaningful than the elements themselves. To some extent, we could trace back to this genre also Calvino's propensity for stressing both the whole and parts alike through the workings of narratives which are modular and yet kept together by means of framing narrative devices (SII 1617). It could be argued, in some sense, that with *Il castello* and in *Se una notte* Calvino reproduces in a single work the sense-making strategies inferred from a whole genre, a whole tradition.

The element of the frame is firstly introduced in a relatively loose version in *Le cosmicomiche*, where each story is introduced by a short caption illustrating some (pseudo-)scientific principle that will be more or less ironically developed in the fictional narrative. Note that, as mentioned earlier, it is precisely with the cosmicomical tales that the stark juxtaposition between a positive view order and a negative view disorder begins to be undermined. Abandoned in *Ti con zero*, the frame returns in *Altre storie cosmicomiche* almost to never leave Calvino's horizon again: in fact, it increases its structural and semantic relevance from *Le città* to *Il castello*, up to its highest point in *Se una notte*.[9] Along with Bonsaver, it thus does not seem out of place to suggest that the macrotext is a narrative mechanism employed by Calvino to negotiate this tension between order and disorder, something working as 'contenitore rigido reso necessario dalla necessità di creare una struttura di supporto in grado di controllare, di dare ordine, alla multiformità della sostanza narrata' (Bonsaver 1994: 182 [a rigid container made necessary by the need to create a scaffolding structure able to control and impose order on the multiformity of the narrated matter]; Camps 2000).[10] In *Il castello*, the macrotext is perfectly exploited as to the first set of cards. With the second set, however, in *La taverna dei destini incrociati* the structure is not as perfect, and at the end it highlights the presence of a void at the centre of the structure: Bonsaver suggests that it is this imperfect application of the constraint that conveys the message that is most interesting as it reveals the epistemological value of the void in the semiotic trilogy as a whole. In *Le città*, the macrotext provides an overarching structure that holds together fragments that have been composed separately and, at the same time, reminds the reader of the multiple possible interpretations of such a peculiar storyworld. In other words, Calvino does not use the macrotext to comfortingly normalise the disturbance of unordered reality: it is a mediating device that, on the contrary, gives the author the opportunity to foreground the issue of the relations among narrative components within a totality. As Simone Tonin (2005) suggests, it might be even argued that these cases clearly show that, for Calvino, space often becomes itself narration, meaning that some of these stories are based less on images and words and more on the relations between elements. It is these mutual spatial relations that ensure the tellability of the narratives.[11]

Also linked to the question of rendering the relationship between the whole and its parts is the utmost care devoted to the graphical structure of *Il castello* and *Le città*. The visual element shows how important it was for Calvino that readers could embrace in one single gaze the design of the work in its entirety so that they could also appreciate the set of constraints operating on it (Milanini 1990: 128). 'Fantasia figurale' is how Calvino calls the capability to grasp this chief quality of spatial configurations — be they conceptual or properly visual — able to gather together antinomies and juxtapositions (SI 705). In space, opposites can co-exist, to the point that Calvino suggests that figural imagination is in fact an irreplaceable tool for both the poet and the scientist for it crystallises composite associations of ideas into something that can be cognitively taken in as a whole (SI 707). Images, in turn, have the capability to capture this property of space. Calvino has explored this idea in many narrative ways, from the Tarot cards in *Il castello*, where each image epitomises a whole story and at the same time has different functions according to its position in a new sequence, to *Le cosmicomiche*, where this condition is creatively turned into the narrative situation of the story 'Tutto in un punto'. The aspect on which I would like to focus my attention is not much the relationship between visual imagination and verbal expression, but rather the potentiality contained in, and conveyed by, the image — a potentiality that refers both to a future, single, unfolding of events and to the multiplicity of possible plural unfoldings. It is on this potentiality and on its virtual nature that I shall focus in the next section.

To recapitulate, the hypothesis of the fractal plot of *Se una notte* not only does make sense within the novel, as my analysis will show, but it also provides a robust critical explanation, when set in the broader context of Calvino's spatially-informed cognitive style, of his reflection on order and disorder and of the narrative strategies he employed to convey them. Fractality is indeed a mode of organisation that embodies the almost paradoxical integration of these two opposites and, by designing a narrative structure that constitutionally relies on variation and repetition, Calvino masterly manages to combine them not only through the content but fundamentally through the form of the narrative.

Calvino's obsession for 'the path not taken'

The discourse on the virtual has been one of the main *fils rouges* of this book. Virtuality, let us remind it ourselves, encompasses all those narrative elements — characters, events, places — that are not fully granted the status of actual facts in the storyworld. The link with spatiality lies in the hypothesis that, since storyworlds are enriched by a complex virtual dimension, in order to make sense of the narrative as a whole readers may be prompted to rely on cognitive strategies usually adopted to make sense of a three-dimensional space, rather than simply consider the chronological linear unfolding of events. All the narratives explored so far variously engage with the dimension of narrative virtuality in order to keep their narrative machineries going.

Throughout his production, Calvino frequently and passionately reflected on the various articulations of virtuality. However, a privileged role is reserved to potentiality and the void, especially in *Se una notte*. After a brief overview of uses of counterfactuality in Calvino, most of the next subsection is devoted to a discussion of potentiality, while the following one examines the void. Finally, in the third subsection I shall consider the concept of hypernovel, how it developed and why it particularly concerns *Se una notte*, since I believe it is significantly linked to the discussion of virtuality.

Counterfactuality and potentiality

If counterfactual and potential events are technically unfulfilled possibilities, counterfactuals are impossible because they missed their chance to be actualised, whereas potentials still retain the chance to be fulfilled at some point. Domenico Scarpa (1999) observes that Calvino already touches on counterfactuality in *Le cosmicomiche*, but then ascribes it a preeminent role in *Ti con zero*, which is pervaded by 'un'ansia rivolta alle cose che potevano essere e non sono state e non saranno mai' (241 [an anxiety for those things that could have been and have not, nor could ever be]).

Such an anxiety may be variously interpreted. To consider what might be its sources, let us look ahead at *Le città invisibili*, whose very title hints at a dimension that struggles to be ascertained as objective:[12]

> Marco entra in una città; vede qualcuno in una piazza vivere una vita o un istante che potevano essere suoi; [...] Ormai, da quel suo passato vero o ipotetico, lui è escluso; non può fermarsi; [...] I futuri non realizzati sono solo rami del passato: rami secchi. [...] L'altrove è uno specchio in negativo. Il viaggiatore riconosce il poco che è suo, scoprendo il molto che non ha avuto e non avrà. [RRII 378–79]

> [Marco enters a city; he sees someone in a square living a life or an instant that could be his; [...] By now, from that real or hypothetical past of his, he is excluded; he cannot stop; [...] Futures not achieved are only branches of the past: dead branches. [...] Elsewhere is a negative mirror. The traveler recognizes the little that is his, discovering the much he has not had and will never have.] [29]

In this excerpt, the obsession with possibility is re-centred on the individual, who becomes aware of the specificities of his/her own identity in relation to what one is *not*, what one has *not* become. From this explicit standpoint, Scarpa looks retrospectively and suggests that the issue of existence at an anthropological scale in *Le città* was already present in *Ti con zero* at a cosmological scale, where Calvino outlines a sort of 'morale della potenzialità' (2008: 95 [ethics of potentiality]) and muses on the unsettling awareness that anything in the universe exists at the expenses of other forms that ceased to be or remained unevolved, unexpressed.

The possibilities yearned for in the excerpt above are clearly counterfactuals, and Calvino ascribes them to the domain of the 'negative'. Far from implying a value judgment, this label rather resembles the concept of typographical matrix, a device that impresses the paper thanks to a pattern of full and empty spaces which create an intelligible meaning. As Calvino states with regard to *Se una notte*, the novel represents 'una specie d'autobiografia in negativo: i romanzi che avrei potuto scrivere e che avevo scartato' (RRII 1396 [sort of a negative autobiography: the novels I could have written which instead I have discarded]). McLaughlin notes, however, that *Se una notte* is as significantly tied to the genres Calvino did not explore as it is to many works he did write (1998: 127–28): counterfactuality, in other words, is often nostalgically craved for by Calvino as it covers an array of potential possibilities. It is therefore on the broader dimension of potentiality that one ought to focus.

Consider the following passage, taken from the fifth intercalated novel of *Se una notte* and representing a full display of the powers of potentiality: 'Sto tirando fuori troppe storie alla volta perché quello che voglio è che intorno al racconto si senta una saturazione d'altre storie che potrei raccontare e forse racconterò o chissà che non abbia già raccontato in altra occasione' (108–09 [I'm producing too many stories at once because what I want is for you to feel, around the story, a saturation of other stories that I could tell and maybe will tell or who knows may already have told on some other occasion, 105]). By making the narrator's intended outcome explicit, this metanarrative passage clarifies the difference between counterfactuals and potentials. Since these stories are simply hinted at by the narrator, they are not fully actualised; however, their lack of actualisation pertains the act of narration only, as they seem to report events that might be actually verified in the storyworld and are simply not known to the reader. They are not counterfactuals because they do not clash with actualised events yet they are not endowed with a full status either, in a way that reminds us of Baricco's use of virtuality in *City* — although the metanarrative intention in the two novels is arguably very different.

Discussing this practice in *Se una notte*, Santovetti associates the regular display of potentiality with the narrative technique of digression. She argues that what is important in the novel is indeed the feeling of saturation of stories, which depends on what it is said as much as on what is left out of the narration (2007: 223). Bonsaver's analogous comment on Calvino's desire to make a novel capable to stand out as the ideal place to show the multiplicity of all possible things (1995: 78) offers the opportunity to stress an important aspect: although I introduced potentiality in relation to a discourse on virtuality, in Calvino it cannot be considered as separate from the issue of multiplicity. The two properties, virtuality and multiplicity, are distinct but irreducibly intertwined. Something potential is such because it has not actualised yet, but also something that, not being actualised, can still co-exist next to its alternatives prior to the specification that follows any choice (Usher 1996: 188).

In her exploration of Calvino's lifelong quest, Hume observes that: 'What the narrator does in this story is explore possibilities' (1992: 30), and indeed in *Se una notte* the intercalated novels offer the chance to all the participants in the narrative experience to try out various solutions. From a creative perspective, Calvino (SII 1874) admits that he deliberately selected the genres of the intercalated novels among those which he thought he would have never approached as an author, thus exploring their stylistic potentiality (Beaudouin 2008: 65). As to readers, different genres and national traditions represent different ways of sense-making, as they involve their own sets of expectations and conventions and therefore different perspectives on storyworlds and consequently different ways of shaping them into narratives. Multiplicity, in other words, emerges as the most suitable scenario for ensuring that different approaches are not excluding each other — thus somehow circumscribing the problem of choice and benefitting from all of the possible options. Perhaps the most charming example of this beautiful variety is represented in *Se una notte* by the final portrait of the seven types of readers and attitudes toward reading, which would deserve to be quoted in full (256–58 [248–50]).

Strongly metanarrative in nature, *Se una notte* is designed to expose the issues surrounding potentiality, both as virtuality and multiplicity. The novel is made of twelve numbered chapters alternated with ten titled incipits of potential novels. The twelve chapters compose the overarching frame that structures the narrative and refer to the same storyworld, within which the incipits are intercalated. With a similar encompassing movement, the titles of the incipits (plus an additional final one) form together a question that could be itself the incipit of an eleventh novel still to be found (260 [252]).

The importance of the incipit for Calvino, both practically and theoretically, is demonstrated by his initial plan to devote one of the Norton Lectures to the topic of 'Cominciare e finire'.[13] In the manuscript, he claims as follows:

> [Cominciare è] un momento decisivo per lo scrittore: il distacco dalla potenzialità illimitata e multiforme per incontrare qualcosa che ancora non esiste ma che potrà esistere solo accettando dei limiti e delle regole. [SI 734]
>
> [To begin is a crucial moment for the writer; to detach oneself from unlimited potentiality and multiformity in order to meet something that does not exist as yet, but which may be able to exist only by accepting certain limits and rules.]

As to its implementation in *Se una notte*, most valuable to our discussion is Chapter Eight, which consists in the journal of the prolific writer Silas Flannery, a character very close to Calvino himself (RRII 1393). Through the technique of *mise en abyme* (on which I will return later), the experimental exploit of the incipit highlights the strategy that chiefly serves potentiality:

> Vorrei poter scrivere un libro che fosse solo un *incipit*, che mantenesse per tutta la sua durata la potenzialità dell'inizio, l'attesa ancora senza oggetto. Ma come potrebb'essere costruito, un libro simile? S'interromperebbe dopo il primo capoverso? Prolungherebbe infinitamente i preliminari? Incastrerebbe un inizio di narrazione nell'altro, come le Mille e una notte? [177]
>
> [I would like to be able to write a book that is only an *incipit*, that maintains

for its whole duration the potentiality of the beginning, the expectation still not focused on an object. But how could such a book be constructed? Would it break off after the first paragraph? Would the preliminaries be prolonged indefinitely? Would it set the beginning of one tale inside another, as in the *Arabian Nights*?] [173]

Confirming the partial overlapping of Flannery's and Calvino's perspectives, Bruno Falcetto (1991) points out that in a partly unpublished piece written by Calvino in 1975 (note that he starts composing *Se una notte* in 1977)[14] we already find those concepts that will constitute the bulk of Silas Flannery's diary in *Se una notte*, in particular the view of the incipit as the epitome of potentiality and the technical difficulties of creating a novel all made of incipits. Two main reasons must be pinpointed here about why such a novel — and, indeed, *Se una notte* — would endorse the powers of potentiality. First, because of the specific nature of the incipit, that is of a beginning. Potentiality is inherent to its openness, which creates the premises for choice(s) but does not force one to its definitiveness (Barenghi 2007: 77–79; Kottman 1996). Secondly, because of the programmatic multiplication of stories: not only beginnings contain in potential an array of unfoldings all equally actualisable, but also the juxtaposition of several different beginnings concretely pursues the plurality that is inherent to potentiality in the first place.

At the end of the quotation above, we can find three envisioned ways to implement potentiality: interruption, prolongation, and embedment. In his response to Angelo Guglielmi's review in *Alfabeta* (1979), Calvino explains that the structure of *Se una notte* is deeply related to the poetics of interruption, or of the 'finito interrotto' (1979a [finished interrupted]). Indeed, Calvino's poetics of interruption is not a poetics of the unfinished. Nor, as Luce d'Eramo (1979) suggests, are the incipits actually concluded short stories.[15] Such a specification is telling because it reveals that the activation of potentiality is not a by-product but a purposely designed effect, a key intended outcome of the narrative. Also, Santovetti (2007) acknowledges interruption as the core technique that, together with multiplicity, ensures the transformative power of the plot in *Se una notte*. Drawing on traditional uses (above all, in popular fiction, the *feuilleton*), Santovetti observes that interruption can consist in either a simple halt in the plot or a halt followed by an interpolation; since this latter is carried out by the narrator, it reveals the narrator's strong presence and power over the narrative (2007: 214). She argues that the principle of interruption constitutes not only a theme of *Se una notte*, but it is also a pivotal device with structuring purposes that impacts upon the reception of the text: on the one hand, it initiates the digression and ensures variety by changing perspective or enabling unexpected turns of events; on the other hand, although frustrating, interruption engages the reader as it teaches one to detach from the text and encourages self-reflection (2007: 217 and 219; Usher 1990).

Interestingly enough, the second solution that Calvino/Silas hypothesises for building a narrative entirely made of incipits is seemingly the opposite of interruption, that is the prolongation of one single continuous incipit. Demonstrating once again his pleasure for paradoxes (as with the integration of order and disorder), in some sense Calvino implements both solutions: the option of multiple interrupted incipits is pursued systematically and thoroughly, yet could not the fact that the titles of the ten intercalated novels all together form an eleventh incipit allow one to see the whole *Se una notte* as one long, prolonged and continuously deferred beginning? Less tentatively, it should be noted that the paradoxical co-validity of two solutions so different also harkens back to another dominant idea of Calvino's — and of Jorge Luis Borges' before him — that is the oscillation between the desire to write all the possible books (or incipits) and write only one, infinite (181). As to the third solution, the long-standing technique of the frame and of embedded narratives, it is another fundamental feature of *Se una notte* which I shall discuss in greater detail in the next section.

Although in the article in *Alfabeta* Calvino identifies an intriguing and Borgesian system of binary possibilities structuring *Se una notte*, one can hardly acknowledge it any substantial programmatic validity. Calvino admits that he himself came to see it as the underlying scaffolding of *Se una notte* only after a 'knowledgeable friend' had made him notice it (RRII 1396).[16] Also Bonsaver (1994, 1995) is sceptical about both the a priori validity of this scheme and that Calvino designed a closed macrostructure to curb down the potentialities of narrative; if any, such a rigorous structure suggests the opposite conclusion, namely its own inability to limit the disorder of reality. Even if we hypothesise that this system of progressive exclusions really was one of the operating constraints at the moment of its composition, the pairs of binary options listed by Calvino are so arbitrary that one could reasonably question whether they actually impact in any way on the readers' understanding and on the elaboration of expectations during reading. In other words, their arbitrariness is such that the process of selection does not configure itself in the reader's eyes as a matter of actual exclusion of some possibilities over others.[17]

Arguably, this is one of the main differences between *Il castello* and *Se una notte*. Although Calvino said that these works are animated by '[l]o stesso principio di campionatura della molteplicità potenziale del narrabile' (SI 730 [The same principle, to sample the potential multiplicity of what may be narrated, *Six Memos*: 120]), they implement this principle in two rather different ways, with significant consequences on plot.[18] In *Il castello*, potentiality is expressed through the creative power of the Tarot set of cards as 'macchina narrativa combinatoria' (RRII 1276 [a combinatorial narrative machine]). The cards provide a finite set of units that can produce a vertiginous yet virtually finite number of combinations; the selection is made by applying reason and thus through the indispensable intervention of the author, who chooses the sequences that are more likely to produce — or had produced over the centuries (for example, the stories of Faust or Parsifal) — some particular meaning when they are processed by the reader's mind (SI 220–21). Infinite indeed is the amount of narratives that the individual can create by building on each sequence, but the number of combinations of cards is mathematically finite. Unlike *Il castello*, *Se una notte* is not technically limited to a definite number of combinations, because its stories are not generated by a finite number of units nor (referring to Calvino's binary structure) by mutually exclusive pairs. The aforementioned arbitrariness of the choices identified by Calvino is such that the novel could have either included half of them or added ten more, and both cases would have been equally viable: 'quanto bastava per comunicare il senso della molteplicità' (RRII 1393 [enough to convey a sense of multiplicity]). My point is that, while *Il castello* has a closed structure and an almost purely instrumental frame, the narrative of *Se una notte* is not inherently finite and has therefore to set the limits of its sample of potential multiplicity in some other way, namely by means of a more binding discursive frame narrative.

Potentiality can also be reformulated in terms of ways to achieve it, either through multiplication and/or through the indeterminate. By manipulating the incipit as narrative element, Calvino fosters potentiality in both ways: through interruption he leaves its unfolding undecided while, by presenting the reader with one beginning after the other, he multiplies such an effect.

However, excessive proliferation of potentials may eventually undermine the narrative itself by exerting too much pressure on its intelligibility. From a feeling of saturation, uncontrolled growth might provoke an 'explosion' of the narrative into an incohesive mass (or, to say it with Hume: magma, paste, flux) of narrative fragments, a risk dreaded but played with by Calvino. In commenting on the section of *Il castello*, 'Tutte le altre storie', Maria Corti (1978: 177) acknowledges this when she writes:

> tutti gli accostamenti di segni essendo possibili, ne consegue che il non senso vale come il senso, produrrà una sequenza dell'irrazionale. Non solo, ma alle sequenze narrative attuate si affiancano quelle affacciatesi alla mente e scartate nel gioco delle combinazioni, cioè quelle che non ci sono, ma potrebbero esserci. Il che equivale a dire che dietro la possibilità infinita di variazioni si cela il dramma a cui alludono alcuni scrittori, come per esempio Borges, per cui una scelta tematica comporta sempre il rifiuto del non scelto.

> [All the combinations of signs being possible, it follows that meaning and the lack thereof are the same thing, it will produce an irrational sequence. Even more, alongside the actualized narrative sequences one will have all those that have been provisionally thought of and then discarded, that is to say those which are not but could have been. Which amounts to say that behind the possibility for infinite variations lies the issue referred to by some writers — Borges, for instance — for whom any thematic choice implies the rejection of what has not been chosen.]

How burning the issue of choice — and, consequently, of discarding the non-chosen — must have been for Calvino emerges in 'La taverna', the second part of *Il castello*. Here, the tale 'Storia dell'indeciso' [The waverer's tale] concludes as follows:

> Ma è davvero lui o non piuttosto un suo sosia, che appena restituito a se stesso s'è visto venire avanti per il bosco?
> — Chi sei?
> — Sono l'uomo che doveva sposare la ragazza che tu non avresti scelto, che doveva prendere l'altra strada del bivio, dissetarsi all'altro pozzo. Tu non scegliendo hai impedito la mia scelta. [RRII 558–59]
> [But is this really he or is it rather a double whom he saw coming through the forest, the moment he was restored to himself?
> "Who are you?"

"I am the man who was to marry the girl you did not choose, who was to take the other road at the crossing, quench his thirst at the other well. By not choosing, you have prevented my choice."] [63]

Interestingly enough, this situation reminds of the passage quoted earlier from *Le città*, where Marco Polo depicts, in a softer yet not less nostalgic atmosphere, the pain one is bound to feel when contemplating the absence of the discarded option. In 'La taverna' the problem appears not to be any less urgent, and Calvino still dreads an ultimate confrontation between two selves who might find themselves comparing the outcomes of their complementary sets of choices: 'ogni scelta ha un rovescio cioè una rinuncia, e così non c'è differenza tra l'atto di scegliere e l'atto di rinunciare' (RRII 552 [for every choice has an obverse, that is to say a renunciation, and so there is no difference between the act of choosing and the act of renouncing, 56]; Scarpa 1999: 244).

To some extent, Calvino seems to have always felt an 'indeciso' himself. Francesca Serra notes that, already in 1946, before he had published his first work, Calvino wrote to a friend as follows: 'Io ho idee per dieci romanzi in testa. Ma in ogni idea io vedo già gli sbagli del romanzo che scriverei, perché io ho anche delle idee critiche in testa, ci ho tutta una *teoria sul perfetto romanzo*, e quella mi frega' (Serra 2006: 337 [In my head, I have ideas sufficient for ten novels; but for each one of them, I already see what's wrong in the novel that I would write because I also have ideas about criticism, I already have a whole *theory of the perfect novel*, and that's what tricks me]).[19] The strength of will that is required and the discomfort that follows any step out of the indeterminate domain of potentiality clearly emerge from 'Cominciare e finire'. With a reformulation of Gadda's belief that 'conoscere [...] è deformare il reale' (quoted in SI 719 [to know is to insert something into what is real, and hence to distort reality, *Six Memos*: 108]), culminated in the character of Palomar, Calvino demonstrates to be fully aware that also narration implies a fundamental deformation of reality: from complex and fluid and indeterminate in its potentiality, it has to be selected and crystallised in order to be narrated. *Se una notte*, with its metanarrative multiplication of incipits, offers the chance to reconcile the necessity of choice with that of exclusion. Such a renunciation to — or better, suspension of — choice as possible outcome of a proliferation of potentialities leads us to the third articulation of virtuality, that is the void.

The void

If virtuality entails the contemplation of alternative possibilities — some of which could be actualised, some of which are never to be — and their infinite multiplication, at the other side of the spectrum there is their annihilation, the void of possibilities. In the cosmicomical tale 'Il niente e il poco', the female character Nugkta turns from worshipping nothingness to the 'wholeness of things', as if the two things were, paradoxically, just one step away from each other, a *coincidentia oppositorum* (Capozzi 1988: 166). This subtle boundary is portrayed, and almost tragically overstepped, also in the tenth incipit of *Se una notte*, where the narrating-I suddenly realises not only that his seemingly only mental deletion of the world around him is indeed real but also that, by doing so, he is actually endorsing the faction of those known for encouraging the addition of things to the world, and that there is no difference between striving for incrementation or destruction (252 [243]).

As already noted, a certain penchant for paradox is not uncommon in Calvino, and it is demonstrated by the short stories of *Ti con zero* ('Ti con zero', 'L'inseguimento', 'Il conte di Montecristo') and by his admiration for the creator of the story of Achilles and the turtle, the Greek philosopher Zeno of Elea, who becomes, by a witty intertextual twitch, the secret recognition password among the two agents in the first incipit of *Se una notte*. For Calvino, the value of paradox lies in that it lays bare the limits of rationality and, consequently, denies the certainty of a definitive and univocal truth or stance on things: to borrow Bonsaver's words, in paradoxes rationality reaches a stalemate ('messa in scacco della razionalità', 1994: 188). In this sense, the taste for paradox reasonably matches with what observed earlier on multiplicity as the solution to Calvino's restlessness on specific stances. According to Barenghi (2007: 63), Calvino is an author who proceeds less by discursive synthesis and more by antinomies, which function as proper thinking instruments. Looking back at what suggested about Calvino's space-informed cognitive style, Barenghi's reference to antinomies could perhaps be read as a tendency to privilege synchronic relations among concepts, multiple possible configurations of ideas that can be geometrically visualised and easily manipulated, unlike discursive argumentations.

Building on Corti's observation quoted above, void is a possible articulation of virtuality that may result from two distinct drives. First, from the inability to acknowledge viable hierarchies in the ascription of meaning: in other words, with *all* the options available, no meaning is as good as any meaning. Secondly, from the refusal to choose anything out of an equal fascination for all other potentials that would become counterfactuals if a definitive choice is made. In other words, it could be suggested that, facing the vastness of virtuality, the former sense is inspired by a retreat of the ordering principle, the latter sense by a fusion with and in the totality, where heterogeneity is so dense that it remains indeterminate to the subject's consciousness.[20] In *Il castello*, the close connection between the two opposites, nothing and everything, is explicitly uttered in the episode of Faust and Parsifal (RRII 582–90). For Faust, the world does not exist as a unitary entity and consists instead of an infinite number of random combinations of elements; Parsifal agrees on the world's non-existence yet not because of its inherent multiplicity but because its ultimate core is an empty space. The empty rectangular identified by Parsifal corresponds to the space left at the intersection of the several sequences of tarot cards as arranged in 'La taverna'. Similarly, in *Le città*, emptiness and reversal appear not only as themes but also at a structural level. Staging a reversal of Thomas More's utopian project — where he describes only the capital, located at the centre of the island, epitome of all the other fifty-four great cities — Calvino describes instead fifty-four cities and reserves the central place of his collection to the empty city of Bauci. Milanini thus observes that '[n]el capovolgimento del modello moreano dobbiamo scorgere molto più dell'assunzione di un'ulteriore *contrainte*: c'è la denuncia di un'assenza e, insieme, una scelta di metodo. C'è, insomma, il rifiuto a prefigurare globalmente ciò che deve essere costruito giorno dopo giorno'

(1990: 144 [to reverse the Morean model is more than creating an additional formal constraint: it means to acknowledge an absence and to take a methodological stance. It means, in other words, to refuse to give a global representation of what should be constructed step by step]; Ossola 1987).

In the semiotic trilogy, Bonsaver (1994: 188) acknowledges the void as a common semiotic and existential concern, a symbolic core and an absence which stands for what is un-rational ('non-razionalizzabile') and untellable ('indicibile').[21] On the one hand, he hints at a possible influence on Calvino's poetics of the void exerted by Jacques Derrida's (1967/1978) deconstructionism and his concept of *différance*. On the other, Bonsaver only cautiously endorses such a connection; in agreement with this last observation, I would suggest that, in the case of Calvino, void might not (univocally) symbolise a continual deferral of meaning but rather the impossibility to settle on a single one: less an impossible meaning, thus, and more a plurality of mutually incompatible meanings, where choice is the hardest part. Bonsaver seems to concur on a similar point when, speaking of *Le città*, he observes that '[a] un'osservazione attenta, anche il vuoto sembra contenere in sé le tracce di una nuova realtà materiale [...] per quanto indicibile e sospesa nel nulla' (1995: 82 [to an attentive observer, even the void appears to retain the traces of a new material reality...no matter how seemingly untellable and up in the air]). In fact, the scholar suggests that familiarising with absence could create a standpoint for a new encounter with the materiality of the world, a view that gains credibility if one thinks of Calvino's following works, *Palomar* and the unfinished *Sotto il sole giaguaro*.[22]

Moreover, to bring *Se una notte* too close with Derrida's post-structuralist theories might imply a risky attitude toward the autonomy of the text and its relationship with the extra-textual. No matter how convincingly Paul Kottman might undermine the interpretation that wants Derrida positing the existence of the text only, to designate Calvino's idea of void as an application of the concept of différance seems to be limiting at best, while at worst it puts one in an ambiguous position concerning the status of extra-textual reality. Against a view of Calvino as crediting only the text with reality (Watson 1988), it should be noted that already in 'Cibernetica e fantasmi' he addresses the duplicity of literature as both the result of a combinatorial process and, still, as something responding to forces that might not be knowable and might reside outside of the limits of language and literature (SI 217). An even more explicit position is expressed in a 1967 interview with Madeleine Santschi, where he asserts that he believes in reality as something that exists independently from the human effort to represent it:

> Io non sono tra coloro che credono che esista solo il linguaggio, o solo il pensiero umano. [...] Io credo che esista una realtà e che ci sia un rapporto (seppure sempre parziale) tra la realtà e i segni con cui la rappresentiamo. [...] Io credo che il mondo esista indipendentemente dall'uomo [...]. [SI 1347]

Finally, in *Se una notte* Silas Flannery admits: 'io non credo che la totalità sia contenibile nel linguaggio; il mio problema è ciò che resta fuori, il non-scritto' (181 [I do not believe totality can be contained in language; my problem is what remains outside, the unwritten, 177]).

Retaining our focus on *Se una notte*, Cesare Segre (1979) was probably the first to spot how all the intercalated novels revolve around the issues of void, nothingness, and absence. I will discuss later how the creation of thematic patterns — including the pattern made of references to void and nothingness — affects the narrative and its understanding, and I shall now concentrate on the consequences of using these specific images. In terms of distribution, it should be noted that, over twenty-two chapters (twelve chapters plus ten intercalated novels), precise references to the void ('vuoto') occur at least once in seventeen of them. Of the chapters where the word 'vuoto' is not included, the intercalated novel 'Sporgendosi dalla costa scoscesa' still revolves around issues such as the end of the world (53 [52]), absence (55 [53–54]), dissolution (63 [62]), and the predominance of the obscurity and the colour black (59 [58]); Chapter Six stages the Reader chasing the elusive Ermes Marana through the correspondence kept by the publishing house, and is dominated by a sense of dissolution beneath the interchange of masks put on by the translator in his game of falsifications. The first reference to void is made in the first incipit, where the character of Madame Marne mentions the empty luggage of her mysterious client (22 [21]); afterwards, the term 'vuoto' appears in every intercalated novel and in almost every chapter of the frame (except for sixth and twelfth).

And yet what is void in *Se una notte*, what does it represent? Before trying to answer this question, we should briefly consider the role and meaning of the void in Calvino's overall production. Without assuming to give a thorough and definitive overview of such a complex concept, I advance a few observations and highlight the underlying tensions within Calvino's elaboration.

The void is an articulation of virtuality for two main reasons. First, because in Calvino's narratives absence and nothingness do impact upon what exist in the storyworld and therefore they have to be appointed a status which, not being actuality, has to pertain to the virtual. Secondly, because the void can present itself as the paradoxical result of excessive plurality. In other words, while it may initially seem that void is something that *is not*, from a theoretical perspective it might be better defined as *undifferentiated*.[23] It belongs to the realm of the virtual because it is undifferentiated potentiality, which, by a paradoxical leap, is configured as nothingness rather than infinite multiplicity. Void as something that is not *yet*, something on which choice does not operate.[24]

Se una notte represents a perfect case study for the exploration of this articulation of virtuality and the discussion of how Calvino's theoretical and nonfictional elaboration of the concept interacts with its fictional narrative counterpart. It has been recorded that the term 'vuoto' occurs for the first time in the first intercalated novel, where it is used to describe an empty luggage that, nonetheless, plays a central role. The fundamental link between importance and emptiness is here tacitly established, which reminds of a nonfictional piece dating back to a journey in Iran in 1975, later published in *Collezione di sabbia* (1984):

> Quello che m'attira [del mihrab] è l'idea di una porta che fa di tutto per mettere in vista la sua funzione di porta ma che non s'apre su nulla; [...] La sua sola qualità è quella di non esserci. [...] la cosa più importante al mondo sono gli spazi vuoti. [SI 611–13]

> [What attracts me [about the mihrab] is the idea of a door that does everything to put on display its function as a door but which opens onto nothing, [...] Its sole quality is that of not being there. [...] the most important things in the world are the empty spaces.] [197–98]

The atmosphere of the first incipit is also meaningful. The description of the physical environment, foggy and dark, together with the repeated statements of the narrating-I concerning his lack of understanding of his own circumstances, contribute to depict a blurred and obscure state of affairs, which is in turn associated with the idea of void, too. This connection is maintained throughout the whole novel by means of reiterated references to the semantic area of 'depth', including 'precipizio' (48 [precipice, 47]), 'precipitare' (55 [plunging, 54]), 'baratro' (69 [chasm, 68]), 'là sotto' (81 [down below, 79]), 'strapiombo', 'voragine' and 'abisso' (82 [gap, chasm, abyss, 80]), 'sotto ogni parola c'è il nulla' (83 [beneath every word there is nothingness, 80]), 'laggiù era ancora oscurità fitta' (114 [down there the darkness was still thick, 110]), 'lottando contro qualcosa d'oscuro' (173 [struggling with something obscure, 169]), 'corda sospesa sul vuoto' (174 [a tightrope stretched over the void, 169]).

Thus, throughout most of the novel, void takes the fictional shape of a dark nothingness that exists all around and beneath the boundaries and the surface of the storyworld. How such a depiction of the void is related to its ascription to virtuality is worth further clarification. Let us consider the first and the last intercalated novels, which adequately represent most of the other instances in the book but also prompt an additional consideration on these two cases specifically.

> ogni volta il muro di buio mi ha ricacciato indietro in questa specie di limbo [...]. La città là fuori non ha ancora un nome, non sappiamo se resterà fuori del romanzo o se lo conterrà tutto nel suo nero d'inchiostro. [14]
>
> [each time the wall of darkness has driven back inside this sort of illuminated limbo [...]. The city outside there has no name yet, we don't know if it will remain outside of the novel or whether the whole story will be contained within its inky blackness.] [13]
>
> Camminando per la grande Prospettiva della nostra città, cancello mentalmente gli elementi che ho deciso di non prendere in considerazione. [...] con la coda dell'occhio li vedo assottigliarsi e svanire in una leggera nebbia. [...] Basta che resti uno strato di crosta terrestre abbastanza solida sotto i piedi e il vuoto da tutte le altre parti. [247, 250]
>
> [Walking along the great Prospect of our city, I mentally erase the elements I have decided not to take into consideration. [...] out of the corner of my eye, I see them shrink and vanish in a faint wisp of fog. [...] A layer of the earth's crust is all that has to remain, solid enough underfoot, and everywhere else, nothingness.] [239, 242]

In the first case, the term 'vuoto' is not directly employed, but the threat of an impending dissolution, a dark nothingness, surrounds the station where the scene takes place; in the second case, the narrating-I deliberately deletes — with his imagination but also, it turns out, actually — increasing chunks of reality around him. The two movements are somehow specular: first, a storyworld is being sketched as still *in fieri* and emerging from the void (Bonsaver 1995: 67), while in the last incipit the storyworld is rapidly disintegrating, and it is only the encounter with the narrator's beloved girl that saves it from annihilation — their meeting like the single grain of sand that remains of the kingdom of Fantasia in *The Neverending Story*, and from which it will arise again.[25]

Calvino's description highlights the artificial nature of the storyworld(s) of *Se una notte*, which indeed fits the overt metanarrative intention of the work. It has been suggested earlier that the void consists in the undifferentiated; along the same lines, Hume argues that Calvino's quest revolves around the need of the intelligence (the cogito) to come to terms with the void,

> be it as empty space, vacuum, nothingness, entropy, or the randomness with which particles collide. When the observer's systems of order are sufficiently powerful to keep particles separable and prevent their merging into a paste (though not so rigid to petrify them), then — in Calvino's words — the void poses no real threat. [1992: 38]

Since Calvino acknowledges narrative fiction as a fully-fledged form of knowledge (Stille 1985), it can be said that *Se una notte* does indeed constitute a complex system of order. Arguably, despite fundamentally relying on this principle, *Se una notte* also directly questions the possibility for narrative to impose order, and it does so by staging multiple ways to create narratives; but it has been already remarked that, for Calvino, the fact that more than one solution exists does not undermine the validity of either. *Se una notte* experiments with different ways of making sense of experience and therefore with different systems of order, epitomised by the ten incipits.

Let us briefly continue the parallelism with *The Neverending Story*. In this novel, people's renunciation to their dreams and imagination in the (fictional) actual world directly feeds the destructive forces menacing Fantasia and hereby takes the much real form (in Fantasia) of the Nothing and the wolf Gmork. In a similar way, Calvino's concept of the void as a theoretical and metaphysical threat, once the threshold of fiction is overstepped, takes the shape of a dark abyss — or 'muro di buio' — that surrounds the storyworld. And by storyworld I mean anything that has assumed a narratively organised form.

It is worth noting that it is at the level of the intercalated novels — not in the frame chapters — that Calvino primarily questions the ontological status of storyworlds. The unwritten void surrounds the written *within* the broader fictional storyworld whose actual world is that of the frame. Chapter One of *Se una notte* implements an engaging metanarrative communication between the narrator and a narratee that has not got yet the features of the Reader. Yet we could argue that the real boundaries of *Se una notte* are established and maintained in quite a traditional manner. While they are not probed until the very end in Chapter Twelve, the boundaries between frame and embedded narratives are constantly pushed, and it is in the interstices between these storyworlds that the void operates.

Calvino stages an incredible metanarrative scaffolding, but he firmly places it in the domain of fictional narrative. In Chapter Nine, he writes: 'Non stacchi lo sguardo dal libro da un aeroporto all'altro, perché al di là della pagina c'è il vuoto' (211 [you do not raise your eyes from the book between one airport and the other, because beyond the page there is the void, 205]). How are we supposed to take this statement? Calvino is very aware of the distinction between the two worlds, one written and one unwritten.[26] The written world is:

> un mondo speciale, un mondo fatto di righe orizzontali dove le parole si susseguono una per volta, dove ogni frase e ogni capoverso occupano il loro posto stabilito: un mondo che può essere molto ricco, magari ancor più ricco di quello non scritto, ma che comunque richiede un aggiustamento speciale per situarsi al suo interno. [SII 1865]

> [a special world, a world made of horizontal lines where words follow one another one at the time, where each clause and paragraph have their own set place; a world that may be very rich, perhaps even richer than the unwritten one, but which, nonetheless, requires one to make a special adjustment in order to situate oneself in it.]

Praised by Calvino for its minimum requirement of intelligibility, the written world is juxtaposed to the unwritten world, with whose interpretation Calvino does not seem equally comfortable. The unwritten world lays itself open to the risk of unintelligibility because it does not provide a fixed semiotic system to process it. The fact that the written world at least clearly employs language as a semiotic system already facilitates the task, and for this reason it exerts an unspeakable appeal on Calvino (SII 1866).

In fact, however, it is not Italo Calvino who pronounces the previous statement about the void lurking just beyond the page: it is the model author, a technical device, a set of textual instructions that mediates the delivery of the narrative (Eco 1994: 14); even if we wanted to anthropomorphise such a set and call it an 'entity', it does not change the fact that it still belongs to the fictional storyworld. The 'special adjustment' that determines the shift from unwritten to written world has already taken place, and it is from such a perspective, internal to the storyworld, that the model author is uttering *its statements.[27] The concept of void embodies for Calvino the indeterminate, that which has not been filtered through any (semiotic) system of order, but it is in the specific fictional storyworld of *Se una notte* that it assumes the shape of a dark abyssal void. Similarly, the statement above does not mean that everything is writing, but that *for a character within a narrative* — an entity whose existence is bound and limited to the written world — what is not told by the narrative itself falls (or remains) within the black void that surrounds the narrated storyworld.

It is perhaps meaningful that in *Se una notte* void never appears to be directly connected to the issue of choice, except for in the first and in the last incipit. I have emphasised how in this novel Calvino designs a trajectory of progressive immersion — a sort of 'plunging' of his speculations about the void into fictional hue — deep into the written world, and thus deep into the mechanisms of fictional narrative. From this perspective, it does make sense to suggest that also the ways void is portrayed slightly change throughout the novel. The first and the last incipits mark the entrance into and the exit from the depths of the fictional emplotment, and as such they are the parts where influences from the unwritten world (in other words, from reality) are stronger. In the first incipit, darkness is pressing upon the storyworld because it mirrors the unusual uncertainty of the narrating-I about whether the storyworld should indeed exist; fictionally staged here is the uncertainty concerning a set of choices to be made by the model author. Drawing a parallel between the last incipit and the storyworld, the latter is on the verge of dissolution because the novel is approaching its ending; as the fictional storyworld gets closer to the level of reality (and the reader gets closer to the moment when s/he shall leave the written world and enter the unwritten world again), the nature of the void as connected to choice emerges again, in the narrating-I's act of deliberate deletion. What becomes fictionally actual void is the actual unwritten world, which from the 'written perspective' is void despite being utterly real, because it cannot be completely rendered into words (SI 1868).

To conclude, again in 'Cibernetica e fantasmi', Calvino speculates on the origins of narrativity, discussing the interrelations between myth and tale and narrativity. He writes that:

> Il mito è la parte nascosta d'ogni storia, la parte sotterranea, la zona non ancora esplorata perché ancora mancano le parole per arrivare fin là. [...] Il mito vive di silenzio oltre che di parola; un mito taciuto fa sentire la sua presenza nel narrare profano, nelle parole quotidiane; è un vuoto di linguaggio che aspira le parole nel suo vortice e dà alla fiaba una forma. [SI 218]

> [Myth is the hidden part of every story, the buried part, the region that is still unexplored because there are as yet no words to enable us to get there. [...] Myth is nourished by silence as well as by words. A silent myth makes its presence felt in secular narrative and everyday words; it is a language vacuum that draws words up into its vortex and bestows a form on fable.] [18–19]

If we cannot posit an affinity between the void and the myth, it is not out of place to suggest though that the two are surely closely related. It is not within the scope of the present discussion to analyse the issue of myth in depth but, starting from the quotation above, I would like to stress three main points. The first comes as a corroboration of what said so far about the paradoxical overlapping of multiplicity and void: the source of infinite stories seems to lie for Calvino in a primeval silence, still undetermined and unapproachable, and the power of myth relies on what remains unsaid as much as on what is uttered. The other two points rather build a bridge with what follows in the core argument of this book, and I shall simply state them briefly here and broaden my discussion of them in the remainder of the chapter: first, the fact that already in 1967 Calvino associates the discourse on narrativity with the void and with the image of the vortex, which will recur in *Se una notte* (256); secondly, that the void can impact not only on the content but also on the structure of the narrative, on the shape of the tale. It is particularly to this point that I revert in the next section on fractality.

Se una notte *as hypernovel*

In the Norton Lecture on 'Molteplicità', which was meant to be delivered in 1985, Calvino advances some theoretical considerations on the concept of hypernovel and overtly associates it with *Se una notte*:

> Ma direi che oggi la regola dello «scrivere breve» viene confermata anche dai romanzi lunghi, che presentano una struttura accumulativa, modulare, combinatoria.
>
> Queste considerazioni sono alla base della mia proposta di quello che chiamo «l'iper-romanzo» e di cui ho cercato di dare un esempio con *Se una notte d'inverno un viaggiatore*. Il mio intento era di dare l'essenza del romanzesco concentrandola in dieci inizi di romanzi, che sviluppano nei modi più diversi un nucleo comune, e che agiscono su una cornice che li determina e ne è determinata. [SI 730]
>
> [But I would say that today the rule of «Keep It Short» is confirmed even by long novels, the structure of which is accumulative, modular, and combinatory.
>
> These considerations are at the basis of what I call the "hypernovel", which I tried to exemplify in *If on a winter's night a traveller*. My aim was to give the essence of what a novel is by providing it in a concentrated form, in ten beginnings; each beginning develops in very different ways from a common nucleus, and each acts within a framework that both determines and is determined.] [120]

The term 'hypernovel' is actually employed for the first time in the short cosmicomical story 'Il conte di Montecristo', published in 1967. Later on, it appears again closely linked to metanarrative and in opposition to the novelistic form when Calvino describes Denis Diderot's *Jacques le fataliste* as a 'antiromanzo-metaromanzo-iperromanzo' (SI 844 [antinovel-metanovel-hypernovel]).[28] In this subsection, I shall disentangle this knot and clarify what properties of *Se una notte* are emphasised when we call it a hypernovel. I will also illustrate how a critical discourse that foregrounds virtuality productively links Calvino's reflections on experimental narrative forms with his scientifically-oriented interests and with his overall view of reality.

Drawing on the passage above and on the view of 'Il conte di Montecristo' as hypernovel, it can be inferred that Calvino ascribes to the prefix 'hyper' the sense of an augmentation, which can be achieved by means of concentration on the one hand (increase of *density*) and multiplication on the other (increase in *quantity*). A hypernovel is therefore something that conveys both the *essence* and the *possible different articulations* of a novel, and it does so through a system of repetitions and variations. As to the core content of *Se una notte*, Calvino himself formulated it in his response to Guglielmi, where he explains that the underlying scheme — that is, the essence — of all the situations narrated in the intercalated novels and in the frame is the following:

> un personaggio maschile che narra in prima persona si trova a assumere un ruolo che non è il suo, in una situazione in cui l'attrazione esercitata da un personaggio femminile e l'incombere dell'oscura minaccia di una collettività di nemici lo coinvolgono senza scampo. [RR 1392]

[a male character, who uses the first-person narration, finds himself to play a role which is not his own, unescapably tangled up in the strong attraction to a female character and the obscure threat exerted by groups of enemies.]

Nevertheless, the prefix 'hyper' does not only entail augmentation, but also possibly envisages the trespassing of a limit, an excess. It has been discussed in the previous subsections how excessive proliferation and void are two steps paradoxically close in Calvino's thought. This paradoxical proximity echoes in Serra's remark, which notes that *Se una notte* presents '[d]ietro all'iper-romanzo, la mancanza del vero romanzo, lo spettro della sua negazione: l'ipo-romanzo' (2006: 337 [the hypernovel hides the lack of the true novel, the ghost of his negation, the hypo-novel]). Serra's argument, though, seems to privilege the sense of a menacing threat beneath this potential reversal of perspective, which leads her to ascribe a negative nuance to the prefix 'hyper' (2006: 294). It could be argued, however, that, while it is true that Calvino's hypernovels envision the ghost of narrative paralysis, 'an artist' as John Barth says, 'doesn't merely exemplify an ultimacy; he employs it' (1984 (1967): 68). In this sense, *Se una notte* does indeed programmatically hint at a multiplicity, at a surplus of stories purposely not pursued but it is precisely because Calvino pushes the limits of the novelistic form to the extreme, up to the very edge of dissolution, that he accomplishes something new, proving that these limits are actually more flexible than they were thought to be.

Se una notte tells a story but also seeks to argue something about narrative itself, about its nature and possibilities, which justifies the label of metanovel or metanarrative work (Bonsaver 1994; Segre 1979). Acknowledging this tendency, Milanini points out that, starting from the abstract short stories of *Ti con zero*, Calvino designs narratives where 'il racconto di un'avventura tende a trasformarsi nell'avventura di un racconto' (1990: 137). The interlinked labels of 'hypernovel', 'metanovel', and 'antinovel' prompts us to consider Calvino's relationship with the novelistic form. Bearing in mind the claim of an archetypal novelist such as Elsa Morante, according to whom 'il romanzo è un'opera poetica d'invenzione che attraverso vicende esemplari, dà intera una propria immagine dell'universo reale' (1988: 1500), Scarpa (1999) suggests that at the heart of Calvino's instinctive distrust lies precisely the aspiration of the novel to capture totality, to convey such a sense of wholeness in a coherent and overarching way. It follows that as *Se una notte* — and the hypernovel — aspires to convey a sense of totality through multiplicity, it is indeed somehow bound to negate the nature of the novel in its more traditional sense and therefore to be, at least to some extent, an 'anti-novel'.

Yet, if Calvino seems to poorly adapt to the novelistic form (SI 730), from other perspectives his narratives fully celebrate its powers.[29] What strongly intrigues him is in fact the 'romanzesco' [the essence of what a novel is], whose centrality in *Se una notte* is explicitly acknowledged (177; cf. Barenghi 2007: 29, Berardinelli 1991, Spinazzola 1987: 512). Historically, the 'romanzesco' is associated to a type of popular narrative which heavily relies on the engagement of the reader through the devices of suspense and surprise, and by stimulating their curiosity about what happens next (RRII 1390). It is no accident that one of the key strategies to create these effects is precisely interruption. In illustrating the importance of digression in *Se una notte*, Santovetti links the rehabilitation of plot in its flexibility to the 'romanzesco' and its popular background (2007: 236). Along the same lines — embracing the 'romanzesco' while fundamentally distrusting the novel — Hume (1992: 3) builds on Scholes' distinction between *fabulator* and novelist, where the first is characterised by taking particular delight in design, and observes that the label fits Calvino perfectly. Most importantly, the natural target of the 'romanzesco' is the lay-reader, who is indeed the Reader of *Se una notte* (RRII 1391). This is to remark that in assessing the proximity of Calvino's work to the novelistic tradition it is important to clearly identify what features are accounted for in the process.

Does the concept of hypernovel add something to our understanding of *Se una notte* or of Calvino's poetics? Where does the concept of hypernovel itself come from? The short answer to the first question is yes, as this label foregrounds the relevance of issue of narrative form and its strong entanglement with broader reflections on order and disorder that have also developed in dialogue with non-literary disciplines such as information theory and mathematics. The second answer needs to be more discursive and its unfolding will provide support for the previous one.

As mentioned, Calvino uses the term for the first time in the 1967 short story 'Il conte di Montecristo':

> l'iper-romanzo *Montecristo* con le sue varianti e combinazioni di varianti nell'ordine di miliardi di miliardi ma pur sempre in numero finito. [...] Disponendo una dopo l'altra tutte le continuazioni che permettono d'allungare la storia, probabili o improbabili che siano, si ottiene la linea a zigzag del *Montecristo* di Dumas; mentre collegando le circostanze che impediscono alla storia di continuare si disegna la spirale d'un romanzo in negativo, d'un *Montecristo* col segno meno. [RRII 355]
>
> [the supernovel *Monte Cristo* with its variants and combinations of variants in the nature of billions of billions but still in a finite number. [...] Arranging one after the other all the continuations which allow the story to be extended, probable or improbable as they may be, you obtain the zigzag line of the *Monte Cristo* of Dumas; whereas connecting the circumstances that prevent the story from continuing you outline the spiral of a novel in negative, a *Monte Cristo* preceded by the minus sign.] [150–51][30]

This short passage clearly shows how deeply the notion of hypernovel is intertwined with virtuality in all its forms: the hypernovel *Montecristo* comprises all the narrative possibilities, probable and improbable alike; the novel that Dumas indeed published represents the (fictional) actuality; all the dead-end sequences that would be incompatible with the continuation of the story constitute the counterfactual realm, the novel in negative.

Another aspect emerging from this excerpt is the influence of Calvino's growing acquaintance with semiotics, combinatorics and information theory, together with his view of the world as particulate, modular, and increasingly decipherable in mathematical terms rather than through historicism and discursive means (Hume 1992). In the 1967 definition, 'hypernovel' seems to specifically designate a novel that gathers together multiple variants and in so doing embraces the full spectrum of (fictional) actuality and virtuality. Corti (1978) observes that card reading, for instance, functions as the symbol of Calvino's semiotic view of narrative creation as a formally constrained process. It follows that deserving the label of hypernovel in this stricter sense are, above all, *Il castello*, with its combinatorial use of the Tarot cards, and *L'incendie de la maison maudite*, which was discussed in the *Atlas de Littérature Potentielle* (Calvino 1981/1986; Pilz 2005: 127; RRIII 1239–45). Obviously, in moving from the hypothetical hypernovel of *Montecristo* to a concrete narrative elaboration such as *Il castello*, Calvino reasonably narrows down the range of infinite possibilities, inclusive of inconsequential and even contradictory ones, and actually selects among the combinatorial sequences a set of stories that somehow strike the reader's imagination and are therefore bestowed a richer poetic meaning:

> la letteratura è sì gioco combinatorio che segue le possibilità implicite nel proprio materiale, indipendentemente dalla personalità del poeta, ma è gioco che a un certo punto si trova investito d'un significato inatteso, [...] tale da mettere in gioco qualcosa che su un altro piano sta a cuore all'autore o alla società a cui egli appartiene. [SI 221]
>
> [Literature is a combinatorial game that pursues the possibilities implicit in its own material, independent of the personality of the poet, but it is a game that at a certain point is invested with an unexpected meaning, [...] activating something that on that second level is of great concern to the author or his society.] [*The Literature Machine*: 22]

Stressing the impact of combinatorics on Calvino's poetics, the stronger relationship with the Parisian intelligentsia — with Barthes and, in particular, with the mathematicians and logicians of the Oulipo such as Perec and Raymond Queneau — influences and guides Calvino's interests from the late 1960s onwards (Ossola 1987). In 1967, Calvino moves to Paris with his family, and it is no accident that a ground-breaking essay such as 'Cibernetica e fantasmi' was published exactly in this year. Next to his interest in narrativity and in the deep structure of stories, Calvino develops a keen curiosity for computing machines and their interrelations with narrative, from both the perspectives of production and reception — a double-edged fascination that indeed emerges from *Se una notte* (Usher 1995).

It should be noticed, however, that Calvino mostly considers the computer less as a medium to convey the narrative and more as a technology supplementing it. In contrast to Pilz's (2005: 128) suggestion, I would argue that Calvino is more concerned with the limits of narrativity rather than of print-bound writing; in other words, the constraint on which Calvino focuses is not the sequentiality of exposition but rather the combinatorial nature of stories. *Il castello*, for instance, capitalises on the specificities of the various permutations rather than on the connections prompted by the re-appearance of the same card (unlike what happens in *Se una notte*, as I shall illustrate).

The fact that one story follows another does not depend on temporal-causal relations but stems from the random decision of the hypodiegetic narrator to approach the geometrical and spatial unfolding of the narrative possibilities from one starting point or the other. What matters is the combinatorial principle behind their creation, and therefore their potential simultaneous co-existence. Similarly, also *Le città* does not depend on a specific reading order and the criteria behind Calvino's selection are still a matter of debate. It is for this reason that a concept such as that of hypertext — which nonetheless has been addressed in scholarship on Calvino — is technically inapplicable to any of Calvino's narratives: while the notion of hypertext is inherently typified by cross-referentiality, Calvino's theoretical explorations rather focus on the issue of non-linearity (Christensson 2006; Gargiulo 2002; Pilz 2005: 126).[31]

My suggestion is that Calvino's notion of hypernovel, however, undergoes significant changes between *Le città* and *Se una notte*. Particularly meaningful in this respect is the idea of 'super-albero' (super-tree), elaborated after a journey in Mexico in 1976 (*Collezione di sabbia*). In 'La forma dell'albero', Calvino recounts his encounter with an almost unique specimen, ancient and enormous, the so-called Tule tree. At first, the tree seems the result of uncontrolled growth, devoid of form, overabundant and redundant in its parts: 'E la mia prima sensazione è quella d'un'assenza di forma: è un mostro che cresce — si direbbe — senz'alcun piano, il tronco è uno e molteplice' (SI 600 [My first impression is of an absence of form: this is a monster that grows — one might say — according to no plan; the trunk is both one and multiple, *Collection of Sand*: 186]). Despite the lack of design, Calvino realises that in such vegetal chaos the viewer can still unmistakably detect the shape of the tree, distinguishing a super-trunk, super-branches, and a super-crown — hence the definition of 'super-albero'. The prefix 'super', in this case, does not merely point at the huge dimension, scaled up to an uncommon size; it designates an augmentation achieved through multiplication and proliferation, a sort of reproduction of the original parts — trunk, branch, crown, tree itself. Contemplating the tree, Calvino elaborates the hypothesis that the best way to express one's nature might be through overabundance and the overstatement of the same message — an idea paradoxically opposed to concision, another quality highly valued by the author (cf. SI 61–75, 'Rapidità and 'Esattezza'). He follows the same thread of thought in the following article on Mexico, 'Il tempo e i rami', where he reports his reflections while looking at a tree painted on the wall of a Dominican sixteenth-century church:

> La profusione barocca delle fronde è una ridondanza apparente, perché il messaggio trasmesso sta proprio in questa profusione, e non si può omettere o aggiungere [...]. Ossia, chi siano e come si chiamino i personaggi del rilievo di stucco importa fino a un certo punto: quello che conta è ciò che attraverso di loro si compie. [SI 604]
>
> [The baroque profusion of branches is only apparently superfluous, since the message transmitted lies precisely in this abundance, and [nothing] [...] can be added or taken away. In other words, who the characters are and what they are called matters only up to a point: what counts is what is achieved through them.] [*Collections of Sand*: 190]

Interestingly, this observation is somehow reminiscent of *Se una notte*. Applying these considerations to the 1979 novel, it could be suggested that the characters appearing in the incipits are not necessarily meaningful per se, nor it is important to fully grasp the exact nature of their fictional affairs: while they are only sketched, sometimes with the seeming purpose of confusing the reader (for example, 'In una rete di linee che s'intersecano'), what matters are the virtual stories that the characters and their vicissitudes prompt in the reader's imagination and, above all, the variations of the same core they represent. As Jonathan Usher argues, 'super-albero' and hypernovel share the fact of being ready to 'sacrifice *parts* (including, of course, the continuation of the *incipits*) for the *whole*' (1996: 181). This means that Calvino deliberately decides to employ only incipits in order to ensure that redundancy would be privileged over variation, while at the same time conveying the sense of threat and creative power of an uncontrolled proliferation of its parts.[32] By identifying networks of recurrent proper names, locations and clusters of objects (for example, 'bavero + alzato' or 'cancello + giardino + vasca', the kitchen, or the situation of the equivocal misunderstanding), Usher stresses the abundance of iterations throughout the whole novel, arguing that they constitute a message in itself and, at the same time, they contribute to connect all the parts together, to create 'an essential narrative continuity between frame and intercalatory sequences' (1996: 195; Ovan 2012: 412).

The notion of hypernovel that Calvino arguably holds in mind as label for *Se una notte* bears witness of both these lines of thought. The major difference from non-hierarchical texts such as *Il castello* and *Le città* is that *Se una notte* is definitely designed to be read sequentially (Pilz 2005: 129). The incipits are interlocked in the frame according to a constraint that compels each intercalated story to implement the type of novel desired by Ludmilla in the frame; moreover, as I pointed out earlier, the first two incipits and the last one display some features that seem to depend precisely on their opening and closing position, respectively. Thanks to the mediation of the notion of 'super-albero', Calvino's late version of hypernovel reconciles the values of multiplicity and potentiality with discursive sequentiality by re-evaluating redundancy.[33] On the other hand, if *Se una notte* inherits from the 'super-albero' the perception of redundancy as a value, it discards its absence of plan or form (Usher 1996).

Nonetheless, as Corti (1978: 174) has pointedly noted, awareness of the virtual multiplicity of the narrative unfoldings lying beneath any specific story is fundamental, in all of the three semiotic works alike. During the linear in-take of *Se una notte* too, virtuality — either in the form of multiplicity or of void — is constantly brought to the fore, thus encouraging the reader to remain aware of the (virtual) presence of the unwritten, and of that each intercalated story is simply one of the many possible permutations available, be it either the basic narrative core formulated by Calvino (1979a) or the potential eleventh incipit made of the titles of the incipits linked together. Reversing my previous statement, if it is true that the incipits are always cued by specific triggers in the frame (in other words, Ludmilla's desires), it is also true that the content of the intercalated novels does not impact in significant ways on the frame, which is the only narrative that follows a chronological development and imposes a linear reading on the reader. It follows that — with the exceptions pinpointed above — the intercalated novels are still independent enough from the frame narrative to convey the sense of potentially infinite proliferation inherent to the original concept of hypernovel, because they still retain their 'sample-like' character: these are the stories being told, but it could have easily been any other.

The intercalated narratives make up a hypernovel as if it were a super-tree, with the frame delineating its overarching border — remember the quotation above from 'Molteplicità': 'una cornice che li determina e ne è determinata' [a framework that both determines and is determined]. Yet the patterns of metamorphosed repetitions individuated by Usher also retain something of the cross-referencing property which is typical of hypertexts. To interpret iteration as a technique that promotes redundancy on the one hand and cross-referentiality on the other might respond to some perplexities raised by Bonsaver (1995) in his stylistic analysis of Calvino's lexicon and syntax. In fact, while Bonsaver registers a steep rise in the use of iterations after *Le cosmicomiche* and initially ascribes it to the need to counterbalance an increasingly fragmented syntax, he also admits that there are instances in *Se una notte* where iteration seems too emphasised and too obsessive to simply serve a clarifying purpose. Bonsaver concludes that the trope of iteration is clearly used to obtain a range of linguistic and semantic effects (130). Indeed, a thorough exploration of the concept of hypernovel, of its origins and development, may shed some new light on the function of iteration, too.

It should be added that in *Se una notte* the labyrinthine cross-referencing, a reminder of the early notion of hypertext, is achieved not only stylistically and through a structural use of virtuality, but also through content (Pilz 2003). The systematic interpolation and exchange, disguise and unmasked falsification and re-attribution of works to their rightful authors via translators contribute to convey an impression of the narrative matter as something magmatic and fluid, which can be arranged in various ways and moulded into various fashions. Yet, they are connected to one another as they ultimately stem from the same source, fictionalised in *Se una notte* by the figure an old man called 'Il Padre dei Racconti' (117 [Father of Stories, 114]).

In this subsection, I have illustrated the full range of meanings behind the label of hypernovel applied to *Se una notte*, stressing its strong links to a discourse on virtuality. I showed that what lies behind the development of the concept of hypernovel and its definitional uncertainties is Calvino's mulled-over reflection on how what is not can still variably and significantly impact on what, instead, is there. *Se una notte* can be regarded as a hypernovel because it explores issues including the combinatorial nature of narrative, the consequent multiplicity of narrative possibilities and the tension it creates against the inherent linearity of the reading process, cross-referentiality, iteration and overabundance. I attempted to discern the theoretical reflections underlying these properties, and I provisionally re-connected them to two main trends, irreducibly intertwined: the research on combinatorics and the techno-scientific discourse on the one hand, and information theory and a revaluation of the continuum on the other. These are epitomised by

Calvino's 1967 version of the concept of hypernovel and by the 1976 image of the 'super-albero', respectively. While the idea of hypernovel was mostly influenced by a combinatorial view of narrative and, by proximity, by the properties of non-linearity and cross-referencing (promoted by the kin-concept of hypertext), the 'super-albero' primarily focuses, instead, on redundancy and iteration. Looking at the hypernovel through the critical lens of virtuality served to clarify the development of the concept, but this concept in turn helps foreground the crucial interrelation between variation and repetition — a problem around which the two aforementioned trends both revolve. The hypernovel seems to foster the aspect of variation whereas the 'super-albero' privileges repetition: as I intend to further explore in the next section by introducing the notion of fractality, this aspect will play a critical role also in relation to *Se una notte*.

Plot as fractal

The notion of fractal, which gives the title to this chapter, is effective in two ways. Firstly, as an image able to aptly convey the nature of the relationship between the novel as a whole and its parts. Secondly, because it expresses the organising principle that guides the reader's understanding of *Se una notte* while she reads.

The *Oxford English Dictionary* defines the fractal as 'a mathematically conceived curve such that any small part of it, enlarged, has the same statistical character as the original'. More suitable to our needs, the term 'fractal' equally describes any object with fractal-like properties. It is on these properties and their conceptual counterparts that I will focus here, rather than on the mathematical discussion. Although the concept has been investigated since the seventeenth century, the term 'fractal' has been used for the first time in 1975 by the mathematician Benoit Mandelbrot (1975/1977). Derived from the Latin *fractus*, it is the past participle of the verb *frangere* and means 'broken', 'interrupted'. In a nutshell, the concept of fractal implies a pattern that repeats itself at different scales: the main properties we are dealing with, therefore, are scalability, self-similarity in repetition, and a peculiar relationship between continuity and interruption — or, to say it in the terms used in the previous section, between repetition and variation.

In what follows, I discuss how these ideas are central to Calvino's reflections and, in particular, how they are typified in *Se una notte*.[34] In the reply to Guglielmi, Calvino reasserts his penchant for paradoxes by writing that *Se una notte* is a closed and calculated work ('opera *chiusa e calcolata*', RRII 1389) that, while parading a seemingly reassuring shape, it actually conceals a vision of the world at its opposite, on the edge of dissolution and chaos. Understanding how this paradoxical message is implemented and conveyed has everything to do with the way plot is processed by the reader. In the first subsection, I expand on the idea that narrative texts can be regarded as complex systems and that they are therefore amenable to be looked at through frameworks usually applied to systems. With this purpose in mind, I shall pinpoint self-reflexivity and non-linearity as the critical properties of *Se una notte* that enable me to establish this theoretical analogy. In the second subsection

I introduce the concept of fractal, which I use in the third subsection to attempt a close reading of Calvino's text. Finally, in the last two sections I build on what has been illustrated throughout the chapter to discuss how the spatial-oriented approach serves to foreground quite a peculiar instance of space of narrative experience: given the strong metanarrative nature of *Se una notte* and the fact that the perspective of the reader — crucial to the definition of the space of narrative experience — is included in the narrative itself, I suggest we can speak of a fictionalised space of narrative experience.

The metanarrative text as complex system

As discussed earlier, *Se una notte* deals with potentiality, combinatorics, and the interplay of repetition and variation. It does so, however, in a way such that the metanarrative reflection is deeply integrated within the act of narration. Bonsaver (1995: 143) identifies *Le città* as Calvino's most experimental text in terms of use of narrative time, and says that subsequent works, *Se una notte* in primis, display a fairer compromise between experimentation and readability. However, I would point out that *Se una notte* has a structure that is all but traditional, and if it comes out as less daring an experimentation than *Le città* it is because Calvino achieves a remarkable integration — rather than a compromise — of technical experimentations with the cognitive processes prompted in the reader.

However, one of the signs of this integration, coming from *Il castello* and *Le città*, is the restoration of a sequential reading.[35] Linear reading, the interrupted and yet finished nature of the intercalated narratives, and the explicit closure of the narrative with its happy ending are arguably among the features that ensure closeness to this work. This section focuses instead on the other half of Calvino's answer to Guglielmi, referring to a vision of the world as something chaotic and on the edge of dissolution.

The concept of complexity is not new to Calvino scholarship, nor it is the connection with the notion of system; acknowledging the centrality of this idea, Milanini writes that Calvino's works arguably strive to draw 'un'immagine del mondo quale «sistema di sistemi»' (1994: xxvi [an image of the world as "system of systems"]). In this study, though, I intend to explore these concepts further and attempt a more technical application to the text. As advanced by Mario Bunge (2004: 372), I suggest that a text can be understood as a semiotic system: a system, because it displays properties that its components (words, sentences, periods, chapters) lack, such as cohesion, structure, and mechanisms; semiotic, because it is a system of signs evoking mental processes. Plot is an emergent property of the text as a system, because it is possessed by the system as a whole but not by its components (Bunge 2004: 377; A. Ryan 2007).

However, it could be argued that if texts are semiotic systems then narrative texts are *complex* semiotic systems — a concept resulting from the application of complexity theory to systems theory.[36] According to Angelique Chettiparamb, 'complexity theory deals with the study of entities that reveal non-linear dynamics; entities that though having determinate properties, yield indeterminate results'

(2014: 6). Complex systems, Chettiparamb continues, 'can exhibit properties not generally observed in linear systems such as self-organisation, leading to the emergence of patterns/order; the coexistence of order and chaos at the same time; resilience or adaptive behaviour in the face of shocks and so on' (2014: 5). It does not seem too far-fetched to suggest that this happens with narrative texts too, since they have objective formal properties that yet may yield indeterminate results in their readers. Chettiparamb observes that complexity emerges from the fact that 'in a complex system, the system is ontologically tied to something other than its structure and the processes between structural components' (2014: 6). Framing this observation within the narrative context, I would suggest that this 'something other', external to and yet involved in the system, is indeed the reader, whose activity continuously changes the outcome of the textual system.

Even though the text as system is not a system of equations, and without disregarding Bunge's (2004: 378) warnings against the risks of too liberal an application of frameworks borrowed from mathematics to literature, I believe that similar infusions of new abstractions into literary theory and criticism might be quite profitable (Pilz 2005: 117; cf. Berressem 2015, Herman 2012, M.-L. Ryan 1999). In the case of Calvino, the use of concepts from complexity and system theory is backed by Calvino's demonstrated acquaintance with mathematical discussions and complexity theories by Ilya Prigogine and Isabelle Stengers (SII 2038–49), which he developed through his experience at the Oulipo and as editor for Einaudi.

In fact, Calvino himself not only muses on crucial concepts such as chaos, chance, and continuity vs. discontinuity, but he also explains some structural aspects of his works — and above all of his *modus operandi* — by resorting to pseudo-mathematical formulations. In a letter to his friend Mario Boselli, he writes: 'Anche per questa struttura potrai trovare una serie di riferimenti in altre narrazioni mie che sono costruite così: con al centro una relazione *a x* data come esemplare, e intorno una raggera [sic] o casistica di relazioni *b x*, *c x*, *d x*, ecc.' (*Lettere* 800 [As to this structure, too, you may find other narratives of mine which are constructed in the same way: at the centre, a relation *a x* which is exemplary, and, all around it, a range of relations *b x*, *c x*, *d x*, and so on and so forth]). I am aware that the non-linearity of the dynamics described by mathematical equations is not the non-linearity of *Se una notte*; that the 'shocks' a textual system bears are quite different from thermodynamic ones. And yet one may wonder whether the metaphor would be ultimately so badly misused if we consider the way in which a reader, when presented with a story, attempts as much as possible to make sense of it as a whole, no matter how fragmented and disrupted or non-linear it might be. Assuming that the story is offered to the reader as a unitary whole, she will process it as a non-linear complex system, attempting to derive a unitary plot from it, as one could attempt to mathematically draw its solution(s).

When Bunge refers to a text as a system, its components are presumably words, sentences, periods, chapters; its levels are the lexical, syntactical, rhetorical level. In the present case, in addition to a more traditional parsing and in line, instead, with the possible-worlds framework adopted in the previous chapters, I claim that a narrative text is a system inasmuch as it is a storyworld made up of different storyworlds, of multiple possible worlds variously interrelated. Starting from this general statement, its components may potentially be defined in a different way from time to time according to the specific features of each narrative. In a work such as Camilleri's *Il ladro*, the textual actual world is the only existing actual world and the narrative relies on the interplay between the characters' private worlds. The characters' private worlds thus constitute the components of this narrative system because it is their interactions that are brought to the fore.

Se una notte, however, displays a more complex ontological structure. Arguably, the frame constitutes the textual actual world to which the various storyworlds instantiated in the intercalated novels are attached and upon which they depend. In spite of their tendency to endless multiplication, the overarching boundary that enables one to recognise the interacting components of the system as something separated from the surrounding environment — a requirement stressed by Chettiparamb (2014) — is not ambiguous from a pragmatic perspective: it is the ultimate boundary between written world and unwritten world. The written world, more specifically, is the one contained within the inked pages and bindings of the object-book entitled *Se una notte d'inverno un viaggiatore* (Barenghi 2007: 202). More blurred and fluid, instead, are the boundaries between the various storyworlds within the textual universe.

One of the properties that *Se una notte* arguably shares with complex systems is non-linearity. Drawing on what I argued earlier about the various storyworlds functioning as the components of Calvino's novel, I suggest that, although it requires sequential reading, this narrative is non-linear because the reader has to shift regularly from the textual actual world (frame) to a series of storyworlds, each instantiated by a new incipit. These hypodiegetic storyworlds are not directly connected with one another, and in fact the reader has to return to the frame to be able to access a new one. Yet, the reader is meant to draw connections between the intercalated novels, as they are indeed interacting with one another in other non-linear ways that I shall explore in the next subsection.

The second key property typical of complex systems and also present in *Se una notte* is self-reflexivity. In his attempt to chart Calvino's multifarious production, Bonsaver (1995: 139) pinpoints *Il cavaliere inesistente* (1959) as a significant turning point and the beginning of Calvino's overt experimentation with textual forms. By overtly referring to the materiality of writing, the narrator of *Il cavaliere* draws attention to its artificiality, marking the outset of a metaliterary and metanarrative investigation that acquires increasing importance in Calvino's following works. Issues concerning the medium of language or narrative communication not only are explored through essayist writing but also become narrative topics themselves. According to Bonsaver, this constitutes a strong *fil rouge* connecting the first experimentations of *Ti con zero* and *Le città* with *Se una notte*. Bonsaver suggests that, before *Ti con zero* in 1967 (with the early exception of *Il cavaliere*), Calvino had probably not aimed at exploring problems of narrativity, as narrative was perceived as a means to be understood in order to be used, rather than as an object of exploration per se. And yet, looking at some of the motifs that dominate the second half of Calvino's production, his semiotic period that in fact coincides with increasing metanarrative interests, we find that they were already being pursued in the 1950s. Bart Van den Bossche (2002), for instance, argues that Calvino's combinatorial view of narrative has probably developed through his early exploration of the genre of the folktale.

Particularly close to Vladimir Propp and to Calvino's own later reflections is the idea of the tale as the archetypal narrative form ('Cibernetica e fantasmi'), characterised by the paradoxical combination of 'infinite variety' and 'infinite repetition'. Again, it is the 'tentacular nature' of the tale (Van den Bossche 2002: 56) that Calvino arguably attempts to reproduce in *Se una notte* by displaying ten narrative articulations of the same narrative core. The narrative core formulated by Calvino is also quite archetypical in itself, since it features conflicting interests and the breaking of some sort of balance, both between individuals and between individual and society (Barenghi 2007: 71). Finally and most overtly connected to the folktale structure are the quest of the Reader staged in the frame and its happy-ending, due less to consolatory intentions and more in obliging compliance with tradition:

> Lei crede che ogni storia debba avere un principio e una fine? Anticamente un racconto aveva solo due modi per finire: passate tutte le prove, l'eroe e l'eroina si sposavano oppure morivano. Il senso ultimo a cui rimandano tutti i racconti ha due facce: la continuità della vita, l'inevitabilità della morte. [261]

> [Do you believe that every story must have a beginning and an end? In ancient times a story could end only in two ways: having passed all the tests, the hero and the heroine married, or else they died. The ultimate meaning to which all stories refer has two faces: the continuity of life, the inevitability of death.] [253]

Reconnecting metanarrative to the property of self-reflexivity, Peter Stoicheff (1991) suggests that metafictional texts share some key characteristics with complex systems.[37] As he questions the role of language as a neutral carrier of meaning, Stoicheff claims that metafiction is self-reflective because it turns its attention to language itself and questions the validity of its own medium, hence constituting 'an investigation of the chaos of meaning's production' (1991: 87).

Stoicheff's essay raises another point which may be interesting in relation to *Se una notte*. He observes that to 'understand' a metafictional text is analogous to understanding a complex system because, in order to do that, one must reject seeing it as a vertical organization of a text's components into a closed order that is interpreted as meaning. Rather, one replaces this view with the recognition of lateral patterns in which disorder becomes order' (93).

Stoicheff's description closely reminds us of an effect that is explicitly prompted by the narrator of *Se una notte* himself: 'Per leggere bene tu devi registrare tanto l'effetto brusio quanto l'effetto intenzione nascosta, che ancora non sei in grado (e io neppure) di cogliere' (19 [To read properly you must take in both the murmuring effect and the effect of the hidden intention, which you (and I, too) are as yet in no position to perceive, 17]). This passage suggests that in *Se una notte* meaning is not only conveyed through the content of words (signified), but it may also reside in the form of their vehiculation — in the disturbance that this communication is subjected to. The difficulty of narration is not simply an unwanted side-effect to be filtered out, but something deliberately designed by the author to acknowledge its inevitability (Bonsaver 1995: 159).[38] In the second part of Stoicheff's quotation, it is worth noticing the concepts of 'laterality' as opposed to 'verticality': not only they are linked to visually-based maps of narrative structures and to Calvino's spatial-informed cognitive style, but their use also reminds us of Baricco's discussion of new (barbarian) as opposed to more traditional modes of sense-making.[39]

In conclusion, in this subsection I have introduced the idea of text as a system and discussed the adequacy of an analogy between *Se una notte* and a complex system. In particular, I focused on the properties of non-linearity and self-reflexivity — the latter focus justified by the strong metanarrative nature of *Se una notte*. The act of narration — its production, commodification and reception, its multifariousness and difficulty — is in fact at the heart of the content and form of this novel. Starting from these premises, in the next subsection I offer a hypothesis regarding how non-linearity and metanarrativity may be designed to be understood in the novel.

Fractals and recurrent symmetries

In mathematics, a system is solved once values are found for each of the unknowns that will satisfy every equation in the system. To 'solve' the complex system of a narrative in literature is, of course, quite a different matter. One point remains, though: in order to understand it, the reader has to be able to process it and to make sense of all of its components as constituents of a whole. In this book, I have referred to this sense-making process of the narrative as plot understanding. The question I want to address now is whether *Se una notte*, which is a narrative influenced by combinatorics and displaying properties such as non-linearity and self-reflexivity, provides some further instructions as to how to combine together the parts (in other words, storyworlds) of which it is made. In more literary terms, is the process of understanding *Se una notte*'s plot affected by the structural properties of the narrative? My answer is yes, and I suggest that the concept of fractality provides a fruitful way to elucidate it.

It is not the first time that fractals are summoned in relation to Calvino. Pilz, for instance, associates them with the narrative technique of *mise en abyme* and with recursivity, arguing that '[t]hrough repeated use of the method of *mise en abyme* the narrative becomes a fractal space of infinite repetitions' (2005: 128). In order to explain this observation further, let us consider how the concept of a fractal can be applied to non-mathematical contexts. Starting from the mathematical definition offered at the opening of this section — in other words, a curve or a geometrical figure, each part of which has the same statistical character as the whole — fractals can be summoned as an effective mode of explanation for systems that exhibit self-reflexivity, or self-similarity, across scales (Chettiparamb 2014). More specifically, fractality may provide a model for the process of plot understanding, or — to use the terminology of complex and systems theory — for the emergence of plot.[40]

In the previous subsection, it was argued that the components of the 'system *Se una notte*' are the storyworlds instantiated by the frame and by the ten intercalated novels. To make this hypothesis work — namely, the hypothesis that *Se una notte* is a complex system characterised by fractality — it should be clarified in what sense the storyworlds are typified by different scales across which self-reflexivity is exhibited. The concept of scale is usually employed to represent the relation between elements belonging to different systems and it is defined by scope and resolution. While resolution indicates the higher (finer) or lower (coarser) degree of detail, scope is an observer-dependent parameter which defines 'the set of components within the boundary between the associated system and its environment' (A. Ryan 2007: 69). It follows that in the intercalated novels, when a different hypodiegetic narrator conveys the narrative, the focus is shifted from the whole system (*Se una notte*) on to one of its components (incipit) and therefore this component becomes the system of interest as the scope has narrowed. This explains why it is possible to speak of both *Se una notte* and each of the intercalated novels as systems (although, technically, the intercalated novels are sub-systems of the main one).

Different scales arise from the diversity of narrative situations implemented in each incipit. Non-linearity, ensured by the fact that, potentially, each (fictional) universe is completely autonomous from the others, guarantees the possibility of adopting completely different scopes and resolutions each time. The properties of each storyworld are determined by the narrative voice and by the genre to which each intercalated narrative belongs. Yet, features and relations recur across storyworlds and it is here that fractality may provide a good description, as it implies recursive repetitive scaling (Chettiparamb 2014: 9; 2005).

Interestingly, the property of recursivity seems to be attached to the hypernovel since its first appearance in Calvino. Already in the short story 'Il conte di Montecristo', the narrator admits that the fortress of If (whose structure mirrors the structure of the hypernovel itself) 'ripete nello spazio e nel tempo sempre la stessa combinazione di figure' (RRII 348 [it repeats in space and time always the same combination of figures, 142]). I shall draw once again on Chettiparamb's application of fractals to planning in order to pinpoint a set of properties of fractals which can be also recognised in *Se una notte*.[41] She argues that:

> Four parameters in particular are advanced: the quality of self similarity; the iterating parameter and a vertical axis that forms from this iteration; the distance between consequent scales in the vertical axis; and a horizontal mechanism that allows the assimilation of scale specific information. [2014: 17]

Since the discussion of the first parameter — the specific type of self-similarity implemented in *Se una notte* — is the more demanding one, let us briefly consider the other three parameters first. Unlike what happens in Chettiparamb's application of fractals to planning, given that iteration is to be appreciated as one proceeds with reading, I would suggest that the axis along which iteration is carried out should be conceived of as a horizontal axis rather than as a vertical axis. Horizontality, in fact, may better represent the temporal dimension of the process which is necessary for plot to emerge and self-similarity between the narrative components to be appreciated. Recursivity involves subsequent chapters, as storyworlds are instantiated in subsequent intercalated novels.

Conversely, the horizontal mechanism mentioned by Chettiparamb becomes a vertical mechanism in the present conceptualisation. In *Se una notte*, such a mechanism, which enables the assimilation of scale specific information, operates by means of the formulations of Ludmilla's desires and through the consequent identification of specific genres or national literary models for each incipit.[42] By prompting the reader to draw on the set of conventions that presumably operate within each intercalated novel, the author encourages the reader to pay attention to specific features varying from time to time, thus adjusting the scope and the resolution of each narrative. To quote from Chettiparamb, this '"[vertical]" mechanism assimilates contextual phenomena that are unique and meaningful to a particular scale. Furthermore, [it] allow[s] the emergent global to be sensitive to the details of the local: [...] the global and the local can get defined simultaneously, and variety and order can coexist at the same time' (2014: 10, 11).

Finally, the regular 'distance' between storyworlds — and therefore between 'levels' of the fractal configuration — is ensured by the frame. Neatly partitioned in numbered chapters composing the frame narrative and titled chapters for the intercalated novels, the paratext of the novel provides an underlying structure that keeps the system components in order and prevents them from collapsing into each other which would hinder the exhibition of self-reflexivity by turning it into a chaotic mass. Each new storyworld is separated from the others by a narrative chapter belonging to the frame, and this also helps manage the ontological boundaries delimiting the parts of the system.

Let us now revert to the first point stressed by Chettiparamb in the definition above. What is iterated throughout *Se una notte*? A process, some referent, a form? In other words, what does self-similarity concern? Following Calvino's indications, the primary and main instance of fractality involves a set of referents and their reciprocal relations that do recur throughout the ten incipits and the frame itself: a male character, displaced from his usual role, finds that he faces a hostile community because of the attraction exerted by a female character. Each time, this quest is re-elaborated through different scenarios and different power relations between the three entities (male character, female character, hostile element). It is also finally epitomised by the story of the Reader who carries out the double-pursuit of the She-Reader Ludmilla and of the ever-changing novel, and finds himself constantly hindered and contrasted along both paths. In fact, in at least one case the antagonistic force is embodied by the same character, Ermes Marana, who opposes the Reader by acting as both Ludmilla's ex-lover and literary forger. Incidentally, it should be noted that the representation of the 'literary system' as Vittorio Spinazzola (2010) intends it, in its multifarious aspects including production, commercialisation, control and reception, does not constitute an instance of recursivity-within-variation. Rather, all these references reveal the elaboration of an underlying theme.

The device of the *mise en abyme* presents some similarities with the concept of fractal (indeed Pilz mentions them together in the passage referred to above). One of its clearest implementations consists in Silas Flannery's project of writing a novel made entirely of incipits. Fractality, however, better represents what happens in *Se una notte* because it not only accounts for these specific episodes, but it also conveys the sense of a continual process taking place through reading. Fractality combines and explains within a purpose-oriented process occurrences of *mise en abyme* and embedded narratives, on the one hand, and the network of interrelated cross-references already emphasised by Usher, on the other.

In his analysis, Usher (1996: 191–92) observes that recurrent nouns acquire different meanings from time to time: the image of the curl, 'riccio', first appears in the shavings of paper produced by the Reader cutting open the pages of the newly bought book, then returns in the 'arricciaburro' (34 [butter curler, 34]), in the 'riccio di mare' drawn by Miss Zwida (58 [sea urchin, 57]), in Lotaria's curly hair (72 [71]) and finally turns into the 'riccioluta crema di nuvole' which the Reader flies through by plane (118 [curly cream of clouds, 115]). The link is established but, considering the dramatic semantic shifts, it is unlikely that Calvino aimed to stress one specific type of 'riccio' (as I suggest later, in this case it is rather the shape of the spiral that is emphasised). Something similar happens with the interplay of proper names. As soon as the Reader starts listening to the novel *Sporgendosi dalla costa scoscesa*, he realises that, apart from the odd coincidence of some identical proper names, the story has nothing to do with the one he had previously started (52 [51]). In this regard, Bonsaver interestingly comments that, particularly in short stories, Calvino often uses proper nouns as textual elements almost devoid of any psychological depth, entities whose functions are predicated on their reciprocal relations and that could be expressed through mathematical formulas (1995: 165). This remark seems quite in line with the use of some recurrent nouns, such as 'riccio' or the colour yellow: what counts is the web of connections they create, rather than the specific sign that concretely establishes the link.

Even more interesting from our perspective are the instances of an intriguing extradiegetic continuation between the intercalated novels and the frame, which, according to Usher, yield consequences for plot understanding (1996: 198). When I described *Se una notte* as a system, I claimed that each intercalated story constitutes a storyworld that can be accessed only from the frame, as the hypodiegetic narrative that instantiates it is accessed by the Reader in the frame story. Boundaries between these storyworlds are therefore supposed to be relatively close because, from the perspective of the (fictional) actuality of the frame, they are construed in stories recounted in different books. And yet Usher's argument cautiously challenges this assumption. He pinpoints a series of details that should reveal a stronger connection among intercalated storyworlds and suggests that each of them somehow impacts on the following ones, thus exhibiting an irreversible process: the first incipit closes with the cryptic news that 'Hanno ammazzato Jan' (24 [They've killed Jan, 22]) and in the second incipit Jan's widow is mentioned in passing (34 [34]); the spicy red pepper that was in Ugurd's kitchen (34 [34]) is ultimately used by Anacleta Higueras for the sauce of her meatballs ('Intorno a una fossa vuota', 227 [220]), and the meatballs themselves have been prepared by Brigd using so many eggs that only one has remained in Ludmilla's fridge (Chapter Seven, 144 [139]); similarly, it is hypothesised that the reason why it took Nacho sixteen years to find his way home lies somehow in the sextodecimo size of a book (25 [24]).

Usher suggests that these reprises are meant to ensure cohesion in a novel with a fragmented structure, in search of a unifying principle (also Segre 1979: 187). I would back his suggestion and reinforce it by proposing that these elements may be interpreted as disguised hinge joints between modules of the narrative structure. The main connection points are provided by the entities that Calvino himself isolates — male character, female character and hostile element. However, through repetition and variation, some elements are made critical and promote the alignment of storyworlds. As Chettiparamb notes, fractality relies on the alignment of the components of system so that 'change in one level can result in a change throughout the system, and the alignments can therefore be important mechanisms for co-evolution. The local and the global in fractal systems can then be co-constitutive' (2014: 9–10).

Segre's words reflect something of the dynamic I describe as fractal-like when he writes that most of the intercalated novels display a spiral-like or funnel-like structure (1979: 205). The spiral is indeed a fractal figure, a curve that progressively converges toward a point — or diverges from it — and creates a shifting movement across different scales that implies a variation in scope and/or resolution. Each storyworld is indeed defined by a different configuration of the core elements that are iterated and varied throughout the whole novel: once this configuration is set and its conditions are designed (affiliation to a specific genre and national literary model), the narrative is run on these settings which uniquely bind the local narrative (the specific incipit) to its initial conditions. Each intercalated novel brings to light the effects of these initial conditions, setting the premises — and the premises only, being all interrupted — for their potential narrative unfolding. The image of the spiral, therefore, captures an aspect related to the aforementioned vertical axis of a fractal structure, the one that connects the details of the local to the global.[43] In a sense, what Segre has described as a spiral-like scheme characterising each incipit individually, Santovetti has explained by formalising Calvino's use of digression (2007: 221–28). According to Santovetti, every incipit constitutes a digression on its own: this departure from the main storyline of the frame may indeed remind of the funnel- or spiral-like convergence along different narrative lines recognised by Segre.

To put the same concept in another way, each incipit dramatises the spiralling down of specific preliminary conditions, which are a variation of the narrative core formulated by Calvino, and each incipit is bound to them. And yet, the initial configuration is the result of fundamentally random variations of the narrative core. By designing a narrative structure of this sort, Calvino manages to combine order and disorder and, above all, gets to reassess through narrative itself one of his key principles: as Scarpa aptly puts it, 'la cosa che Calvino ha detto per tutta la vita è che nella vita è impossibile dire una cosa sola' (1999: 93 [The only thing Calvino has kept on repeating all his life is that, in life, it is impossible to say just one thing]). Fractality is a mode of organisation (of narrative matter, in this case) that embodies this almost paradoxical idea, as it constitutionally relies on repetition and variation. As I argue in this section, fractality accounts for isolated narrative phenomena within a broader sense-making *process*, and this is probably as close as one can get to a representation of totality according to Calvino's beliefs; referring to *Se una notte*, Calvino affirms that is thanks to its circularity that the novel gets closer to the idea of totality (RRII 1396–97).

The ten intercalated novels represent an arbitrary selection of the narrative core's possible configurations: the added value introduced by fractality is that, by 'kaleidoscoping' points of view and simulating multiple alternatives (Segre 1979: 204), it also emphasises their interdependence and prompts one to appreciate their being 'facce d'un medesimo cristallo, giacché rimodulano un'unica situazione esistenziale' (Milanini 1990: 158 [different faces of the same crystal, as they are reformulations of the same existential knot]) without restraining them within a rigidly closed structure. Or better, the novel does find closure, thanks to the traditional happy ending and the fact that the Reader is depicted while finishing to read the novel itself. Both things, though, disguise a sort of anomaly.

As to the happy ending, the swiftness of the final resolution inevitably stresses its artificiality and, consequently, the arbitrariness of the closure itself: 'Poi fulmineamente decidi che vuoi sposare Ludmilla' (261 [Then, in a flash, you decide you want to marry Ludmilla, 253]). This might even be a case of implicit authorial metalepsis (Genette 1980: 234; cf. Cohn 2012, Pier 2016), where the author pretends to raffishly intervene into his characters' vicissitudes. As to the final lines of the novel, they bring about such a blatant collapse of storyworlds — a possibility that was often ambiguously hinted at but never unequivocally accomplished before — that closure becomes almost inevitable:

> Ludmilla chiude il libro, spegne la sua luce, abbandona il capo sul guanciale, dice: — Spegni anche tu. Non sei stanco di leggere?
>
> E tu: — Ancora un momento. Sto per finire *Se una notte d'inverno un viaggiatore* di Italo Calvino. [263]
>
> [Ludmilla closes her book, turns off her light, puts her head back against the pillow, and says, "Turn off your light, too. Aren't you tired of reading?"
> And you say, "Just a moment, I've almost finished *If on a winter's night a traveller* by Italo Calvino."] [254]

Barth (1984 (1967)) identifies a similar short-circuit in Borges' invention of the 602nd night of *The One Thousand and One Nights*, when Sheherazade tells the story of the *One Thousands and One Nights* itself: the King, however, fortunately interrupts her, or there would be no 603rd night ever (cf. SI 395). Barth observes that these instances 'disturb us metaphysically [because] when the characters in a work of fiction become readers or authors of the fiction they're in, we're reminded of the fictitious aspect of our own existence' (73). The strategies employed to prepare closure happen so quickly that one cannot avoid the impression that the author, here, has rapidly stitched up a potentially continuing narrative. Yet, this operation is anything but improvised. On the contrary, I suggest that both the rapid escalation toward the happy ending and the disturbance caused by the fuzziness of the ontological boundaries as performed in the final lines are operations designed to attract the reader's attention to the arbitrariness of the act of closure itself. The implicit suggestion is thus that the narrator artificially put an end to a narration that could have easily continued (Asor Rosa 2001: 146; De Toni 2007: 188).

Fractals, too, have an ordered structure and yet admit potentially infinite continuity. The affinity of this hypothesis with the Calvinian idea that no position could ever be definitive but only an infinite approximation adds to the suitability of fractals as a profitable mode of explanation of the type of plot understanding designed in *Se una notte* (SI 229–37, SI 381–98). In this sense, infinite approximation is due to the infinite potential perspectives (in fractals: scales) that could be adopted in representing reality. However, close to the idea of infinite approximation by addition, there is also the idea of infinite divisibility, another concept fractal in nature: as soon as the scale changes and the resolution increases, one finds the same structures, reproduced. The same *regressus ad infinitum* is contemplated by another paradox dear to Calvino, the aforementioned example of Achilles and the Tortoise, by Zeno of Elea. A connecting line can therefore be traced between *Se una notte*, its fractal plot structure, and *The One Thousands and One Nights*, as they all explore potential continuity in this double sense: on the one hand, they are made of a finite — though, arbitrary — number of parts (variation); on the other, they potentially continue in a recurring self-mirroring and self-reproduction, *ad infinitum* (repetition).

Se una notte's *plot as fractal*

Fractality thus provides us with a profitable framework to account for narrative strategies such as embeddedness or *mise en abyme*, and the programmatic use of patterns of repetitions. Most importantly though, it affords us a suitable description of the underlying process connecting them together and, therefore, a description of the sense-making strategy that guides the reader in understanding the narrative as a whole. From chapter to intercalated novel to chapter again: the reader shall look for familiar elements (repetition) while at the same time searching for any direction that the narrative may follow next (variation), in order to orient her expectations. Fractality as a mode of organisation may adequately represent the reader's strategy of sense-making of the narrative, building on returning and variable elements. In the close reading that follows, I seek to substantiate my hypothesis by pinpointing those elements and events that support a reading of plot understanding in *Se una notte* as modelled on fractality.

The novel opens with Chapter One. The first feature that arguably catches the reader's attention is the use of second-person narration, which not only is uncommon but also has the effect of stimulating quite a direct engagement of the reader. Expectations immediately enter the picture, confirming their crucial role in the relationship that is being established between narrator and readers. By mentioning expectations, the narrator arguably prompts readers to interrogate themselves about their own. Furthermore, the reference to 'bisogni di nuovo e di non nuovo (del nuovo che cerchi nel non nuovo e del non nuovo che cerchi nel nuovo)' (6 [your desires and needs for the new and the not new (for the new you seek in the not new and for the not new you seek in the new, 6]) neatly evokes the principle of reading dynamics as grounded in a balance between novelty and reassurance of one's expectations. Already in Chapter One, the narrator contemplates multiple counterfactual or potential possibilities, as if browsing them:

> Forse è già in libreria che hai cominciato a sfogliare il libro. O non hai potuto perché era avviluppato nel suo bozzolo di cellophane? Ora sei in autobus, in piedi [...] O forse il libraio non ha impacchettato il volume; te l'ha dato in un sacchetto. Questo semplifica le cose. Sei al volante della tua macchina, [...]. [7]

> [Perhaps you started leafing through the book already in the shop. Or were you unable to, because it was wrapped in its cocoon of cellophane? Now you are on the bus, standing in the crowd [...] Or perhaps the bookseller didn't wrap the volume; he gave it to you in a bag. This simplifies matters. You are at the wheel of your car] [7]

As expressed by the disjunctive coordination, the first two paragraphs exhibit counterfactuals: the reader (not yet officially the Reader) has the book either wrapped or not; is either on the bus or in his car. Some expressions used by the narrator ('Vediamo come comincia', 7; 'Vediamo', 9 [Let's see how it begins, 7; Let's see, 9]) cue the reader into thinking that the novel the narrator is talking about is still to begin, and it will begin the following chapter.

The following chapter abandons the numeric sequence and simply bears the title 'Se una notte d'inverno un viaggiatore'. At this point, some readers might even think that what they just finished reading was a catchy foreword authored by the person Italo Calvino, rather than the first chapter of a metanarratively complex work delivered by a model author (Eco 1994). Some signs contribute to ensure a sense of continuity between Chapter One and this new chapter. In other words, what are the instances of not-new in the new? First of all, the confirmation of what anticipated by the narrative voice: there, the narrator was inviting the reader (at that point, presumably the narratee — on which, see below) to begin the reading; here, such beginning is dramatised with the first line reading: 'Il romanzo comincia in una stazione ferroviaria' (11 [The novel begins in a railway station, 10]).[44] Secondly, the continuation of a metanarrative discourse maintains the narrator in a position to some degree external to the narrated matter: he still metanarratively refers to chapters, paragraphs, pages recounting the unfolding story.[45]

On the other hand, new elements also emerge. Some of them are newly introduced, as are the setting of the station and all the narrative details pertaining the specifics of 'Se una notte': Mr and Madame Marne, the chief-inspector Gorin, the mysterious agents the narrating-I is supposed to meet and those he answers to, the missed luggage exchange. Other elements, instead, progressively reveal themselves to be variations of prior ones: the main instance of variation within continuity concerns metanarrativity. If it initially ensured continuity with Chapter One, as soon as the chapter proceeds it becomes clear that the narrating-I's lack of knowledge encompasses not only the circumstances of a potential reader but also the very narrative of which he is a part. Narrating-I and author overtly uncouple, as suggested by sentences such as, 'O forse l'autore è ancora indeciso' (13), 'Forse per questo l'autore accumula supposizioni su supposizioni in lunghi paragrafi senza dialoghi' (15), 'questo qualcosa d'altro che rende rischioso identificarsi con me, per te lettore e per lui autore' (16) [Or perhaps the author still has not made up his mind, 12; Perhaps this is why the author piles up supposition on supposition in long paragraphs without dialogue, 14; this something else that makes it risky to identify with me, risky for you the reader and for him the author, 15]. Furthermore, the strategy of displaying counterfactual possibilities, already employed in Chapter One, aims here to highlight the gap between the reader's expectations and the narrative (fictional) actuality:

> Tu lettore credevi che lì sotto la pensilina il mio sguardo si fosse appuntato sulle lancette traforate come alabarde d'un rotondo orologio di vecchia stazione [...]. Ma chi ti dice che i numeri dell'orologio non s'affaccino da sportelli rettangolari e io veda ogni minuto cadermi addosso di scatto come la lama d'una ghigliottina? [13–14]
>
> [You, reader, believed that there, on the platform, my gaze was glue to the hands of the round clock of an old station, hands pierced like halberds [...]. But who can say that the clock's numbers aren't peeping from rectangular windows, where I see every minute fall on me with a click like the blade of a guillotine?] [12]

Arguably, these ambiguities signal that we are not simply facing a continuation of the narrative situation designed in Chapter One and that the new one is re-employing the metanarrative device at a different narrative level, with different premises and agents. The first instance of fractal structure emerges, although it is not recognisable as such at this point.

Another passage should serve to demonstrate how frequently Calvino includes the issue of readerly expectations in his narrative machinery:

> La tua attenzione di lettore ora è tutta rivolta alla donna, è già da qualche pagina che le giri intorno, che io, no, che l'autore gira intorno a questa presenza femminile [...], ed è la tua attesa di lettore che spinge l'autore verso di lei, e anch'io che ho tutt'altri pensieri per il capo ecco che mi lascio andare a parlarle [...]. [20]
>
> [Your attention, as reader, is now completely concentrated on the woman, already for several pages you been circling around her, I have — no, the author has — been circling around the feminine presence [...], and it is your expectation, reader, that drives the author toward her; and I, too, though I have other things to think about, there I let myself go, I speak to her] [19]

In this excerpt, too, the distinction between narrating-I and author is confirmed. Together with the mysteriously attractive female figure, the dangerous and potentially hostile group makes its appearance: 'L'organizzazione è potente. Comanda alla polizia, alle ferrovie' (24 [The organisation is powerful. It can command the police, the railroad, 23]). Immediately after this sudden escalation, the chapter ends.

The first anomaly in the following chapter is that it reprises the numbering as Chapter Two, while being technically the third chapter of the novel. The storyworld featuring (or 'priming', to use Emmott's (1997) contextual frame theory terminology) the station and the luggage exchange is abandoned (or 'unprimed'), and arguably it does not take long to the reader to realise that the content of the chapter 'Se una notte d'inverno' constituted an embedded narrative delivered via a damaged book. It becomes undeniable over the following few pages that the book 'Se una notte' is physically not the same book the actual reader is reading. An attentive analysis might have already spotted some signs (such as the fact that the narrating-I is referring to paragraphs and lines that the actual reader cannot actually access — 'è già un paio di pagine che', 12; 'ma invece solo pochi elementi affiorano dalla pagina scritta', 21 [For a couple of pages now, 11; but instead only a few elements surface on the written page, 19]). Yet, until page 26, the situation remains utterly ambiguous. Even though Chapter Two opens with the line 'Hai già letto una trentina di pagine' [You have now read about thirty pages] and the actual page is 25, the reader might well admit an approximation. It is at page 29 that the Reader as a character is named for the first time, concomitant with the appearance of the She-Reader ('Lettrice'): this marks the final disjunction between the 'reader who reads', namely the real reader, and the 'reader who is read', that is the character Reader (Segre 1979: 179). Critical views differ on this issue: while Ian Rankin (1986: 125) argues that the Reader is a proper fictional character, Waugh (1984) maintains instead that through the second person Calvino is addressing the real reader.[46] It is legitimate yet inconclusive to wonder whether either a shift (or a narrowing down) of addressees has occurred between Chapter One and Two — from reader to Reader — or the narratee of Chapter One was already the Reader as a character. The following excerpt from Chapter Two seems to endorse the latter hypothesis, if any, because it starts to employ the masculine form consistently and the man who is now named 'the Reader' is the same man who was said to hold certain beliefs earlier: 'uomo che credevi finita l'epoca in cui ci si può aspettare qualcosa dalla vita. [...] Ecco come sei già cambiato da ieri' (31 [a man who thought that the period when you could still expect something from life had ended. [...] But something has changed since yesterday, 31]).

Without expecting to solve the ambiguity, I venture a second hypothesis: reverting to Chapter One, one can retrospectively detect a caesura, or a sort of double beginning. The novel opens by addressing the reader in their own room, prompting them to find a suitable posture, regulate the light and prepare anything they might need during reading so they do not have to interrupt it. After commenting on the reader's low expectations, the first contextual-frame shift is instantiated, introduced by a single word: 'Dunque' (5 [So, 4]). With a partly exhortative partly summarising function, the word 'dunque' marks a shift in space and time to the moment and the place of the purchase of the book; the chapter ends with a circular return to the reader's room, finally facing the novel. I would suggest however that it is the 'dunque' that pragmatically triggers a shift through the ontological border of storyworld, and with it the passage from reader to Reader.[47]

The metanarrative discourse carried out by the narrator ensures a certain continuity throughout the first three chapters, even though at least two distinct narrating entities have intervened so far, the narrator of Chapter One and the narrator of 'Se una notte'. The reprise of the numbering in Chapter Two seems to vouch, at least provisionally, for the hypothesis that its narrator might be the same one of Chapter One. Another element of continuity is provided by a new female character entering the story, after Madame Marne of 'Se una notte'. Her relevance is immediately emphasised: 'Ecco dunque la Lettrice fa il suo felice ingresso nel tuo campo visivo, Lettore' (29 [And so the Other Reader makes her happy entrance into your field of vision, Reader, 28]). What fades away in this chapter, instead, is the narrator's tendency to browse through counterfactuals, of which we find no instance in Chapter Two. Rather, the narrator explicitly leaves some details unspecified: 'Chi tu sia, Lettore, quale sia la tua età, lo stato civile, la professione, il reddito, sarebbe indiscreto chiederti. Fatti tuoi, veditela un po' tu' (31–32 [Who you are, Reader, your age, your status, profession, income: that would be indiscreet to ask. It's your business, you're on your own, 31]). As far as variation and novelty are concerned, Chapter Two takes a significant narrative turn by fully admitting the fictional nature of the Reader as character and recounting the events leading to the beginning of his quest. When the following incipit is introduced, the narrator makes immediately clear that a new storyworld is to be instantiated. The reader is aware that 'Fuori dall'abitato di Malbork' is a new embedded narrative and should be ready to grasp clues that could guide their understanding of it. The narrator is quite explicit in outlining the narrative atmosphere and the style: 'Qui è tutto molto concreto, corposo, designato con sicura competenza, o comunque l'impressione che dà a te, Lettore, è quella della competenza' (33 [Here everything is very concrete, substantial, depicted with sure expertise; or at least the impression given to you, Reader, is one of expertise, 33]). In fact, this style had been already anticipated by Ludmilla's opinion expressed in Chapter Two (29), but it might well be that the regular connection between the She-Reader's desires and the following intercalated novels has not been intuited by the reader yet.

Storyworld and narrative style thus change, but the position of the narrative voice toward the narrative seems to initially remain the one exhibited in Chapter Two: there are still metanarrative comments ('Olio di colza, è specificato nel testo, dove tutto è molto preciso', 33 [Rape oil, the text specifies; everything here is very precise, 33]) and the Reader is directly addressed, as if the narrative voice is recounting a reading experience rather than creating the premises for it to take place. However, at some point a second homodiegetic narrator emerges, and the two voices continue to awkwardly converge and overlap throughout the chapter, as proved by the shift from third- to first-person narration within the same sentence: 'Ogni momento scopri che c'è un personaggio nuovo, non si sa in quanti *siano* in questa nostra immensa cucina, è inutile contar*ci*, *eravamo sempre* in tanti' (34, my emphases [Every moment you discover there a new character, you don't know how many people there are in this immense kitchen of ours, it's no use counting, there were always many of us, 34]). This ambiguity will remain a constant feature throughout the whole novel. The smoothness with which shifts between narrative voices are constantly implemented is remarkable: in fact, it may be argued that by blurring the boundaries between narrators and by not making them exactly coincide with the paratextual boundaries of the chapters, fluidity and continuity are actually enhanced rather than hindered.[48]

Along with this strategic use of the narrative voice, the next point ensuring variation within continuity is given once again by the female figure and the relation between her and the male character. The narrative core is dramatised in this case through a double doubling: the homodiegetic narrator Gritzvi and his rival Ponko, and the blond Brigd and her dark-haired counterpart Zwida Ozkart; toward the end of the chapter, the hostile community takes the shape of an old and mysterious rivalry between the Ozkart family and the Kauderers. Calvino does not miss the opportunity to metanarratively foreground this mechanism: the homodiegetic narrator Gritzvi finds himself thinking of his pseudo-replacement with the new apprentice Ponko. This is exactly what happens more broadly in the fractal narrative structure of *Se una notte*, where different characters (carriers of full sets of local features, attached to the various storyworlds) become the nodes of a set of recurring relations and seem to step seamlessly into one another's shoes.[49]

Once the reader approaches Chapter Three, they should arguably begin to sense the pattern between a returning narrative — the frame — and the embedded stories, if any, thanks to the paratextual hints. The return of narrative focus onto the practical activity of cutting the pages, mentioned at the end of Chapter Two, presumably does not take the reader by surprise. It is likely that the systematic employment of interruption has not yet been detected at this point, but the iteration of a similar situation — that of the typographical mistake — does catch one's attention.

From Chapter Three onwards, the frame progressively assumes its own narrative autonomy, keeping its focus on the quest of the Reader and the She-Reader against the array of obstacles that hinder them more or less intentionally. As the novel proceeds, the reader presumably learns to expect the regular alternation between the embedded stories conveyed by the different manuscripts found and lost by the Reader (here, too: variation and repetition) and the narrative continuum delivered in the numbered chapters of the frame. As anticipated, the frame enucleates the basic directions that shall guide the upcoming incipit, which are always dictated by Ludmilla's reading wishes. Interestingly, it can be noted retrospectively that in the first incipit, not yet guided by Ludmilla's predictive captions, the reader is indeed uncertain, 'anche tu lettore non sei ben sicuro di cosa ti farebbe più piacere leggere' (13 [just as you, reader, for that matter, are not sure what you would most like to read, 12]). Starting from these brief descriptions, the reader is usually provided with the necessary interpretive tools to collocate the incipits and account for each distinctive atmosphere and style.

Without going into the same degree of detail for the whole novel, I shall attempt to sketch the basic structure of variations and repetitions that arguably guides the reader through a fractal-like continuum, across the scales represented by each new storyworld. Chapter Three ends in a similar way to Chapter Two, anticipating that 'Sporgendosi dalla costa scoscesa' is no continuation of the previous story: awkwardly enough, only the proper names of characters do recur — which is a first overt and yet mysterious sign of continuation. Around a handful of returning signifiers, a completely different narrative unfolds: Miss Zwida is an elegant young lady sojourning in the small seaside resort of Pëtkwo, who spends her days drawing inanimate objects; she attracts the attention of the narrator, a guest of the nearby Kudgiwa Pension (no longer a farm), recovering from some illness. The main action revolves around the location of the meteorological observatory, usually directed by professor Kauderer (no longer a farmer) and temporarily passed on to the narrator's supervision. While the narrator and Miss Zwida are the recurring male and female characters, the hostile community is impersonated by the two mysterious men looking for Mr Kauderer and by Kauderer himself. Through these specific characters, a few new elements are added to the fractal-like semantic continuum: the motif of obsessive sign-reading (for example, 53, 59 [52, 58]; this builds on a similar feeling of paranoia experienced by the narrator of 'Se una notte') and the importance of form.

In Chapter Four, the character of Lotaria returns and with her a 'bearded man' (perhaps recalling the bearded fugitive appeared at the end of last incipit?), Professor Galligani. Continuity is ensured, paradoxically, by the first theoretical discussion of a poetics of interruption and of its positive aspects, advanced by Uzzi-Tuzii. It could be also suggested that the militarist attitude surrounding Lotaria's seminar and her cold and over-analytical interpretive grids aptly prepare the ground for the setting of the following intercalated novel.

The pseudo-Marxist critical paradigms listed at the end of Chapter Four are transposed into the fictional left-oriented revolution staged in 'Senza temere il vento e la vertigine'. The male-female pair and the Other that interposes between them is here exhibited by the threesome relationship between the narrator Alex Zinnober, his friend and love rival Valeriano, and Irina; the hostile element is represented by the anonymous and body-less entity of the Revolutionary Army, ultimately embodied with a dramatic turn of events by Valeriano himself, who is carrying a message ordering the narrator's death sentence. In addition to the tone, continuity is ensured by the return of the proper name Kauderer, now the owner of a munitions factory, while the meteorological observatory is indirectly resurrected through Irina's reference to the profession of the astronomer (' — Fa l'astronomo? — No, un altro genere d'osservatorio -', 83 [— Are you an astronomer? — No, another kind of observer, 81]). Like the replacement between Ponko and Gritzvi in the second incipit, here too Irina hopes for a change of power roles between genders (86 [84]). In fact, along with their subversion, the story introduces the idea of a fluidity of roles, where even juxtaposed roles may overlap and co-exist ('Irina è insieme l'officiante e la divinità e la profanatrice e la vittima', 87 [Irina is at once priestess and divinity, profaner and victim, 85]).

Chapter Five recounts the Reader's arrival at the publishing house, where he meets the editor Dr Cavedagna and discovers the plagiarist activities of Ermes

Marana. The frame story fully integrates the motifs of role replacement and of fluidity between — in this case — narratives, and exploits it to explain the messy relationships connecting the various incipits. Also the idea of receiving and interpreting messages, introduced in 'Sporgendosi', is retrieved and applied to the discussion of the editing activity as something completely other from reading for pleasure ('i veri libri [...] erano per lui come messaggi d'altri mondi', 101 [true books for him [...] were like messages from other worlds, 98]).

The themes of disguise and reinvention introduced by Marana in the frame are dramatised in the fifth incipit through the obsessive transformations of Ruedi the Swiss. Instead of concerning plagiarism, though, the issue triggers a reflection on multiplicity in relation to interruption and renewed beginning — that is what the reader is experiencing in *Se una notte*. From the offence of plagiarism, the story expands toward the context of illegality and criminality by staging a murder. The complicity that the Reader seems to be developing with Ludmilla is distorted, in the intercalated novel, into a criminal connivance, and the She-Reader's intellectual independence, slightly resented by the Reader (93 [90]), takes the hypofictional shape of Bernadette's ambiguous pursuit of her own interests to Ruedi's expenses. In 'Guarda in basso', the idea is introduced that interrupting something (for instance, a narrative) does not at all guarantee that its consequences and effects will equally cease to exist: far from simplification, new beginnings result into a multiplication of the consequences that must be escaped (105–06 [102–03]).

Chapter Six marks an interesting turning point in *Se una notte*: the narrative levels begin to interact with one another. While so far the embedded stories were accessed only in the intercalated chapters, here the Reader directly accounts for Marana's correspondence with the publishing house, thus inserting further hypodiegetic narrative fragments within the frame chapters. These stories, moreover, exhibit several details linking them to previous intercalated novels (perhaps reasonably, since it looks like they might be acknowledged a shared paternity in the figure of Marana):[50] the motherland of Ruedi the Swiss returns as one of Marana's past addresses (118 [115]); the zinc canopy where Marana was held hostage (119 [116]) reminds of the canopy of the meteorological observatory in 'Sporgendosi' (53 [52]); the Sultan's wife is the Oriental queen mockingly evoked by Alex Zinnober in 'Senza temere' (85 [83]). The spy motif, also introduced in 'Senza temere', in Chapter Six becomes critical as the plagiaristic activity of Marana is placed within a broader and even more entangled network of conflicting interests, where transformation and disguise cease to be creative forces and become signs of deception, corruption, and mutual espionage.

It could be argued that Chapter Six aims at deliberately producing an effect of deep confusion. Syntactically, the fragmentary and disordered state of Marana's correspondence — and consequently the Reader's difficulties in making sense of it — is rendered through the frequent use of suspension dots, blank spaces in between excerpts, and sometimes paragraphs starting with lower case letters. Semantically, this claim seems justified by the way Dr Cavedagna introduces the whole situation, remarking that Marana's accounts are incredibly messy (115 [112]). Metanarratively,

I suggest that this state of confusion, displayed both at the level of mimesis and of narrative structure, has in fact been anticipated in the fourth intercalated novel. Although I will revert later to the analogy established between characters' actions and the geometrical concept of line, I would like to raise here a point advanced in 'Senza temere':

> Avvicinandosi al centro della scena le linee tendono a contorcersi, a diventare sinuose come il fumo del braciere [...], ad attorcigliarsi — sempre le linee — come la corda invisibile che ci tiene legati [...]. [...] una lenta danza in cui non è il ritmo che importa ma l'annodarsi e lo sciogliersi di linee serpentine. [87, 88]

> [Near the centre of the scene, the lines tend to twist, to become sinuous like the smoke from the brazier [...], to twist — the lines again — like the invisible rope that binds us [...]. [...] a slow dance where it is not the rhythm that counts but the knotting and loosening of serpentine lines.] [85, 86]

The impression that the degree of confusion increases halfway through the novel may not be accidental. It is worth recalling an observation on the first incipit, already quoted, which exhorts the reader to 'take in both the murmuring effect and the effect of the hidden intention, which you (and I, too) are as yet in no position to perceive' (17). Both this sentence and the passage quoted above seem to encourage the reader to take into account the overall effect, somehow leaving aside its exact components (namely, the precise agendas and allegiances among the several groups mentioned in Chapter Six, even more in Chapter Nine). The exponential absurdity of the circumstances of the Reader's quest follows an increasing degree of asymmetry in the structure of the frame chapters. All Chapters from Two to Five end by anticipating that the upcoming narrative would not be the expected one, thus building the reader's expectations and clarifying that the storyworlds instantiated were going to be different hypodiegetic worlds (32, 52, 75, 102 [32, 51, 73, 99]). Chapter Six breaks this pattern of repetition, and the fact that 'In una rete di line che s'allacciano' is an altogether different novel from the previous one is only confirmed a posteriori in Chapter Seven (141 [136]); the pattern is then restored in Chapter Seven (160 [156]), partly in Chapter Eight (where the information is given not at the end but at page 196 [191]), and changed again in Chapter Nine, where the protean female character of Corinna-Gertrude-Ingrid gives the Reader a book in exchange for the one he has been confiscated, but readily admits soon afterwards that it is an apocryphal too (213 [207]). As to Chapter Ten, Arkadian Porphyritch passes on to the Reader 'Quale storia laggiù attende la fine?' as an Ircanian adaptation of Bandera's novel.

Yet, despite the internal escalation of disorder that undeniably characterises the second part of the novel (for example, 218–19 [212–14]), the fractal structure still holds. Let us revert to the outline of the fractal structure of repetitions and variation that arguably underpins the reader's understanding of *Se una notte*. I have already pointed out a few elements of continuation from the previous incipit that appear in Chapter Six. There is still the character of Marana, but the threat represented by his plagiaristic compulsion extends to wider and shadier entities and institutions, such as OEPHLW and APO. A new character, Silas Flannery is introduced.

The title of the following intercalated novel, 'In una rete di linee che s'allacciano', retrieves almost literally the image offered in 'Senza temere'. From this perspective, these last three incipits — 'Senza temere', 'Guarda in basso', and 'In una rete' — build on one another in an interesting way: 'Senza temere' introduces the conceptualisation of sequences of events or individual actions as intersecting lines (79 [77]); 'Guarda in basso' does not explicitly use the image of the line but stresses the multiplication of Ruedi's entangled alternative lives; 'In una rete' combines the two images: the telephones around the narrator are connected into a web of interrelated lines that tightens around him, thus also prolonging the atmosphere of impending conspiracy triggered in Chapter Six. As to the female component of the recurring narrative core, the duplicity of the character of Bernadette — helper of the narrator who might, though, change allegiances in the end — returns in the twofold view of Marjorie, abducted victim and yet temptress in the narrator's eyes.

In Chapter Seven, Ludmilla's involvement in Marana's plagiaristic scheme is revealed, as it is ascertained that its first motive lies in Marana's jealousy of the authorial ghost behind every novel that used to absorb Ludmilla's attention. The following incipit, 'In una rete di linee che s'intersecano', still foregrounds the taste for geometry via the narrator's fascination for mirrors and catoptrics. An element of variation, instead, is represented by the shift of role of the narrator, who in the previous novel played the part of a sort of unaware instigator whereas here he is a proudly over-controlling businessman, busy deflecting his many enemies' threats and, in turn, constantly plotting against them. Although the narrator exhibits a degree of self-control that his predecessor lacked, he finds himself in a similar situation when he is put in the same cell with Lorna (here, an actual lover rather than a failed flirt), who believes to have been abducted by the narrator himself. Unlike in the previous incipit, in this case the likely actual responsible is the narrator's wife, Elfrida.

Chapter Eight is a further proof of the deepening interaction between narrative planes outlined above, as it wholly consists of an excerpt from Silas Flannery's diary, written in the first person. The central chapter of the frame is the one that most closely shares the fictional nature of the intercalated novels and has been recognised as an overt *mise en abyme* of the whole novel (Everman 1988; Milanini 1990), where Calvino gives voice to some of the core ideas that firstly prompted it. I would suggest that the last passage of the chapter has an interesting double function. The first part is a proper *mise an abyme* of the narrative strategy implemented at the beginning of the novel:

> M'è venuta l'idea di scrivere un romanzo fatto solo d'inizi di romanzo. Il protagonista potrebb'essere un Lettore che viene continuamente interrotto. Il Lettore acquista il nuovo romanzo A dell'autore Z. Ma è una copia difettosa, e non riesce ad andare oltre l'inizio... Torna in libreria per farsi cambiare il volume...
> Potrei scriverlo tutto in seconda persona: tu Lettore... [197]
>
> [I have had the idea of writing a novel composed only of beginnings of novels. The protagonist could be a Reader who is continually interrupted. The Reader buys the new novel A by the author Z. But it is a defective copy, he can't

> go beyond the beginning... He returns to the bookshop to have the volume exchanged...
> I could write it all in the second person: you, Reader...] [193]

In the paragraph that follows, however, the perspective of Silas Flannery the character becomes predominant as he imagines to arrange his hypothetical narrative in a way that is meant to favour the character of the writer over the Reader.[51] Even though in this novel such a plan will turn out to be unsuccessful, with this strategy Calvino provides the reader with a useful interpretive key and a horizon of expectations to guide the remainder of the reading:

> Ma non vorrei che per sfuggire al Falsario la Lettrice finisse tra le braccia del Lettore. Farò in modo che il Lettore parta sulle tracce del Falsario [...], in modo che lo Scrittore possa restare solo con la Lettrice.
> Certo, senza un personaggio femminile, il viaggio del Lettore perderebbe vivacità: bisogna che incontri qualche altra donna sul suo percorso. La Lettrice potrebbe avere una sorella... [198]
>
> [But I wouldn't want the young lady Reader, in escaping the Counterfeiter, to end up in the arms of the Reader. I will see to it that the Reader sets out on the trail of the Counterfeiter [...], so that the Writer can remain alone with the young lady, the Other Reader.
> To be sure, without a female character, the Reader's journey would lose liveliness: he must encounter some other woman on his way. Perhaps the Other Reader could have a sister...] [193]

'Sul tappeto di foglie illuminate dalla luna' offers a further re-elaboration (possibly, a preview) of this possibility: the male protagonist is attracted to the young daughter of his mentor Okeda, but is ultimately involved in a physical intercourse with the girl's mother. This happens under the disturbing acquiescence of Mr Okeda himself, who uses his knowledge and the protagonist's guilt to further bound him to his will. Moreover, as to other iterations harking back to the previous incipit, the Japanese name of Kawasaki (motor-bike brand in 'In una rete', surname of a rival professor here) and the motif of the female rivalry (lover vs. wife and mother vs. daughter) are worth mentioning.

The sketch outlined by Silas Flannery guides the reader through the series of forgeries, replacements, and disguises staged in Chapter Nine: the degree of confusion achieves its apex. The fact that the Reader's initial recognition of Lotaria does match with Silas' hypothetical story arguably contributes to confirm it to the reader, who skims through the vertiginous number of roles and counter-roles of the woman. In the end, the Reader gets involved in an equivocal situation similar to that of the male protagonist of 'Sul tappeto', as he is unexpectedly seduced by the combative hyper-spy.

After the turmoil concluding Chapter Nine, the beginning of 'Intorno a una fossa vuota' marks an abrupt change of narrative tone. The scene shifts from computers and cables to starry dawns, vultures, and horses; together with a slower-paced syntax, this reminds of a more traditional form and topic of storytelling. The motif of the search for the unknown mother somehow draws back toward the origins, both existential and narrative. Yet, in line with the dominant dynamic of the novel, replacements still dominate the story, albeit framed within a more conventional and familiar pattern of swopped mothers and sisters (instead of spies and counter-spies and counter-counter-spies in a *regressus ad infinitum*). As ventured by Flannery, sisterhood retains its problematic nuance in the protagonist's eyes: attracted to both Amaranta and Jacinta, he lays himself open to the risk of incest. The element of mystery that is usually embodied by a hostile community, carrier of a power unknown to and escaping the control of the male protagonist, is represented here by the unnatural return of a young Faustino Higueras. He may or may not be the same Faustino who was allegedly killed by Nacho's father; as he might as well be Faustino's son, who bears the same name, Nacho, that don Anastasio was going by in his youth.

Chapter Ten illuminates the delicate equilibrium behind the system of global literary censorship, filtered through the clarity of vision of the General Chief of the National Police Archives, Arkadian Porphyritch. The Reader's dream of the travellers reading all the books he did not manage to finish, together with Ludmilla's reading wish referring to the end of the world, work as omens of the upcoming conclusion of the Reader's adventure and of the novel itself. A progressive deliberate deletion dominates the intercalated novel 'Quale storia laggiù attende la fine?'. A passage at its outset could refer to both the hypodiegetic storyworld of this embedded story and to the novel as a whole, crammed with the multiple storyworlds and storylines accumulated so far: 'Il mondo è così complicato, aggrovigliato e sovraccarico che per vederci un po' chiaro è necessario sfoltire, sfoltire' (247 [The world is so complicated, tangled, and overloaded that to see into it with any clarity you must prune and prune, 239]). Arguably, such a statement fits into a trajectory toward a restoration of order — or better, an alleviation of confusion — that achieves its highest degree in Chapter Nine after some chapters and incipits of increasing disorder. In 'Quale storia', not only the physical storyworld but also its core interrelations are winnowed down to their barest structure: the male protagonist and the anonymous relentless officials of Section D meet on 'una distesa piatta e grigia di ghiaccio compatto come il basalto' (250 [a flat, gray expanse of ice, as compact as basalt, 242]); although their actions may seem similar, their purposes are clearly juxtaposed and their relationship overtly antagonistic; the attraction to the female character, Franziska, is the narrator's only firm point and it is only by reaching her that the final dissolution of the storyworld is escaped.

As explicitly admitted by the narrator, Chapter Eleven is an arrival point: 'Lettore, è tempo che la tua sballottata navigazione trovi un approdo' (255 [Reader, it is time for your tempest-tossed vessel to come to port, 247]). After browsing several storyworlds instantiated by the ten intercalated novels, the reader is likely to expect some sort of closure for the Reader's quest staged in the frame. The pattern of variations and repetitions is emphasised once again through a series of alternative views on reading, its modes and purposes (256–59 [248–50]).

In this regard, it is worth remarking that the argument elaborated in this book does not deny a variable phenomenology of reading. Rather, it attempts to outline how the text is designed to prompt a certain interaction with the reader. If the underlying assumption is that storyworlds are produced and co-constructed by readers, we can therefore infer that the text has to include tools and instructions to carry out such a co-construction. The fractal-like narrative structure I have illustrated in this section, with its patterns of variations and repetitions, its horizontal axis running through the frame and vertical axes guiding the understanding of each embedded narrative, is arguably the main strategy implemented by the author via the text to guide the reader's understanding of the narrative in its parts and as a whole. I have suggested that the type of closure provided by the novel is a satisfactory and yet arbitrary one. This does not contradict the potentially infinite fractal structure of the narrative, as its conclusion in this case amounts more to a summary of its parts, followed by its sudden conclusion brought about by an overt authorial interference, rather than merely the inescapable exhaustion of the possibilities offered by its mechanism.[52]

The space of narrative experience, fictionalised

In Chapter 2 of this book, I suggested that plot understanding pertains to the higher-level space of narrative experience, which draws on the virtual space made up of the characters' private worlds and their interrelations on the one hand, and include the perspective of the reader on the other. In Calvino's *Se una notte*, however, the perspective of the reader is programmatically included in the narrative itself in a decidedly metanarrative way. Given that the concept of *space of narrative experience* is inherently informed by the reader's experience and given that, in this case, the reader's experience is directly called upon and itself turned into a story, I suggest that *Se una notte* presents an instance of fictionalisation of the space of narrative experience.

The narrative You

When I discussed how Baricco's *City* engages with the reader's virtual body, I argued that embodiment of contextual-frame shifts leverages a view of storylines as something to be almost (virtually) physically entered, and that, in doing so, their spatial nature was strongly emphasised. I also noted that the large number of contextual-frame shifts highlights the overarching power of the narrator, and hence the deliberateness of the act of narration. Comparing *City* with a novel so deeply metanarrative as *Se una notte*, however, prompts us to look at the differences between the strategies of sense-making implemented by Baricco and Calvino respectively.

Following Caracciolo's terminology, it has been said that in *City* the reader is prompted 'to take on, in [her] imaginative engagement with the story, the fictional body of a character' (2014a: 158). The passage thereby analysed featuring Diesel and Poomerang is placed at the high-level end of Caracciolo's scale of fictionalisation of the reader's virtual body, because the reader's virtual body is aligned with the fictional body of two characters. As I remarked, all the ontological doubts raised during the reading of *City* are ultimately resolved, and the reader is not left facing an ontologically subverted storyworld.

Se una notte does not present a situation as straightforward. The main reason for such increased complexity is the employment of the second-person narration. If we look briefly at its uses in the tradition, of which Calvino was surely aware, worth mentioning is his 1979 foreword to the *Metamorphoses*. Calvino points at Ovid's use of the apostrophe to the narratee (SI 904–16) and dates it back to the earlier Greek novel (Reardon 1969). Overall, the occasional address to the narratee is a well-established device in the novelistic tradition: it has been widely discussed by the scholarship and multiple examples have been identified in English, French and Italian literature (for example, Henry Fielding's *The History of Tom Jones, a Foundling*, 1749; Michel Butor's *La modification*, 1956; and Italo Svevo's *La coscienza di Zeno*, 1923).[53] As an interesting case in point for our discussion, when Butor's use of 'narrative you' was (wrongly) welcomed as an unprecedented novelty, American Professor W. M. Frohock observed that it produced a 'novel narrational dimension' (Morrissette 1965: 2). Even though the device is by no means new, I agree that it can impinge on narrative comprehension by promoting the visibility of what, in fact, I define as the space of narrative experience in its three-dimensional nature.

In his postclassical reformulation, Herman rethinks the concept of narratee within his discussion of contextual anchoring — that is, the 'process whereby a narrative, in a more or less explicit and reflexive way, asks its interpreters to search for analogies' between the narrative storyworlds prompted by the text and the readers' mental models of the world they live in and from which they try to make sense of the narrative (2002: 331). In our attempt to define the ontological status of the 'you' in *Se una notte*, Herman's and Caracciolo's theories can supplement one another. The relevance of investigating the ontological status of the entity referred to as 'you' becomes clear as we adopt Herman's observation that the 'narrative *you* produces an ontological hesitation between what is actual and what is virtual within the storyworld' (2002: 338), which perfectly describes what happens in *Se una notte*. Caracciolo's concept of readers' virtual body, then, helps illuminate the cognitive operations triggered by the specific formal designs adopted by Calvino to guide the readers of *Se una notte* through this fuzzy situation.[54] In other words, Herman's study of contextual anchoring clarifies why and how the text manages to achieve this ontological ambiguity; Caracciolo's contribution serves to explain how Calvino manipulates this ambiguity throughout *Se una notte*, and how he enables readers to make sense of shifts across this ontological continuum and to get to plausible (though not definitive) solutions which ultimately allow narrative comprehension.

Accounts of second-person narrative basically posit two possible situations, either an intradiegetic or an extradiegetic narratee. Herman's study takes Monika Fludernik's (1993) reformulation as point of departure for a restructuration of the whole issue, enriching it through research on deixis (Margolin 1984; Zubin and Hewitt 1995). Herman diversifies the possible uses of the pronoun *you* by isolating its grammatical form and deictic profile. If these two functions are uncoupled, then we have either cases where the pronoun *you* actually entails a deictic transfer from the *I*, or a pseudo-deictic *you* (Furrow 1988: 372), that is an impersonal or generalised *you*. Otherwise, if grammatical form and deictic profile converge, then the address function of the pronoun is highlighted, and we have two types of address: a 'fictionalised' or 'horizontal' address, if it refers to another member of the fictional world, and an 'actualised' or 'vertical' address, if it refers to an entity belonging to another ontological (nonfictional) domain (Herman 2002: 341). Narrative situations, however, are rarely that clear-cut. Uri Margolin (1984) addresses the problem and points out that textual indicators can be deliberately used in a way such to stretch or blur the scope of the address functions attached to textual *you*. More specifically, a certain use of *you* may cue the superimposition of the two deictic roles, one internal and one external to the storyworld, thus prompting the situation called of 'double deixis'. Double deixis is therefore a hybrid case, characterised by 'a merely partial (dis)agreement between form and functions of *you*' (Herman 2002: 352–53).

Surely any schematisation of the meanings and uses of the textual *you* ought to be arranged into a scalar taxonomy rather than into a binary one or rigidly divided into types. Potentially, each and every occurrence of *you* could bear differently on contextual anchoring, and therefore cue readers to slightly adjust their self-positioning toward the storyworld. With reference to the frame in *Se una notte*, my suggestion is that three main phases can be identified, each characterised by a dominant use of narrative *you*: preceding the appearance of the Reader, referring to the Reader (main body of the novel), and a hybrid version in the last chapter. Overall, the fluidity of functions of the textual *you* should be acknowledged, and with it the fact that these different functions can operate at a higher or lower degree in various moments throughout the narrative. In particular, by impacting on deictic dimensions, different configurations of functions underlying the narrative *you* at some specific moments can be responsible for situations where the boundary between textual and extra-textual is particularly porous.

In the first two chapters and half of *Se una notte*, up to the point where the Reader is officially introduced, Calvino designs textual features to cue an apostrophic address, which prompts readers 'not to virtualize, but rather to actualize the entity references by *you*' (2002: 359; Habermas 1988; Kacandes 1993). It is a case of 'vertical address' because it is meant to break through the boundaries of the storyworld and directly address the real reader. The apostrophic address designed by Calvino, though, constitutes quite a borderline case insofar as, referring to Herman's model, it straddles apostrophic address and double deixis.

The official introduction of the Reader marks a watershed in readers' comprehension of the pronoun *you*. As I discuss below, readers' confidence in attributing a clear extradiegetic deictic referent was already undermined by the reading experience of the first incipit. In Chapter Two, then, it is made explicit that what had been allegedly understood as an apostrophic address is in fact a fictionalised address, his target being the intradiegetic Reader. Throughout the narrative, the Reader's profile is increasingly specified as his status as fully-fledged character internal to the storyworld is reinforced.

Albeit this change of perspective surely casts a retrospective ambiguity upon the prior status of the discourse model, it is my belief that this is not enough to classify the narrative *you* of Chapter One as a case of double deixis. To argue that the textual *you* produces a doubly deictic context fundamentally bears on the ontological structure of the storyworld, in that it makes it hard to neatly distinguish between what is internal and what is external to the storyworld. However, although we could register an 'interference pattern between two or more competing deictic fields' (Herman 2002: 364), as soon as the Reader appears it is no longer true that there is no ultimate reference point to orient the deictic transfers: to the best of my knowledge, until Chapter Twelve the vast majority of the occurrences of narrative *you* in the frame deictically refer to the Reader as a character. What I would rather argue, and what I expand on in the next subsection, is that the projection relations between readers and the character are made denser not by the compromised boundary between virtual fictional protagonist (the Reader who is read) and the actual reader (the reader who reads), but thanks to the reinforced alignment with the reader's virtual body, as explained by Caracciolo's framework. If any, additional ambiguity is produced by the insertion of embedded narratives which also employ the narrative *you*. By doing so, not only do they severely hinder the reader's comprehension of their hypodiegetic nature, at least at the beginning, but they might also interfere with the function of the Reader as deictic centre.

One last significant shift occurs at the very end of *Se una notte*, in Chapter Twelve. Here, the narrator describes the Reader and the She-Reader, happily married, reading in bed before going to sleep. While in the first lines the narrative *you* still clearly refers to the fully-specified and intradiegetic Reader ('Ora siete marito e moglie, Lettore e Lettrice', 263 [Now you are man and wife, Reader and Reader, 254]), the last instance causes an unexpected reversal: 'E tu: — Ancora un momento. Sto per finire *Se una notte d'inverno un viaggiatore* di Italo Calvino' (263 [And you say, "Just a moment, I've almost finished *If on a winter's night a traveller* by Italo Calvino.", 254]). However, one of the first adjustments required at the outset of Chapter Two, and concomitant with the appearance of the Reader, had concerned precisely the fact that, within the fictional storyworld to which the Reader belongs, 'Se una notte d'inverno' is not the same novel the real reader is reading, but only the first incipit started by the Reader and never completed. Representing the Reader as he finishes reading *Se una notte* not only denies that prior re-adjustment but also suddenly restores a relation of identity — now perceived as incompatible — between reader and Reader. In this sense, I suggest that, for this instance only, the textual *you* serves as a proper double deixis, as it determines an 'ontological interference pattern' 'produced by two or more interacting spatiotemporal frames — none of which can be called primary or basic relative to the other(s)' (Herman 2002: 345).

To recapitulate, it should be remembered that readers interpret the deictic function of *you*, (dis)agreement with its grammatical form, and the modal status (actuality vs. virtuality) of its referents in a gradient and ever-adjusting way, along a continuum where the pronoun *you* takes on at one end 'strictly referential functions, and at the other strictly the function of address' (2002: 350). At the outset of the narrative, the textual *you* most probably serves an apostrophic function, addressing the extradiegetic actual reader; the fact that the narrator diversifies the potential context from which real readers might be making sense of the storyworld seems to endorse the apostrophic function, as an attempt to maximise its chances to meet analogous profiles among them. As soon as the Reader enters the storyworld, the narrative *you* is re-inflected as a fictionalised address: the range of probable actual profiles is narrowed down to one intradiegetic profile, which is progressively specified. Only at the very end of the novel, with a swift subversion of the storyworld ontological boundaries, the deictic force of narrative *you* is suddenly doubled, as it evokes at the same time the fictional Reader (as he responds to the question of another intradiegetic character, Ludmilla) and the real reader. Even more strikingly, the profile of real reader referred to in this last line arguably matches with each and every real reader, something which could not been guaranteed for all real readers of Chapter One: here, the text encodes a profile specified uniquely by the fact of being reading the ending of *Se una notte*, and the very fact of getting to read that line means that the reader is indeed reading the end of the novel. Also amongst second-person narratives, *Se una notte* presents a technically interesting case study because, whereas it initially seems to be the virtual body of the narratee that reaches out in order to align itself with the stance of actual readers, as soon as the Reader is identified the perspective turns inside-out. While assuming to be pulling something out from the diegetic context, the actual reader has actually been 'pulled into' the storyworld.

The self-reflective character of *Se una notte* is further reinforced by the use of narrative *you*, as it transforms the monitoring process of the ways in which the storyworld matches the context in which it is reconstructed, 'from an automatic into a conscious interpretive activity' (Herman 2002: 350). After all, *Se una notte* as a whole exhibits a strong metanarrative commitment. It would thus not seem out of place to suggest that Calvino might have taken up second-person narration to further explore, as Herman hopes, through 'an irreducibly plural *you*' the potentialities and issues of narrative itself.

The R/reader's virtual body

Apart from passages of stronger ambiguity at the beginning and at the end of the novel, in the frame of *Se una notte* the narrative *you* encodes a fictionalised address to the intradiegetic character of the Reader. I claimed that, despite the sometimes fuzzy distinction between what is external and what is internal to the storyworld, I would resist classing it as double deixis because, in the frame, the textual *you* remains anchored to an increasingly specified character.

Nevertheless, the (overall) absence of ambivalence concerning the function of the second-person narration does not mean ambiguity is effaced in general. The brief analysis carried out in the previous section simply considered the grammatical form and deictic function of textual *you*, and excluded that these specific textual aspects should be carriers of further ambiguities. Yet we cannot ignore that this intradiegetic and characterised entity is called the Reader, and since real readers are readers too, this profile analogy does encourage a certain superimposition.

In order to analyse the mechanisms employed by the text to cue this superimposition of fictional Reader's and reader's deictic fields, I draw again on Caracciolo's concept of readers' virtual body. My suggestion is that, even when the second-person pronoun refers grammatically and functionally to the Reader, an expansion of the scope of *you* is promoted via the bodily-perceptual capabilities of the virtual body attached to it. As far as *Se una notte* is concerned, I believe that the concept of readers' virtual body enables one to account for the ways in which such an ambiguous and powerful engagement of the reader can be achieved through the text. In the previous section, I discussed how with the appearance of the Reader readers experience a shift in the narratee's identity: from a generic and underspecified reference to real readers, to the fictionally actual character of the Reader. This re-assessment, I suggest, is also followed by a change of allegiances of the readers' virtual body.

Before the Reader officially enters the storyworld, the virtual body of the reader is aligned with the narratee. Referring to Caracciolo's scale of fictionalisation, the narratee initially addressed by the narrator is closer to a 'deputy focalizor' — that is, a persona that can access the fictional world without being a character (2014a: 163). Although, unlike E. M. Foster's 'anonymous visitor' in *A Passage to India* (which Caracciolo employs to explain this concept), the narratee of *Se una notte* is directly addressed in the second person, which prompts a deeper and more immediate engagement of the actual reader. In fact, it is the narrating-I who seems willing to adapt the narratee's profile to any potential real reader, rather than the other way round. The variety of physical actions the narratee performs while getting ready for the reading experience and the description of the number of attitudes one might take on entering a bookstore increase the chances for actual readers to project models of their own current context onto the narratee's position. The attention paid by Calvino to the intellectual (the taxonomy of book types in a bookstore, 5–6 [5–6]) and physical (the range of bodily positions and material preparations that surround the reading activity, 3–4 [3–4]) phenomenology of reading emphasises the embodied nature of the reader's virtual body and favours its alignment with that of the narratee. As Segre points out, however, the major novelty of *Se una notte* is less the second-person narration per se and more the overlapping of 'you-narratee' and 'you-protagonist' (1979: 203). To draw on Herman's terminology, we witness a shift in the deictic function of the textual *you*, moving from an apostrophic address to a fictionalised address. When the character of the Reader is introduced in Chapter Two, the reader's virtual body is expected to reassess its allegiance: from an alignment with the deputy focalizor to an alignment with the fictionally actual body of the Reader. Although I do not label the narrative *you* used in the frame as a double deixis, I do agree with Segre (1979: 203) when he argues that:

> Calvino ha [portato] entro il quadro ciò che sta al di fuori di esso; perciò eliminare, non di fatto, perché è impossibile, ma con una volizione suggestiva, il limite tra esterno e interno, tra vissuto o vivibile o esperibile e scrittura, letteratura.
>
> [To bring inside the frame what was outside of it; therefore, to eliminate, not actually — as it would be impossible — but imaginatively, the boundary

between outside and inside, between what is or could be lived or experienced, and writing, literature.]

Segre's comment on how the discourse situation designed in *Se una notte* 'brings inside the frame what is outside of it' closely brings to mind what I suggested earlier about the reader's virtual body being 'pulled into' the storyworld.

Let us look more closely at the dynamics of fictionalisation of readers' virtual body in *Se una notte*. Both situations implemented in Calvino's novel — alignment with a deputy focalizor and with a fully-fledged character — imply that the narrating-I provides the reader with a perspective highly encoded in the text, as chiefly demonstrated by the use of second-person narration. In other words, the text prepares a position for the readers' virtual body to accommodate in, which is so overtly formalised that the narrating-I even addresses it directly with the textual *you* (irrespective of the change in the type of entities specified by the pronoun). In his theorisation, Caracciolo ascribes the highest degree of fictionalisation to the deputy focalizor, even though characters are endowed with fully-fledged fictional bodies, and should therefore be expected to allow for the easiest option for the reader to re-position their virtual body. By proposing this hierarchy, instead, Caracciolo concurs with Herman that 'the projection relations between reader and narratee are likely to be denser in the case of extradiegetic narratees than in the case of intradiegetic ones', as the former type is less specified (2002: 333). It follows that the type of alignment required to readers in *Se una notte* would shift down along Caracciolo's scale of fictionalisation, from a higher degree of fictionalisation of the virtual body to a slightly lower degree, described as 'strict focalisation' (Jahn 1999), because it identifies with the body of a specific character in the narrative. Technically, therefore, this represents a risk of decreased engagement, since readers' bodily-perceptual identification with fully-fledged characters could be hindered by the interference of the characters' consciousness-attribution (Caracciolo 2014a: 166). I suggest however that this is not the case in *Se una notte* because other strategies intervene as counterbalance.

First of all, the use of second-person narration and of the present tense still exerts a strong invitation to readers to blend their virtual body with the Reader's fictionally actual body. Secondly, constant reference to the bodily-perceptual experience of the reading activity, both in general and as the Reader lives it at present, creates a strong connection with the physical sensations of readers who are (probably) holding in their hands the physical object of the book. Thirdly, to address the character as 'Reader' has a twofold effect: the lack of a proper name deprives the character of an essential property, which makes it easier for readers to accommodate their virtual bodies in its place; moreover, to emphasise critically his function over his identity calls for an immediate and blatant superimposition of his role and that of real readers. The naming choice has significant impact on the way readers manage to maintain a deep engagement with the narrative when it comes to intercalated novels. Whenever a new storyworld is instantiated, the readers' engagement is continuous but the storyworld's organisational principle and specifics change. To be bound to an entity whose function is (partly) privileged over his individuality highlights the Reader's role as mediator and ensures a better alignment between real readers and characters of the intercalated novels.

As it is, the Reader works as both a filter and a vessel for readers to access the hypodiegetic narratives, and the text is designed to co-construct the ideal connection to enable a full narrative experience. At the outset of *Se una notte*, real readers are cued a) to identify the deictic field of the narratee with their own via the apostrophic use of *you*, and b) to align their virtual body with the extradiegetic narratee. Then, the extradiegetic narratee turns into (or turns out to be) the intradiegetic character of the Reader; due to the reasons discussed above, the alignment with the readers' virtual body is not broken but re-assessed, maintaining robust but flexible projection relations between interpreters and the storyworld. Real readers find themselves prompted to strongly identify with a fictionally actual body which is replicating their own position at a different level (note again the fractal-like pattern), using the storyworld of the frame as point of departure to access several hypodiegetic storyworlds. Every time a new intercalated novel begins, a deictic shift is required (Duchan, Bruder and Hewitt 1995; Herman 2002: 271–74). I argue, however, that the entity that projects its virtual body into the hypodiegetic storyworld is not the real reader, but rather the Reader, who thus becomes an unavoidable experiential filter. It functions as a hinge joint that connects the real reader with the hypodiegetic storyworlds. It could be argued that actual readers do not access the intercalated storyworld directly (or, at least, not always in an unmediated way), but they rather access the Reader's experience of his own imaginative projection into that storyworld.

For instance, when in 'Se una notte' the narrator remarks that 'tu lettore non hai potuto fare a meno di distinguermi tra la gente che scendeva dal treno' (15 [If you, reader, couldn't help picking me out among the people getting off the train, 14]), the reference does not exactly match with any narrative passage the actual reader has directly read about the man leaving the train. When we 'find' him, he is already at the café of the station. This means that real readers have accessed only the Reader's filtered understanding of the embedded narrative. Analogous passages are scattered throughout all of the incipits, in the form of metanarrative comments delivered by the narrating-I:

> I personaggi prendono corpo a poco a poco dall'accumularsi di particolari minuziosi e di gesti precisi, ma anche di battute, brandelli di conversazione [...]. [34]
>
> [The characters take on form gradually in the accumulation of minute details and precise movements, but also of remarks, shreds of conversations] [34]
>
> La prima sensazione che dovrebbe trasmettere questo libro è ciò che io provo quando sento lo squillo d'un telefono, dico dovrebbe perché dubito che le parole scritte possano darne un'idea anche parziale [133]
>
> [The first sensation this book should convey is what I feel when I hear the telephone ring; I say "should" because I doubt that written words can give even a partial idea of it] [129]

Inasmuch as he is a fictional character eagerly compliant to the needs of the story (even too compliant: the narrating-I itself exhorts him not to accept what is expected of him passively, and indeed also his final desire to marry Ludmilla is ultimately dictated by the conventions of narrative), the Reader serves as a receptive antenna, perfectly and flexibly synchronised to adjust to each hypodiegetic narrative — he is, in other words, an ideal reader. It is thanks to the Reader's alignment to the hypodiegetic narrator of each story that real readers also manage to align their virtual body in turn. *Se una notte* could be regarded as a novel that capitalises on the various ways in which readers can experience storyworlds. The novel pays homage to the array of experiences the same reader can have, thus making a point of the enriching power of reading.

A certain continuity of readers' engagement is also promoted by the peculiar position of the narrator (De Toni 2007; Ricci 1982). While the frame arguably maintains the same one, different narrating-Is are produced for each intercalated novel. Yet, Calvino ensures a stable connection — both among narrating-Is and between narrating-stance and recipients — by always employing the first-person narration and by ascribing to all narrating-Is the same peculiar metanarrative position. As Waugh notes, the narrating-I of *Se una notte* 'is also an "I" who talks to the characters *in* the novel, and therefore exists at the level of the story *and at* the level of discourse' (1984: 134).[55]

The irreducible ambiguity of contextual anchoring in *Se una notte* is a designed outcome, not a by-product. Furthermore, the constant re-assessment it demands of real readers forces them to question the reasons behind this ambiguity. *Se una notte*, I suggest, provides a very good case for endorsing Herman's hypothesis that 'stories not only assume a relation between text and context but sometimes work to reshape it' (2002: 336). In this light, this narrative also makes a point of how plot understanding is a moment-by-moment process that is constantly impinged by features of the text.

The reader makes her entrance

In a draft for a conference presentation at Columbia University in 1983, Calvino writes:

> Un libro (io credo) è qualcosa con un principio e una fine (anche se non è un romanzo in senso stretto), è uno spazio in cui il lettore deve entrare, girare, magari perdersi, ma a un certo punto trovare un'uscita, o magari parecchie uscite, la possibilità d'aprirsi una strada per venirne fuori. [RRII 1361]
>
> [A book (I believe) is something with a beginning and an end (even if it is not a novel in the strict sense), a space where the reader can enter, roam around, maybe even get lost, but at a certain point finds an exit, or even several exits, the possibility of opening up for himself a route to come out.][56]

Apart from registering the striking resemblance of the excerpt with Baricco's description in the blurb of the experience of writing and reading *City* as a joint exploration for himself and his readers ('Ci ho viaggiato per tre anni, in *City*. Il lettore, se vorrà, potrà rifare la mia strada' [I have travelled through *City* for three years. The reader, should she wish, is welcome to retrace my steps]), one thing that comes to mind is an affinity of what expressed here with the way Calvino designs *Se una notte*'s closure. As I observed earlier, the ending of this fractal novel comes abruptly, thanks to a fairly overt intervention of an authorial entity that suddenly takes control of the unfolding of events. What emerges is an idea of closure as something that does not ensue directly and necessarily from the narrated matter, from the content, but rather as a formal need imposed by the dynamic of narrative itself, functional to the success of the narrative experience.

The second point worth emphasising is the concept of the narrative as a space for readers to navigate and to move through. It should not take us by surprise by now, but it is still significant to pinpoint the overt references Calvino makes in this direction. I would like to expand on this idea, building on the concept of readers' virtual body and on the evidence of its evocation in *Se una notte*, with the purpose of reconnecting this reflection also to the hypothesis of fractal plot. My suggestion is that making sense of *Se una notte*'s plot as fractal not only stems from the analytic elaboration of patterns of variation and repetition, but it is also reinforced by a supplementary response elicited by leveraging the readers' bodily-perceptual experience.

The possibility that memories of bodily-perceptual experience may impact upon higher-order meanings — namely, plot as higher-order macrodesign — is explicitly entertained by Caracciolo (2014a: 158). In this light it could be argued that, starting from the assumption that fractals are primarily characterised by self-reflexivity across scales, by aligning their virtual body with the fictionalised body of the Reader's and consequently with different elements of the narrative core, by trying out different angles on similar situations, readers arguably experience such a self-reflexivity. This alignment alone would not probably justify an interpretation of the process of plot sense-making as fractal; yet, when concomitant with other elements, the overlapping of readers' virtual body and the Reader's fictionally actual body does promote such a reading.

Overall, to acknowledge the importance of readers' bodily engagement allows for a deeper appreciation of the full array of narrative strategies implemented by Calvino in *Se una notte*. Moreover, it might add a point to the debate around the view that sees Calvino's as an emphatically 'mind-centred' author (for example, Hume's reading of Calvino's thought as cogito vs. cosmos). In fact, many research strands sparked from Calvino's oeuvre — for example, the salience of desire (Bonsaver 1995) — already grant relevance to issues that are not purely disembodied and abstract. Rather than challenging an interpretation of Calvino as an author pre-eminently interested in the mind's workings, my contribution adds a further perspective, aiming to emphasise the complexity of Calvino's reflection, which brings to the fore the precise nature of the mind as embodied. On the one hand, this study re-asserts the overarching power of Calvino's spatially-informed cognitive style; on the other, it also shows how embodiment still crucially affects the narrative enterprise as a means to enable a shared experience between Calvino's mind and the readers' minds.

As already noted, the space of narrative experience designates the dimension where plot emerges and it equally depends on the virtual worlds encompassed in the storyworld and on the reader's perspective. Whenever one of these aspects is somewhat leveraged by the narrative design, there may be interesting consequences for the space of narrative experience itself. Following the analyses of the previous two subsections, I suggest that in *Se una notte* the reader's perspective exhibits complex and ambivalent features that impact on this additional virtual space. More specifically, the readers' perspective is programmatically included in the narrative via manipulations of the deictic function of *you* and engagement of readers' virtual body, which leads me to hypothesise that we could speak of fictionalisation of the space of narrative experience.

In 'Cibernetica e fantasmi', Calvino observes that in contemporary narrative writing is less a matter of telling and more a matter of telling that one is telling. If this statement is not per se unprecedented, it is instead interesting that he describes the resulting metanarrative effect with a spatial image, in terms of *literature squared* or *cubed* (SI 208). Refining the analogy, I suggest we could actually distinguish between literature squared — that is, 'conventional' metanarration — and literature cubed, which defines instances of narrative such as *Se una notte* or the cosmicomical short story 'L'origine degli Uccelli'. These are narratives that do not merely stage acts of storytelling, but specifically reach out from the written world and toward the real reader. Literature cubed, we could say, amounts to the breaking of the fourth wall in theatre, and implies the inclusion of an additional dimension. Also Santovetti (2007: 190) refers to Calvino's all experimental texts — *Le città* and *Il castello*, in addition to *Se una notte* — as 'three-dimensional mazes', although she does not explain the expression further. It could be suggested that, in relation to *Se una notte*, the label of hypernovel conveys a sense of augmentation, not necessarily of plot ramifications, but rather of 'levels of reality' that, by being crossed and interpenetrated, gain an extra dimension and become a sort of three-dimensional space. A sense of three-dimensionality — as opposed to a simpler system of concentrically embedded narratives — is promoted by the cross-referencing practice between different levels discussed in Usher's (1990) study.[57]

What is more interesting in *Se una notte* is that the creation of an additional dimension able to accommodate readers' perspective is not simply a theoretical condition accounting for a peculiar narrative design. I describe it as 'fictionalised' because Calvino turns this emerging dimension into a subject for narration itself:

> Sto tirando fuori troppe storie alla volta perché quello che voglio è che intorno al racconto si senta una saturazione d'altre storie che potrei raccontare e forse racconterò o chissà che non abbia già raccontato in altra occasione, uno spazio pieno di storie che forse non è altro che il tempo della mia vita, in cui ci si può muovere in tutte le direzioni come nello spazio trovando sempre storie che per raccontarle bisognerebbe prima raccontarne delle altre, cosicché partendo da qualsiasi momento o luogo s'incontra la stessa densità di materiale da raccontare. [109]

> [I'm producing too many stories at once because what I want is for you to feel, around the story, a saturation of other stories that I could tell and maybe will

tell or who knows may already have told on some other occasion, a space full of stories that perhaps is simply my lifetime, where you can move in all directions, as in space, always finding stories that cannot be told until other stories are told first, and so, setting out from any moment or place, you encounter always the same density of material to be told.] [105]

The spaces the narrating-I(s) directly looks at are not mimetic spaces in the proper sense of the word. Rather, they are spaces created by the movement of the narrative, co-constructed on the basis of conditions, which are set at the outset of each incipit according to a pattern of variation and repetition. 'Lo scrivere è un'operazione di movimento' (SII 2693 [writing is movement]), and these spaces are fictionalised renderings of the space of the narrative experience.[58] In the first quotation, for instance, there are no oblique lines physically circumscribing an actual fictional space where the characters are confined: the lines represent geometric stylisations of actions and objects (parading tanks, banners, workers demonstrating in the streets — which somehow remind us of the intentional trajectories of characters discussed in Chapter 2 of this book) occurring at different times. They define a standard type of setting for the multiple interactions of the protagonists, and, at the same time, they symbolise how historical and social and private events converge toward a state of affairs that should produce some crucial conditions for the life of the characters (namely Irina's power over Valeriano and Alex, and Alex's possible death sentence for treason). Calvino describes the proximity to the crucial events or moments as proximity to a space, and the actions or events leading toward it as trajectories, lines, that by existing create a geometric virtual space. The second quotation conveys the sense of a seething virtual multiplicity of stories pressing against the single storyline that constitutes the narrating-I's actual present. It epitomises the way in which virtuality, when foregrounded, is likely to prompt the cognitive elaboration of an additional dimension to the narrative storyworld.

Se una notte exhibits a particularly high degree of fictionalisation of the space of narrative experience. Referring to *Le città*, Simonetta Noé argues that the images of the city, the Khan's garden as well as the chessboard are in fact metaphoric representations of a space of the mind wherein everything is integrated in an orderly manner (1982: 92; Hume 1992: 183).

I suggest, however, that *Se una notte* represents a step further because this space is no longer crystallised in a static image that functions as ordering grid for modular pieces of narrative. Rather, the operation of narrative integration and fictionalisation is such that the space becomes a dimension which one can imaginatively interact with and move through. By cuing readers to align their virtual body with the Reader's, the novel invites use for the cognitive strategy of body tour (Herman 2002: 280–81), not through the mimetic storyworld but through the space of narrative experience itself, through the space of the plot of each specific intercalated novel.

As Barbara Tversky claims, 'Switching perspectives carries cognitive costs, at least for comprehension' (1996: 469): there is no doubt that the constant renewal of perspective brought about by new incipits does initially disorient readers; yet the alignment with the Reader's virtual body (as the Reader himself accesses the embedded narratives with his own virtual body) ensures that this link — and comprehension — is never truly undermined. The fictionalisation of the virtual body contributes to ensure interpretive coherence to the overall storyworld.

It should be clear by now that spatialisation of the narrative experience and self-reflexivity do enhance each other: while self-reflexivity often brings about an additional virtual dimension, instances of spatialisation like in *City* are likely to highlight the artificiality of narrative. Although, in this self-reflexive act, narrative may focus both on the storytelling process and on its own materiality. At the outset of the first incipit, the reader seems to participate in a storyworld that is a work in progress, which is construed in front of, and around, the R/reader (Segre 1979): 'O forse l'autore è ancora indeciso [...]. La città là fuori non ha ancora un nome, non sappiamo se resterà fuori del romanzo' (14 [Or perhaps the author still has not made up his mind [...] The city outside there has no name yet, we don't know if it will remain outside of the novel, 12–13]). As observed earlier, it is no accident that the first and the last incipit instantiate storyworlds in construction and under impending dissolution, respectively. In other incipits, however, it is not the storyworld itself that is presented in an *in fieri* status, but it is rather the Reader who is placed below the ideal knowledge threshold — in other words, it is made clear that he should always know more than he actually does about the storyworld in which he is immersed.

I suggest that this narrative strategy should be classified under the rubric of metalepsis, which according to Gérard Genette designates the act of 'taking hold of (telling) by changing level' (1980: 235). Indeed, the narrating-I, here, is not narrating directly the storyworld but rather the process of its co-construction operated by the reader as they read. Arguably, this metanarrative operation causes an ontological uncoupling between the reader and the storyworld she is immersed into: on the one hand, she is part of the diegesis (in other words, she is directly addressed by the narrating-I and her expectations and false assumptions become themselves narrative matter); on the other, she is aware of its artificial nature in a way that is not shared by the other components of the storyworld. By putting some ontological distance between reader and storyworld, the narrative is positing a larger space that should accommodate at least these two ontologically different entities.

Another feature of this process of metaleptic construction concerns the awareness of its materiality, that is the fact that the narrator does not conceal that the storyworld is firstly constructed through an act of writing (nor that it is then re-constructed via an act of reading — Bonsaver 1995: 160):

> uno sfiatare di stantuffo copre l'apertura del capitolo, una nuvola di fumo nasconde parte del primo capoverso. [...] Un fischio come di locomotiva e un getto di vapore si levano dalla macchina del caffè che il vecchio barista mette sotto pressione come se lanciasse un segnale, o almeno così sembra dalla successione delle frasi del secondo capoverso [...]. [11]

> [steam from a piston covers the opening of the chapter, a cloud of smoke hides part of the first paragraph. [...] A whistling sound, like a locomotive's, and a cloud of steam rise from the coffee machine that the old counterman puts under pressure, as if he were sending up a signal, or at least so it seems from the series of sentences in the second paragraph] [10]

Similar instances are scattered all over the intercalated novels (for example, 'Un odore di fritto aleggia ad apertura di pagina', 33; 'Anche il racconto deve sforzarsi di tenerci dietro, di riferire un dialogo costruito sul vuoto', 83; 'Il mondo è ridotto a un foglio di carta dove non si riescono a scrivere altro che parole astratte, come se tutti i nomi concreti fossero finiti', 254 [An odour of frying wafts at the opening of the page, 33; The story must also work hard to keep up with us, to report a dialogue constructed on the void, 80; The world is reduced to a sheet of paper on which nothing can be written except abstract words, as if all concrete nouns were finished, 246]). Usher (1996: 192) describes this as an 'interpenetration of plot and page', which is quite an original feature if one considers that it is carried out throughout the whole novel. As an isolated device, though, it is not totally new for Calvino, who adopts it already in the cosmicomical tale 'Il conte di Montecristo' and 'L'origine degli Uccelli' (both in *Ti con zero*, 1967). Bonsaver (1995: 65) notes that the material and typographical nature of writing is emphasised for the first time in *Il barone*: 'Quel frastaglio di rami e foglie [...] era un ricamo fatto sul nulla che assomiglia a questo filo d'inchiostro, come l'ho lasciato correre per pagine e pagine, zeppo di cancellature, di rimandi, di sgorbi nervosi, di macchie, di lacune' (RRI 776–77 [That mesh of leaves and twigs [...] was embroidered on nothing, like this thread of ink which I have let run on for page after page, swarming with cancellations, corrections, doodles, blots and gaps, 284]). The significant turning point though is marked by *Il cavaliere*, which presents some authentically metanarrative parts: here, not only the theme of writing is central, but through the character of Suor Teodora/Bradamante the suspension of disbelief is fully (if temporarily) broken.

In *Se una notte* the situation is slightly more complex, and not just because the strategy is spread over a longer narrative. Calvino does not merely refer to writing as a linguistic and material vessel that cues the co-construction of the mental model of the storyworld; the two levels — that of material signs and that of the mental images they prompt — interact with each other. The hypothesis advanced earlier may thus provide a plausible explanation to this phenomenon, too: arguably, real readers access the hypodiegetic narratives not in an unmediated way, but via the narrative experience of the Reader.[59] Material features of the narrative are presented to real readers as themselves mental images of the page, with its ink and written words ('uno spessore di piombo fitto e opaco', 15 [a thick, opaque layer of lead, 14]), and as such they can interact and interfere with the mental images of the storyworld as they are re-constructed by the Reader.

In this fundamental ambiguity, perhaps, is grounded the illusionistic element identified by Segre (1979: 203). I have already quoted in full the passage where the scholar points at the interrelations between frame and intercalated novel, describing Calvino's attempt to seemingly erase discontinuities between what is internal and what is external to the storyworlds. To conclude my discussion, I would like to link this effect and its 'illusionistic' properties with the particular spatial image of the Moebius strip, that is a 'one sided, one edged, nonorientable surface with boundary' (A. Ryan 2007: 71). Even though the Moebius strip is evoked by Marìa

Calvo Montoro (2008) to study the structure of *Le città*, I believe the image could be interesting also in relation to *Se una notte*. Building on a suggestion by Varese and Calvino (1973), Calvo Montoro advances the Moebius strip as a concept that suitably captures the permanent discontinuity ('formula «immanente e discontinua»') and the convergent and divergent discourses adopted by Calvino in talking about the reception of the book (2008: 73). It is likely that Calvino was acquainted with the Moebius figure: he was a reader of *Scientific American* and probably met the model via Martin Gardner's first introduction of the concept in 1968 (for example, *Mathematical Puzzles and Diversions*) or in the 'Mathematical Games' section of the journal; moreover, in April 1972 the Oulipian author Luc Ètienne presented in Paris some 'models of moebiusation'. Calvo Montoro claims that the features of a Moebius strip which may bear on the conceptual structuring of *Se una notte* (even more than *Le città*) are its paradoxical bipolarity, its infinite continuity in time and space, its visual representation, and circularity (2008: 75 and 77). Although Calvino's re-adaptations of mathematical models and processes — from the Moebius strip to fractals — may not serve as rigidly inescapable structuring principles, it is still meaningful to assess the doubtless analogies between these models and processes and his narratives.

★ ★ ★ ★ ★

In this chapter, I have investigated Calvino's 1979 novel *Se una notte*, claiming that its plot is designed to be apprehended as a fractal. Or, more precisely, I suggest that the concept of fractality effectively renders the way interpreters are invited to make sense of the novel's plot as they read it. I am not arguing that the fractal was the image Calvino intentionally and univocally had in mind in designing *Se una notte*: rather, that the fractal seems to meet most of the constraints and underlying values that Calvino attempted to comply with in the novel, above all the relationship between order and disorder. Among other properties, for instance, the fractal adequately expresses the Calvinian principle that complexity should be conveyed through multiplicity, as a constellation of infinite approximations (Milanini 1994); it endorses heterogeneity as a value, provided that it is also framed within an ordered (if provisional) consistent unity; further, fractality constitutionally includes a dynamics of repetition and variation, which is typifying of Calvino's whole oeuvre and which any scholar working on the author's text has to confront.

If *Se una notte* lends itself as a suitable case study for an investigation of plot as bearing spatial properties, the elements I foreground are not isolated instances. In fact, they often are either the result of a life-long technical and critical research on Calvino's part, or traits that actually recur — perhaps under different vests — also in previous works. My argumentative effort, thus, illustrates the fact that these strategies and features usually stem from Calvino's specifically cognitive style, which has irreducibly informed and has developed in continuous and silent dialogue with his critical and philosophical stances.

Notes to Chapter 3

1. Quotations from *Se una notte* refer to the Einaudi 1979 edition. For all the other works by Calvino, I refer to *Romanzi e racconti* or *Saggi*.
2. McLaughlin (1998) cites Zena il Lungo in *Il sentiero dei nidi di ragno*, and other short stories ('La stessa cosa del sangue', 'Il giardino incantato', 'Pranzo con un pastore', 'I figli poltroni', and 'Il gatto e il poliziotto') where readers do not feature metanarratively but as a detached or intellectualised figures in the story. Indubitably, a crucial moment is marked by *Le città invisibili*, where the character of Marco Polo observes that 'Chi comanda al racconto non è la voce: è l'orecchio' (RRII 473 [It is not the voice that commands the story: it is the ear]).
3. Although semiotic works in the strict sense usually include only *Il castello dei destini incrociati* (1969/1973), *Le città invisibili* (1972), and *Se una notte* (1979), if we foreground the metanarrative and metaliterary propensity then we could find several connections also with previous works, starting from *Il cavaliere inesistente* (1959) through to several cosmicomical tales (*Le cosmicomiche*, 1965; *Ti con zero*, 1967; *La memoria del mondo e altre storie cosmicomiche*, 1968).
4. The term 'model' is also often employed by Capoferro (2006) and by Calvino himself in *Lezioni americane*.
5. For an overview of the Oulipo see Baetens (2012) and the volume edited by Motte (1986b); on Calvino's relationship with this group, see Aragona (2008), Barenghi (1991b), Bénabou (2008), Botta (1997), Cannon (1979), Motte (1986a), Perroud (1981).
6. From now on, *Il castello*. The first version of *Il castello* was published in Samek Ludovici and Calvino (1969), as a narrative accompanying the analysis of the set of Tarot cards. In 1973, Einaudi published a revised and broadened version of Calvino's previous work, also accompanied by *La Taverna dei destini incrociati* and an afterword.
7. Cf. Barenghi (RRII 1359–65), Milanini (1990: 130–31), Ossola (1987).
8. I selected *Se una notte* instead of *Le città* as main case study because my chief concern lies in the impact of spatiality upon plot and plot understanding. While *Le città* should definitely be included in a broader discussion of Calvino's spatially-informed cognitive style (Beltrami, in preparation), it distinctively lacks plot in the sense that it offers no affordances to readers to create any kind of expectation about the unfolding of the narrative. As I aim to illustrate how spatiality actively impacts on readers' understanding, to demonstrate how the plot of *Se una notte* is governed by spatially-oriented strategies constitutes a more significant example of the far-reaching productiveness of the approach endorsed in this book.
9. In *Palomar* the narrative frame is less developed, but it remains crucial that all the stories revolve around the same character as well as the ordering effort explicated through the paratext.
10. Hence Bonsaver's (1994: 182–83; 1995: 75–76; Musarra Schrøder 2012) suggestion that architecture — due to its combination of geometry and art — should be the best suited discipline to provide useful images and concepts to analyse Calvino's work, from that of 'container' to 'modularity'.
11. Tonin (2005) recognises an increasing centrality of spatiality, with *Marcovaldo* (1963) as turning point preparing the ground for more inherently spatial works, such as the cosmicomical tales and *Le città invisibili* (from now on, *Le città*).
12. Claudio Varese suggests that *Le città*, through its form, attempts to make the invisible visible (Varese and Calvino 1973: 125).
13. Barenghi (SI 734) reports that we still have the completed manuscript of the intervention, even though Calvino ultimately decided to eliminate the lecture and to rearrange its material in the sixth unfinished lecture on 'Consistency' (dated 22 February 1985). As, to my knowledge, no translation of the draft for the sixth 'memo' has been published, the translation of the following passage is mine.
14. This is the preface Calvino wrote for a volume on painter Giulio Paolini, entitled 'La squadratura'.
15. Sabrina Ovan (2012: 416) draws in this respect a connection with Barthes' (1966/1989) concept of *jouissance* as the pleasure (distinctive of writerly texts) derived from a sense of interruption, a break or a gap, where something unexpected occurs.
16. An alternative — and still *a posteriori* — scheme is based on the employment of Greimas' semiotic squares, illustrated in Calvino (1984).

17. As a matter of fact, the same criticism has been advanced to Greimas' structural semantics as a whole. The pairs identified by Calvino for Guglielmi (each pair always stems from a bifurcation of the second term of the previous pair) are: 'il minimo vitale' vs. 'la ricerca della pienezza > 'nelle sensazioni' vs. 'nell'io' > 'rivolto verso il dentro' vs. 'rivolto verso il fuori' > 'la storia' vs. 'l'assurdo' > 'l'identificazione' vs. 'l'estraneità' > 'l'angoscia' vs. 'lo sguardo che scruta' > 'la trasparenza' vs. 'l'oscuro' > 'nell'uomo' vs. 'nel mondo' > 'le origini' vs. 'la fine del mondo' > 'il mondo finisce' vs. 'il mondo continua'. The last option, 'il mondo continua', is presumably meant to close the structure in a circular way.
18. With the due distinctions, the difference is analogous to that expressed by John Barth's shift from literature of exhaustion (1984 (1967)) to literature of replenishment (1984 (1980)).
19. Quotation from a letter to Silvio Micheli, 8 November 1946 (*Lettere*, 68; my translation).
20. For a psychoanalytical reading of the theme of the void in *Se una notte* and *Le cosmicomiche*, see Spackman (2008).
21. JoAnn Cannon defines *Se una notte* as 'poised between two voids, the absence of the subject and the absence of the object' (1989: 59).
22. For a Derridean reading of *Se una notte*, see Belpoliti (1996), Kottman (1996), Markey (1999).
23. In *Il castello*, the same meaning is ascribed to the forest, 'regno dell'indifferenziato e del continuo' (Milanini 1990: 141 [domain of the undifferentiated and continuous]).
24. Another meaning of the void, which should not be dismissed and yet shall not be investigated because it does not pertain virtuality, is linked to the principle of lightness. Calvino remarks that 'la mia operazione è stata il più delle volte una sottrazione di peso; ho cercato di togliere peso ora alle figure umane, ora ai corpi celesti, ora alle città; soprattutto ho cercato di togliere peso alla struttura del racconto e al linguaggio' (SI 631 [my working method has more often than not involved the subtraction of weight. I have tried to remove weight, sometimes from people, sometimes from heavenly bodies, sometimes from cities; above all I have tried to remove weight from the structure of stories and from language, *Six Memos*: 3]).
25. Interestingly, also Michael Ende's *Die unendliche Geschichte*, with which *Se una notte* shares some fascinating features, is first published in Germany in 1979.
26. It is in relation to these issues that a certain diffidence toward a view of void as Derridean différance arises. In *Se una notte* Calvino initiates a programmatically metanarrative discourse, and one should be careful not to mistake literary reflections concerning the fictional nature of narrative for philosophical statements about the nature of reality. Calvino is perfectly aware of the distinct levels of reality that intervene in the literary system, including that 'il lettore è *acquirente*, che il libro è un oggetto che si vende sul mercato' (RRII 1391 [the reader is a *buyer*, and that books are objects which are sold on the market]).
27. As set of textual instructions that mediates the delivery of the narrative, Eco prefers to use the neutral pronoun in referring to the model author (1994: 14).
28. See R. Bertoni (1993) for a discussion of Diderot's novel as one of the models of *Se una notte*.
29. I am thinking here not only of the semiotic trilogy but also of earlier works: apart from the collections of short stories, the *Our Ancestors* trilogy barely fits the genre of the novel and rather straddles those of 'racconto lungo' and *conte philosophique* (Milanini 1991; Starobinski 1991).
30. In the light of the discussion proposed here on the relationship between 'super-tree' and 'hypernovel', it is interesting that Weaver decided to translate the Italian 'iper-testo' as 'supernovel'.
31. Coined by Ted Nelson in 1965 to designate forms of non-sequential writing, the term 'hypertext' holds non-linearity as one of its primary features insofar as it describes 'a text composed of blocks of words (or images) linked electronically by multiple paths, chains, or trails in an open-ended, perpetually unfinished textuality described by the terms *link*, *node*, *network*, *web* and *path*' (Landow 1997: 3).
32. For a discussion of redundancy in linguistics and literature, see among others Phelan (2001) and Suleiman (1980).
33. This position is arguably different from Pilz's conclusion, as she proposes that hypertext 'is thus a medium that reconciles the discontinuous with the continuous as every independent text is potentially linked to the whole' (2005: 131).

34. For other uses in literary criticism see Harris (2015), who adopts the concept of fractal to describe the literary operations of the American novelist David Mitchell, characterised by a 'fractal imagination'.
35. I speak here of a re-integration because the re-evaluation of sequentiality, while still questioning it, fully ascribes *Se una notte* to Barth's (1984 (1980)) literature of replenishment. Literature of replenishment is opposed to the category of literature of exhaustion (1984 (1967)), with which perhaps *Il castello* could be associated.
36. For discussion of complexity applied to narrative studies, see Grishakova and Poulaki (2020) and Walsh and Stepney (2018).
37. In fact, Stoicheff speaks of metafictional texts, but I suggest that his argument equally holds for metanarrative texts.
38. Probably derived from information theory, the concept of 'brusio' refers either to an unclear communication, because it is whispered or overlapping with other voices, or to the noise produced by something moving quietly; in both cases, clear understanding is hindered. Information theory is a discipline variously concerned, according to the field of application, with the transmission of information over a 'noisy' channel; it starts thus from the premise that information is not purely emitted and received, but has to pass through a medium that always interacts (and interferes) with it to some extent (Paulson 1991).
39. The other two properties shared by metanarrative texts and complex systems are irreversibility and self-organisation. As irreversibility can be related to the sequential reading, this property could be still applied to *Se una notte*. Self-organisation, instead, poses a more complicated issue. Since a text is an artistic product designed by an author, when patterns of order emerge it cannot be actually called self-organisation: it is only in the mind of the reader that a system seemingly chaotic may go through leaps of sense-making, perhaps when two apparently unrelated semantic elements suddenly become significant in relation to each other. My suggestion, however, is that these cases could be discussed more productively in terms of self-reflexivity.
40. While plot is an emergent property, emergence is the process of how emergent properties arise. Theoretically, emergence could arise through assembly, breakdown or restructuring of a system (A. Ryan 2007: 73); in the case of plot, I suggest it emerges through assembly — that is, by adding interactions between the components of a system, thereby changing the cardinality of their set. This process of assembly consists in the reading process.
41. Chettiparamb's study offers a useful precedent for the present work, inasmuch as she does not include any mathematical representations in her application of the concept of fractal or of complexity and system theory.
42. Also Santovetti (2007: 216) acknowledges Ludmilla's desires as one of the main links between frame and intercalated novels. This view of intercalated storyworlds as fractal configurations somehow corroborates McLaughlin's (1998: 82–83) and Bonsaver's (1996) argument of desire as key motive force of the (Calvinian) universe: Ludmilla's desires do express the parameters of variation for each new configuration, and variation is one of the two drives operating in fractality, together with repetition.
43. The link with fractality is further corroborated by Segre's additional suggestion that the spiral-shaped scheme is epitomised by the seventh incipit, 'In una rete di linee che s'intersecano', in which he observes that catoptrics is also the symbol of the relationship between micro- and macrocosm (1979: 205). Catoptrics is, indeed, the carrier of the other significant element I stress in the fractal, self-reflexivity.
44. Interestingly, it is precisely *the beginning of a narrative* that is dramatised: the narrator emphasises all the aspects that, according to a folk-phenomenology of reading, a reader should be paying attention to, in order to make sense of the story ('Tutti questi segni convergono nell'informare che', 11 [All these sings converge to inform us that, 10]).
45. The male pronoun is used here not in reference to Calvino, but in relation to the narrating-I of the first incipit who turns out to be a homodiegetic male narrator.
46. In fact, Rankin acknowledges instances when Calvino actually addresses the real reader (for instance, when he considers the risk of identification); however, he remarks that on those occasions Calvino does not use the second person. Rankin's conclusion is that 'Calvino lays

bare the relationship between author and reader not to break down the barriers but rather to re-establish his own supremacy, [...] substantiating the hold of the author *over* the reader' (129).

47. It should be noted that this remains mostly a retrospective speculation, since pragmatically I would mainly rely on the paratext and the separation of chapters and intercalated novels to settle the boundaries among systems of the fractal-like structure.
48. From the second incipit onwards, the reader should arguably start to notice an increasingly overt pattern of recurrent nouns, already stressed and discussed earlier.
49. Cf. also with another interesting statement, where the connection between the various female figures is emphasised: 'Ora poi le reazioni del professore al nome di Ludmilla [...] creano intorno alla Lettrice una curiosità apprensiva non dissimile a quella che ti lega a Zwida Ozkart, nel romanzo di cui stai cercando il seguito, e anche alla signora Marne nel romanzo che avevi cominciato a leggere il giorno prima' (49 [Now, moreover, the professor's reactions at the name Ludmilla [...] create about the Other Reader an apprehensive curiosity not unlike that which binds you to Zwida Ozkart, in the novel whose continuation you are hunting for, and also to Madame Marne in the novel you had begun to read the day before, 48–49]).
50. And, perhaps, a shared maternity through Ludmilla's desires?
51. Admittedly, this can be fully realised retrospectively, when the reader discovers that, in fact, the writer's plan fails and the Reader does ultimately manage to conquer the She-Reader.
52. By suggesting that *Se una notte* outlines a way out of the dead end represented by postmodernist fiction, Carl Malmgren (1986: 106) seems to agree with this position; Valérie Beaudouin (2008: 68), instead, argues that in *Se una notte* Calvino exhausts the narrative possibilities offered by its structure.
53. For a theoretical discussion of the narratee, see Genette (1980), Prince (1982: 57; 1985), B. Richardson (2006). For research with specific focus on second-person narration see Fludernik (1993), Herman (2002), Morrissette (1965). For discussion of the second-person narration in Calvino, see Bonsaver (1995: 160 ff.), Habermas (1988), Lavagetto (1980).
54. The concept of fuzzy logic, programmatically employed by Herman to introduce multivalence as opposed to bivalence (e.g. 2002: 212), is originally proposed by Black (1937) and Zadeh (1965).
55. For Waugh, the purpose of confusing ontological levels and blurring the boundaries author/narrator and implied reader/reader is to break the alleged separation between an 'inventing' author and a passive reader, therefore stressing the necessary collaboration and interrelation between the two entities through the text (1984: 47). Although I concur with Waugh's analysis, I am not sure I agree with her interpretation, which is that in this way Calvino suggests that 'the language in this sense refers ultimately to itself' (47). In fact, Calvino stated on multiple occasions his belief in the existence of a world outside, connected to — although not perfectly representable through — language.
56. 'Cominciare e finire' has not been officially translated into English; this translation is from Bartezzaghi (2007: 136).
57. See also Calvino's 1959 definition of a novel: 'Il romanzo è *un'opera narrativa e fruibile e significante su molti piani che s'intersecano*' (SI 1525).
58. My hypothesis may not be too different from the point advanced by Santovetti when she argues that in *Se una notte* 'what is important is the space [...] full of stories where the reader can move in all directions' (2007: 223). My chapter gives further credit to this analogy and outlines a theoretical framework able to justify the cognitive and fictionally virtual existence of such a space.
59. This would be the case also in the first incipit, even though the character of the Reader has not yet been introduced. This is why the first incipit is more disorientating and presents a bigger cognitive challenge to real readers.

CONCLUSIONS

The research that produced this book was sparked by a dissatisfaction with the explanatory power of current definitions of plot. Action-based as they are, most of the extant plot theories offer few parsing instruments to grasp the peculiarity of narratives that do not predominantly rely on the principles of causality and temporality to ensure coherence.

With the purpose of addressing this significant lacuna, the case studies I explored make the argument for spatiality as a potential alternative organising principle for narrative. At the same time, foregrounding spatiality enabled me to tap into psychological and cognitive frameworks that stress the embodied nature of cognition and storytelling practices. For this reason, spatiality became an ideal entry point for a model of narrative understanding based on a view of cognition as embodied, thus paving the way for endorsing an embodied narratology. On the one hand, spatiality can impact on the narrative structure and on the mimetic content at a semantic level. On the other hand — and more interestingly for my argument — spatiality plays a crucial role in relation to the types of knowledge and the sense-making strategies that readers are prompted to call upon as part of the process of narrative understanding during reading. In other words, some narratives are designed in such a way that readers are encouraged to comprehend them by drawing on strategies originally developed through their experience of space.

In fact, these case studies are particularly effective because they rely on spatiality to such an extent that they cue readers into conceiving the narratives' plots as spaces themselves. The image schemata of map, trajectory, and fractal capture the specific ways in which readers are invited to organise the narrative information as they take it in. My underlying claim, therefore, is that spatiality critically impacts on the form and processes of abstract thought — like plot understanding — rather than being limited to issues concerning mimetic setting.

The novel *City* by Baricco has been explored an as example of narrative that invites readers to understand its plot as a (dynamically) static space, to be made sense of in the same way individuals set out to explore a given territory. Conventional crime fiction narratives and Camilleri's *Montalbano* series are characterised by plots which ought to be explored as a means to reach a goal, and therefore, compared to the first type of narratives, they are more target-oriented and forward-driven: the goal to which crime plots tend is the outcome of the investigation, which consists in a specific configuration of states of affairs and agents' intentions. Again, one should be mindful that whether the achievement of this goal is successful or not does not impinge on the expectations and comprehension strategies implemented by readers, who still strive toward it as they make sense of the plot in its unfolding. Finally, Calvino's *Se una notte* stands out as a narrative whose material is arranged according to an order that is expressed by the figure of the fractal as epitome of complex patterns of repetition and variation.

In this study, I have demonstrated how a focus on spatiality serves to illuminate aspects of these narratives that would have otherwise gone unnoticed. The new features that this approach helped to emphasise have been subsequently built on in each chapter to elaborate reoriented readings of the text (as in the case of Baricco); to highlight the specificities of an author's narrative style as well as to better describe the conventional comprehension procedures prompted by a particular genre (as in the case of Camilleri and crime fiction respectively); to draw innovative connections between works by a specific author and to hypothesise overlooked patterns operating below the surface of some narratives (as in the case of Calvino).

Methodologically, this work shows how the focus on reception and the view of narrative as production and co-construction of storyworlds may unveil new textual patterns, in addition to offering fresh readings. The spatially-oriented perspective I endorse in this book, however, is not expected to produce novel interpretations automatically. My ultimate intention is rather to encourage more diverse thought about the organisational strategies people might use to construct a story — an attempt to go beyond straightforward causality. It is possible that these alternative sense-making patterns operate unconsciously and then are harnessed to various extents through narrative solutions that an author comes to perceive as particularly well-suited. Although this hypothesis needs further corroboration, I have partly showed how this might be the case for Calvino and Baricco, who arguably present distinctively spatially-oriented cognitive styles. In other instances, foregrounding spatiality may be a viable way of deliberately overshadowing causality. In his *Narratori delle pianure* (1985), for instance, Gianni Celati uses the spatial progression from Milan to the Po delta to organise otherwise unrelated stories. Sometimes, instead, writers or more generally storytellers come up with more radical and narratologically complex applications, such as Michael Cunningham in *The Hours* (1999) or, again, Baricco with *Tre volte all'alba* (2012): in both cases, the narrative structure is comprised of multiple storylines analogically yet nor causally interconnected. With this research, I have laid the foundation for an exploration of spatiality as the organising principle that might help us better understand how these kind of narratives work.

The purpose this study strives towards is to open up a debate in narrative theory by providing evidence in support of a still-to-be outlined approach to narrative understanding crucially hinging upon spatiality. In order to do so, I explored three case studies and demonstrated how the focus on spatiality and on the process of narrative understanding contributed to the scholarship on each author or text. At the same time, I suggested alternative frameworks and concepts for narrative analysis, made available by a perspective that foregrounds the embodied mind and the activity of narrative understanding as a mental process textually encoded and yet not necessarily fully propositional in nature. Although the use of these theoretical and analytical tools (for example, contextual-frame shift theory, possible-worlds theory, concepts such as storyworlds and readers' virtual body) has been initially tailored on the specificities of my case studies, the study of their theoretical groundings and reasons for applicability sought not only to justify their employment with regard to these case studies specifically, but also to show how these frameworks and concepts constitute the scaffolding of a coherent and integrated approach to narrative understanding that could potentially be used to explore other works.

This book, therefore, built on the three case studies along two main and interrelated directions. First, I preliminarily isolated a set of narrative features that are likely to endorse a spatial narrative understanding and can thus function as signs of or criteria for assessing the productive applicability of an approach focused on spatiality. The criteria that emerged from my analysis include: (a) the engagement of virtuality; (b) the semantic references to spatiality; (c) the embodiment of comprehension strategies; (d) self-reflexivity; (e) the fictionalisation of the reader's virtual body. The works of Baricco, Camilleri and Calvino all exhibit and implement these characteristics to various degrees and in various ways. As they are differently combined and framed within a variety of authorial contexts, the same features can lead to quite different reading effects — as epitomised by the three image schemata. Although these might not be sufficient criteria for applying a spatially-oriented approach, it seems reasonable to argue that, if a text presents several of these features combined, this could be taken as an indicator of a pre-eminent role played by spatiality, and encourage the critic to further investigate it under this new light.

Secondly and in relation to the task of isolating applicability criteria, this study seeks to pave the way for the design of a flexible yet better defined spatially-oriented approach to narrative understanding. This would primarily entail the outline of the theoretical principles and premises on which such an approach ought to be based; in a second phase, it would require a more in-depth and systematic discussion of the frameworks and models that enable the shift from a theoretical exploration to the elaboration of effective analytical tools to be employed in the interpretive practice of narrative works.

As to the bases of a spatially-oriented approach, this work clarifies that it ought to be rooted in a non-fully-propositional view of thought and in a notion of the mind as embodied. These two principles represent the theoretical pillars of such an approach because, on the one hand, they usher in a way of working on narrative understanding that is textually and verbally encoded yet also crucially factors in the reader's world knowledge; on the other, they bring the embodied nature of human thought to the forefront and therefore prepare the ground for a cognitive study of human strategies of plot understanding that are also influenced by the strategies that the body has developed to make sense of the space around it. As far as a systematic outline of the frameworks involved in a spatially-oriented approach is concerned, this work, albeit not exhaustive nor definitive, still takes some initial productive steps. From the research carried out so far, it emerges that possible-worlds theory and the enactivist view of narrative understanding are rather fruitful models on which a spatially-oriented approach could rely. They provide the necessary conceptual and analytical instruments, together with a philosophically well-grounded theoretical background, to explore two crucial ways in which spatiality impacts on the narrative: the involvement of virtuality in all its various forms (counterfactuality, potentiality, absence), and the active engagement of the reader and her virtual body during the process of co-construction of the storyworld.

Narrative theory cannot be developed in a void, outside of a dialogue with actual narrative works. Yet, attempts toward a systematisation of comprehension practices and their underlying dynamics sometimes give illuminating insights into innovative patterns that may emerge from a specific text or link together previously unrelated works. This book makes a contribution to narrative studies and literary criticism alike. While offering a fresh perspective on the narrative works of Baricco, Camilleri and Calvino, it also aims to explore the hypothesis of a spatially-oriented theoretical approach to narrative understanding, thus opening up a fascinating path for future research in both fields. Indeed, there is much scope for further work to be carried out in both directions. The investigation of additional case studies would ascertain the applicability of the set of analytical features pinpointed in this study, thus confirming and/or refining their representativeness and effectiveness in the individuation of spatially-oriented plots. Moreover, although this work individuated plot types in order to draw more general critical guiding lines to be applied to other narratives, as far as literary criticism is concerned it is my impression that a spatially-oriented approach would have the most innovative outcomes in the elaboration of new readings of specific works and authors' oeuvres, rather than in the definition of literary or narrative macro-categories.

At the same time, it will be interesting to proceed with the theoretical articulation of the spatially-oriented approach advanced here by expanding and organising a comprehensive range of models and frameworks to be applied in a flexible way to different narratives. Such an approach would include a set of analytical and conceptual tools that scholars could consult and employ whenever they wish to adopt a spatially-oriented critical perspective. In addition to endowing literary critics with new analytical power, this theoretical model would also interestingly contribute to the exploration of our cognitive practices as readers, and provide scientific scholarship with invaluable insights into the thinking strategies and processes prompted by artefacts as chronologically and culturally ubiquitous as narratives.

BIBLIOGRAPHY

ABBOTT, EDWIN A. 1884. *Flatland* (London: Seeley)
ABBOTT, H. PORTER. 2011. 'Narrativity', in *the living handbook of narratology*, ed. by Peter Hühn et al. (Hamburg: Universität Hamburg) <https://www.lhn.uni-hamburg.de/node/27.html> [accessed 1 March 2021]
—— 2007. 'Story, Plot, and Narration', in *The Cambridge Companion to Narrative*, ed. by David Herman (Cambridge: Cambridge University Press), pp. 39–51
ADLER, H., and S. GROSS. 2002. 'Adjusting the Frame: Comments on Cognitivism and Literature', *Poetics Today*, 23.2: 195–220
ALBER, J., and M. FLUDERNIK. 2010. *Postclassical Narratology: Approaches and Analyses* (Columbus: Ohio State University Press)
ALLEN, WALTER. 1954. *The English Novel* (New York: Dutton)
ALMANSI, GUIDO. 1971. 'Il mondo binario di Italo Calvino', *Paragone*, 22.258: 95–110
AMENDOLA, GIANDOMENICO. 1997. *La città postmoderna. Magie e paure della metropolis contemporanea* (Bari: Laterza)
ANTONELLO, PIERPAOLO. 2004. 'The Myth of Science or the Science of Myth? Italo Calvino and the "Hard Core of Being"', *Italian Culture*, 22.1: 71–91
ARAGONA, RAFFAELE. 2008. 'Calvino e il potenziale', in *Italo Calvino. Percorsi potenziali*, ed. by Raffaele Aragona (Lecce: Manni), pp. 11–17
ASOR ROSA, ALBERTO. 2001. *Stile Calvino* (Turin: Einaudi)
AUGÉ, MARC. 2000. *Disneyland e altri nonluoghi* (Turin: Bollati Boringhieri)
—— 1995. *Non-Places: Introduction to an Anthropology of Supermodernity* (London: Verso)
BAETENS, JAN. 2012. 'OuLiPo and Proceduralism', in *The Routledge Companion to Experimental Literature*, ed. by Joe Bray, Alison Gibbons, and Brian McHale (London: Routledge), pp. 115–27
BAKHTIN, MIKHAIL MIKHAILOVIC. 1981 (1937). *The Dialogic Imagination. Four Essays* (Austin: University of Texas Press)
BAL, MIEKE. 1997. *Narratology: Introduction to the Theory of Narrative* (Toronto: University of Toronto Press)
—— 1981. 'Notes on Narrative Embedding', *Poetics Today*, 2.2: 41–61
BARENGHI, MARIO. 2007. *Italo Calvino, le linee e i margini* (Bologna: Il Mulino)
—— 1995. 'Introduzione', in *Saggi: 1945–1985*, ed. by Mario Barenghi (Milan: Mondadori), I, pp. ix–lxxiii
—— 1991A. 'Il castello dei destini incrociati. Note e notizie sui testi', in *Romanzi e racconti*, ed. by Mario Barenghi and Bruno Falcetto (Milan: Mondadori), II, pp. 1366–80
—— 1991B. 'Poesie e invenzioni oulipiennes. Note e notizie sui testi', in *Romanzi e racconti*, ed. by Mario Barenghi and Bruno Falcetto (Milan: Mondadori), III, pp. 1239–45
BARICCO, ALESSANDRO. 2012. *Tre volte all'alba* (Milan: Feltrinelli)
—— 2008. *I barbari. Saggio sulla mutazione* (Milan: Feltrinelli; originally published as series of articles in *La Repubblica*, 12 May–21 October 2006; first publ. as a collection, Rome: Fandango, 2006)
—— 1999. *City* (Milan: Rizzoli)

—— 1993. *Oceano mare* (Milan: Rizzoli)
—— 1991. *Castelli di rabbia* (Milan: Feltrinelli)
BARONI, RAPHAËL. 2011. 'Tellability', in *the living handbook of narratology*, ed. by Peter Hühn et al. (Hamburg: Universität Hamburg) <https://www.lhn.uni-hamburg.de/node/30.html> [accessed 1 March 2021]
BARRY, JACKSON G. 1990. 'Narratology's Centrifugal Force: A Literary Perspective on the Extensions of Narrative Theory', *Poetics Today*, 11.2: 295–307
BARTEZZAGHI, STEFANO. 2007. 'Calvino at Play: Rules and Games for Writing in Space', in *Image, Eye and Art in Calvino: Writing Visibility*, ed. by Birgitte Grundvig, Martin McLaughlin, Lene Waage Petersen (Cambridge: Legenda), pp. 122–40.
BARTH, JOHN. 1984 (1980). 'The Literature of Replenishment', in *The Friday Book: Essays and Other Non-Fiction* (London: Johns Hopkins University Press), pp. 193–206
—— 1984 (1967). 'The Literature of Exhaustion', in *The Friday Book: Essays and Other Non-Fiction* (London: Johns Hopkins University Press), pp. 62–76
BARTHES, ROLAND. 1966/1989. *Le Plaisir du Texte* (Paris: Seuil); *The Pleasure of the Text*, trans. by Richard Miller (New York: Noonday Press)
—— 1966/1975. 'Introduction à l'analyse structurale des récits', *Communications* 8; 'An Introduction to the Structural Analysis of Narrative' (trans. by Lionel Duisit), *New Literary History*, 6: 237–72
BARTLETT, FREDERICK. 1932. *Remembering: A Study in Experimental and Social Psychology* (Cambridge: Cambridge University Press)
BEAUDOUIN, VALÉRIE. 2008. 'Incontro tra due iper-romanzi: *Se una notte d'inverno* e i *Voyage d'hiver*', in *Italo Calvino. Percorsi potenziali*, ed. by Raffaele Aragona (Lecce: Manni), pp. 63–71
BECKWITH, MARC. 1987. 'Italo Calvino and the Nature of Italian Folktales', *Italica*, 64.2: 244–62
BELL, IAN A. 2003. 'Eighteenth-century Crime Writing', in *The Cambridge Companion to Crime Fiction*, ed. by Martin Priestman (Cambridge: Cambridge University Press), pp. 7–18
BELLAVIA, ELISA. 2001. 'La lingua di Alessandro Baricco', *Otto-Novecento*, 25: 135–68
BELPOLITI, MARCO. 1996. *L'occhio di Calvino* (Turin: Einaudi)
BELTRAMI, MARZIA. 2019. 'Urban Space as Cognitive Metaphor? Suggestions from Alessandro Baricco's *City*', in *Cross-Disciplinary Approaches to Italian Urban Space*, ed. by Giulio Giovannoni and Silvia Ross (Firenze: DIDA), pp. 253–78.
BÉNABOU, MARCEL. 2008. 'L'Oulipo tra Francia e Italia: l'esempio Calvino', in *Italo Calvino. Percorsi potenziali*, ed. by Raffaele Aragona (Lecce: Manni), pp. 19–31
BERARDINELLI, ALFONSO. 1991. 'Calvino moralista. Ovvero restare sani dopo la fine del mondo', *Diario*, 9: 37–58
BERARDINELLI, A., G. FERRONI, F. LA PORTA, and M. ONOFRI. 2006. *Sul banco dei cattivi. A proposito di Baricco e di altri scrittori alla moda* (Rome: Donzelli)
BERNAERTS, L., D. DE GEEST, L. HERMAN, and B. VERVAECK. 2013. *Stories and Minds: Cognitive Approaches to Literary Theory* (Lincoln: University of Nebraska Press)
BERNINI, MARCO. FORTHCOMING. *Beckett and the Cognitive Method: Mind, Models and Exploratory Narratives* (Oxford: Oxford University Press)
BERSELLI, EDMONDO. 2006. 'Il caso Baricco, i libri e la critica come nasce un best seller', *La Repubblica*, 3 March
BERRESSEM, HANJO. 2015. '"Secret Integrations": Leibniz, Mathematics, and Literature', *Anglia*, 133.1: 105–24
BERTONI, CLOTILDE. 1998. 'Ritorno all'intreccio', http://www.vigata.org/bibliografia/ritorno.shtml [accessed 1 March 2021]

BERTONI, ROBERTO. 1993. *Int'abrigu int'ubagu. Discorso su alcuni aspetti dell'opera di Italo Calvino* (Turin: Tirrenia)
BJORNSON, RICHARD. 1981. 'Cognitive Mapping and the Understanding of Narrative', *SubStance*, 10.1: 51–52
BLACK, MAX. 1937. 'Vagueness: An Exercise in Logical Analysis', *Philosophy of Science*, 4: 427–55
BLACKMORE, S., G. BRELSTAFF, K. NELSON, and T. TROSCIANKO. 1995. 'Is the Richness of our Visual World an Illusion? Transsaccadic Memory for Complex Scenes', *Perception*, 24.9: 1075–81
BONINA, GIANNI. 2007. *Il carico da undici* (Siena: Barbera)
BONSAVER, GUIDO. 2001. 'La carne, la morte, il chewing gum nella narrativa di Baricco', *Nuova Prosa*, 28: 121–29
—— 1995. *Il mondo scritto: forme e ideologia nella narrativa di Italo Calvino* (Turin: Tirrenia Stampatori)
—— 1994. 'Il Calvino "semiotico": dalla crisi del romanzo naturalistico all'opera come macrotesto', *The Italianist*, 14.1: 160–69
BORDWELL, DAVID. 1985. *Narration in the Fiction Film* (Madison: University of Wisconsin Press)
BORSELLINO, NINO. 2004. 'Teatri siciliani della storia. Da Sciascia a Camilleri', in *Il caso Camilleri. Letteratura e storia*, ed. by Antonino Buttitta (Palermo: Sellerio), pp. 48–53
—— 2002. 'Camilleri gran tragediatore', in *Storie di Montalbano*, ed. by Mauro Novelli (Milan: Mondadori), pp. x–lvii
BOSELLI, MARIO. 1979. 'Italo Calvino: l'immaginazione logica', *Nuova corrente*, 26.78: 137–50
BOTTA, ANNA. 1997. 'Calvino and the Oulipo: An Italian Ghost in the Combinatory Machine?', *MLN*, 112.1: 81–89
BRAFFORT, PAUL. 2008. 'Italo Calvino o il guerriero rigoroso', in *Italo Calvino. Percorsi potenziali*, ed. by Raffaele Aragona (Lecce: Manni), pp. 55–61
BREMOND, CLAUDE. 1973. *Logique du récit* (Paris: Seuil)
—— 1966/1980. 'La Logique des possible narratifs', *Communications*, 8: 60–76; 'The Logic of Narrative Possibilities' (trans. by Elaine D. Cancalon), *New Literary History*, 11.3: 387–411
BRIDGEMAN, TERESA. 2007. 'Time and Space', in *The Cambridge Companion to Narrative*, ed. by David Herman (Cambridge: Cambridge University Press), pp. 52–65
BROOKS, PETER. 1984. *Reading for the Plot. Design and Intention in Narrative* (Cambridge, MA: Harvard University Press)
BROWN, ALISTAIR. 2015. 'Communication Technology and Narrative: Letters, Instant Messaging, and Mobile Phones in Three Romantic Novels', *Poetics Today*, 36.1–2: 33–58
BROWN, G., and G. YULE. 1983. *Discourse Analysis* (Cambridge: Cambridge University Press)
BRUNER, JEROME. 1991. 'The Narrative Construction of Reality', *Critical Inquiry*, 18.1: 1–21
BUCCIANTINI, MASSIMO. 2006. *Italo Calvino e la scienza. Gli alfabeti del mondo* (Rome: Donzelli)
BUNGE, MARIO. 2004. 'Clarifying some Misunderstandings About Social Systems and their Mechanisms', *Philosophy of the Social Sciences*, 34.3: 371–81
BURKE, M., and E. TROSCIANKO (eds). 2017. *Cognitive Literary Science* (Oxford: Oxford University Press)
BUTOR, MICHEL. 1957. *La modification* (Paris: Éditions de Minuit)
BUTTITTA, ANTONINO (ed.). 2004. *Il caso Camilleri. Letteratura e storia* (Palermo: Sellerio)
CAIRNS, H. S., W. COWART, A. D. JABLON. 1981. 'Effects of Prior Context upon the Integration of Lexical Information during Sentence Processing', *Journal of Verbal Learning and Verbal Behavior*, 20: 445–53
CALABRESE, STEFANO. 2017. *La letteratura e la mente. Svevo cognitivista* (Milan: Meltemi)

—— 2013. 'Neurogenesi del controfattuale', *Enthymema*, 8: 96–109
CALABRÒ, ANTONIO. 2004. 'L'identità siciliana e la lezione di Camilleri', in *Il caso Camilleri. Letteratura e storia*, ed. by Antonino Buttitta (Palermo: Sellerio), pp. 31–41
CALVINO, ITALO. 2000. *Lettere. 1940–1985*, ed. by Luca Baranelli (Milan: Mondadori)
—— 1995. *Saggi. 1945–1985*, ed. by Mario Barenghi, 2 vols (Milan: Mondadori)
—— 1991. *Romanzi e racconti*, ed. by Mario Barenghi and Bruno Falcetto, 3 vols (Milan: Mondadori)
—— 1987 (1984). 'Comment j'ai écrit un de mes livres', *Nuova Corrente*, 34.99: 10–28
—— 1981/1986. 'Prose et anticombinatoire', in *Atlas de littérature potentielle* (Paris: Gallimard), pp. 319–31; 'Prose and Anticombinatorics', in *Oulipo. A Primer of Potential Literature*, ed. by Warren F. Motte (Lincoln: University of Nebraska Press), pp. 143–52
—— 1979A. 'Se una notte d'inverno un narratore', *Alfabeta*, 1.8: 4–5
—— 1979B. *Se una notte d'inverno un viaggiatore* (Turin: Einaudi)
CALVO MONTORO, MARÌA J. 2008. '*Le città invisibili*: prosa con metamorfosi per il nastro di Möbius', in *Italo Calvino. Percorsi potenziali*, ed. by Raffaele Aragona (Lecce: Manni), pp. 73–87
CAMILLERI, ANDREA. 2016. *L'altro capo del filo* (Palermo: Sellerio)
—— 2015. *La giostra degli scambi* (Palermo: Sellerio)
—— 2012. *Una lama di luce* (Palermo: Sellerio)
—— 2010. *Il gioco degli specchi* (Palermo: Sellerio)
—— 2009. 'Montalbano. Strategia seriale', in her *Ancora tre indagini per il commissario Montalbano* (Palermo: Sellerio) <www.vigata.org/bibliografia/ancora3.shtml> [accessed 1 March 2021]
—— 2007. *La pista di sabbia* (Palermo: Sellerio)
—— 2002. *La paura di Montalbano* (Milan: Mondadori)
—— 2000A. *Biografia del figlio cambiato* (Milan: Rizzoli)
—— 2000B. *La gita a Tindari* (Palermo: Sellerio)
—— 1999. *Gli arancini di Montalbano* (Milan: Mondadori)
—— 1998. *Un mese con Montalbano* (Milan: Mondadori)
—— 1997. *La voce del violino* (Palermo: Sellerio)
—— 1996A. *Il cane di terracotta* (Palermo: Sellerio)
—— 1996B. *Il ladro di merendine* (Palermo: Sellerio)
—— 1995. *Il gioco della mosca* (Palermo: Sellerio)
—— 1994. *La forma dell'acqua* (Palermo: Sellerio)
—— 1980. *Un filo di fumo* (Milan: Garzanti)
CAMPS, ASSUMPTA. 2000. 'Principio senza fine: l'iper-romanzo di Italo Calvino', *Annali d'Italianistica*, 18: 309–26
CANDEL BORMANN, DANIEL. 2016. 'Possible Worlds in the History of the Novel', *Poetics Today*, 37.1: 107–36
CANNON, JOANN. 1989. *Postmodern Italian Fiction: The Crisis of Reason in Calvino, Eco, Sciascia, Malerba* (Rutherford: Fairleigh Dickinson University Press)
—— 1979. 'Literature as Combinatory Game: Italo Calvino's *The Castle of Crossed Destinies*', *Critique: Studies in Contemporary Fiction*, 21.1: 83–92
CAPECCHI, GIOVANNI. 2000. *Andrea Camilleri* (Fiesole: Cadmo)
CAPOZZI, ROCCO. 1988. 'Mitopoiesi come ripetizione e differenza: *Cosmicomiche vecchie e nuove*', *Studi novecenteschi*, 15.35: 155–71
CAPOFERRO, RICCARDO. 2006. '*Le città invisibili*. Lo spazio urbano come modello di conoscenza', *Fictions*, 5: 41–48
CARACCIOLO, MARCO. 2014A. *The Experientiality of Narrative: An Enactivist Approach* (Berlin: De Gruyter)

—— 2014B. 'Tell-Tale Rhythms: Embodiment and Narrative Discourse', *StoryWorlds. A Journal of Narrative Studies*, 6.2: 49–73
—— 2011. 'The Reader's Virtual Body: Narrative Space and its Reconstruction', *StoryWorlds: A Journal of Narrative Studies*, 3: 117–38
CARACCIOLO, M., C. GUÉDON, K. KUKKONEN, and S. MÜLLER. 2017. 'The Promise of an Embodied Narratology: Integrating Cognition, Representation and Interpretation', in *Emerging Vectors of Narratology*, ed. by Per Krogh Hansen, John Pier, Philippe Roussin, and Wolf Schmid (Berlin: De Gruyter)
CARLONI, MASSIMO. 1994. *L'Italia in giallo. Geografia e storia del giallo italiano contemporaneo* (Reggio Emilia: Diabasis)
CASADEI, ALBERTO. 2007. *Stile e tradizione nel romanzo italiano contemporaneo* (Bologna: Il Mulino)
—— 2002. '1994: i destini incrociati del romanzo italiano', *Italianistica*, 2/3: 269–76
CAVALLARO, DANI. 2010. *The Mind of Italo Calvino* (Jefferson, NC: McFarland)
CAWELTI, JOHN G. 1976. *Adventure, Mystery and Romance: Formula Stories as Art and Popular Culture* (Chicago: University of Chicago Press)
CELATI, GIANNI. 1985. *Narratori delle pianure* (Milan: Feltrinelli)
CHAMBERS, ROSS. 1984. *Story and Situation: Narrative Seduction and the Power of Fiction* (Minneapolis: University of Minnesota Press)
CHATMAN, SEYMOUR. 1978. *Story and Discourse. Narrative Structure in Fiction and Film* (Ithaca: Cornell University Press)
CHETTIPARAMB, ANGELIQUE. 2014. 'Complexity Theory and Planning: Examining "Fractals" for Organising Policy Domains in Planning Pratice', *Planning Theory*, 13.1: 5–25
—— 2005. 'Fractal Spaces in Planning and Governance', *Town Planning Review*, 76.3: 317–40
CHILTON, PAUL. 2014. *Language, Space and Mind: The Conceptual Geometry of Linguistic Meaning* (Cambridge: Cambridge University Press)
CHRISTENSSON, PER. 2006. 'Hypertext Definition', *TechTerms* <https://techterms.com/definition/hypertext> [accessed 1 March 2021]
CITATI, PIETRO. 1959. 'I racconti di Calvino', *Il punto*, 7 February
CLARK, ANDY. 2001. *Being There: Putting Brain, Body, and World Together Again* (Cambridge, MA: MIT Press)
CLARK, A., and D. CHALMERS. 1998. 'The Extended Mind', *Analysis*, 58.1: 7–19
CLAUSI, M., D. LEONE, G. LO BOCCHIARO, A. PANCUCCI AMARÙ, and D. RAGUSA. 2007. *I luoghi di Montalbano. Una guida* (Palermo: Sellerio)
COCCIA, ANDREA. 2014. 'É tornato Alessandro Baricco, re del Midcult', *Linkiesta*, <https://www.linkiesta.it/it/article/2014/%2011/07/e-tornato-alessandro-baricco-re-del-midcult/23432> [accessed 1 March 2021]
COHN, DORRIT. 2012. 'Metalepsis and Mise En Abyme', *Narrative*, 20.1: 105–14
—— 1990. 'Signposts of Fictionality: A Narratological Perspective', *Poetics Today*, 11.4: 775–804
CORTI, MARIA. 1978. 'Trittico per Calvino', in *Il viaggio testuale* (Turin: Einaudi), pp. 201–20
CREMANTE, R., and L. RAMBELLI. 1980. *Teoria e analisi del racconto poliziesco* (Parma: Pratiche)
CULLER, JONATHAN. 1975. 'Defining Narrative Units', in *Style and Structure in Literature*, ed. by Roger Fowler (Oxford: Blackwell), pp. 123–42
CUNNINGHAM, MICHAEL. 1999. *The Hours* (London: Fourth Estate)
DANNENBERG, HILARY. 2008. *Coincidence and Counterfactuality* (Lincoln: University of Nebraska Press)
—— 2005A. 'Plot', in *Routledge Encyclopedia of Narrative Theory*, ed. by David Herman,

Manfred Jahn, and Marie-Laure Ryan (New York: Routledge), pp. 435–39
―― 2005B. 'Plot Types', in *Routledge Encyclopedia of Narrative Theory*, ed. by David Herman, Manfred Jahn, and Marie-Laure Ryan (New York: Routledge), pp. 439–40
DAVIS, NICK. 2012. 'Rethinking Narrativity: A Return to Aristotle and Some Consequences', *StoryWorlds: A Journal of Narrative Studies*, 4: 1–24
DE CERTEAU, MICHEL. 1980/1984. *Arts de faire* (Paris: Gallimard); *The Practice of Everyday Life*, trans. by Steven F. Rendall (Berkeley and Los Angeles: University of California Press)
DEMONTIS, SIMONA. 2001. *I colori della letteratura. Un'indagine sul caso Camilleri* (Milan: Rizzoli)
DENNETT, DANIEL C. 1991. *Consciousness Explained* (Boston: Little, Brown)
D'ERAMO, LUCE. 1979. 'Intervento su *Se una notte d'inverno un viaggiatore*', *Il Manifesto*, 16 September
DERRIDA, JACQUES. 1967/1978. *L'écriture et la différence* (Paris: Seuil); *Writing and Difference*, trans. by Alan Bass (Chicago: University of Chicago Press)
DE TONI, MARIA. 2007. 'Cornice narrativa e dissoluzione del *récit* in Italo Calvino', *Studi novecenteschi*, 34.73: 169–94
DI BARI, ISABELLA. 2008. *L'idea di letteratura in Alessandro Baricco. Il rapporto con la critica, la narrativa, l'esperienza cinematografica* (Patti: Kimerik)
DI GRADO, ANTONIO. 2001. 'L'insostenibile leggerezza di Andrea Camilleri', *Spunti e Ricerche*, 16 <http://www.vigata.org/bibliografia/leggerezza.shtml> [accessed 1 March 2021]
DIJK, TEUN A. VAN. 1979. 'Cognitive Processing of Literary Discourse', *Poetics Today*, 1.1: 143–59
DOLEŽEL, LUBOMIR. 1998. *Heterocosmica: Fiction and Possible Worlds* (Baltimore: Johns Hopkins University Press)
―― 1976. 'Narrative Modalities', *Journal of Literary Semantics*, 5.1: 5–14
DORFLES, PIERO. 2004. 'Montalbano e altri poliziotti anti-istituzionali', in *Il caso Camilleri. Letteratura e storia*, ed. by Antonino Buttitta (Palermo: Sellerio), pp. 54–60
DORFMAN, MARCY H. 1996. 'Evaluating the Interpretive Community: Evidence From Expert and Novice Readers', *Poetics*, 23.6: 453–70
DOWNS, R. M., and D. STEA. 1977. *Maps in Minds. Reflections on Cognitive Mapping* (New York: Harper & Row)
DUCHAN, J., G. BRUDER, and L. E. HEWITT (eds). 1995. *Deixis in Narrative: A Cognitive Science Perspective* (Hillsdale, NJ: Erlbaum)
ECKERT, ELGIN. 2008. 'Murder in Sicily: Commissario Montalbano Talks about his Author's Literary Traditions', in *Differences, Deceits, and Desires*, ed. by Mirna Cicioni and Nicoletta Di Ciolla (Newark: University of Delaware Press), pp. 67–79
ECO, UMBERTO. 1994. *Six Walks in the Fictional Woods* (Cambridge, MA: Harvard University Press)
―― 1980. *Il nome della rosa* (Milan: Bompiani)
―― 1979. *Lector in fabula* (Milan: Bompiani)
―― 1962. *Opera aperta* (Milan: Bompiani)
EDER, JENS. 2003. 'Narratology and Cognitive Reception Studies', in *What is Narratology? Questions and Answers Regarding the Status of a Theory*, ed. by Tom Kindt and Hans-Harald Müller (Berlin: De Gruyter), pp. 277–302
EMMOTT, CATHERINE. 2005. 'Narrative Comprehension', in *Routledge Encyclopedia of Narrative Theory*, ed. by David Herman, Manfred Jahn, and Marie-Laure Ryan (New York: Routledge), pp. 351–52
―― 1997. *Narrative Comprehension. A Discourse Perspective* (Oxford: Clarendon)
ENDE, MICHAEL. 1979. *Die unendliche Geschichte* (Stuttgart: Thienemann)

ENTRIKIN, NICHOLAS J. 1991. *The Betweeness of Place* (Baltimore: Johns Hopkins University Press)
EVERMAN, WELCH D. 1988. 'The Reader Who Reads and the Reader Who is Read: A Reading of Italo Calvino's *If on a winter's night a traveler*', in his *Who Says This? The Authority of the Author, the Discourse, and the Reader* (Carbondale: Southern Illinois Press), pp. 111–27
FALCETTO, BRUNO. 1991. 'Se una notte d'inverno un viaggiatore. Note e notizie sui testi', in *Romanzi e racconti*, ed. by Mario Barenghi and Bruno Falcetto (Milan: Mondadori), II, pp. 1381–401
FARRELL, JOSEPH. 2011. 'Literature and the *Giallo*: Gadda, Eco, Tabucchi and Sciascia', in *Italian Crime Fiction*, ed. by Giuliana Pieri (Cardiff: University of Wales Press), pp. 48–72
FAUCONNIER, GILLES. 1997. *Mappings in Thought and Language* (Cambridge: Cambridge University Press)
FAUCONNIER, G., and M. TURNER. 2008. *The Cambridge Handbook of Metaphor and Thought* (Cambridge: Cambridge University Press), pp. 53–66
—— —— 2002. *The Way We Think. Conceptual Blending and the Mind's Hidden Complexities* (New York: Basic)
—— —— 1998. 'Conceptual Integration Networks', *Cognitive Science*, 22.2: 133–87
FERLITA, S., and P. NIFOSI. 2004. *La Sicilia di Andrea Camilleri. Tra Vigàta e Montelusa* (Palermo: Kalòs)
FERRONI, GIULIO. 2006A. 'Caro Baricco, io la recensisco ma lei non mi legge', *La Repubblica*, 2 March
—— 2006B. 'L'insostenibile leggerezza di Baricco', *La Stampa*, 6 September
—— 2005. *I confini della critica* (Napoli: Alfredo Guido Editore)
FERSTL, E. C., and W. KINTSCH. 1999. 'Learning From Text: Structural Knowledge Assessment in the Study of Discourse Comprehension', in *The Construction of Mental Representations During Reading*, ed. by Herre van Oostendorp and Susan Goldman (Mahwah, NJ: Erlbaum), pp. 247–78
FIELDING, HENRY. 1749. *The History of Tom Jones, a Foundling* (London: Millar)
FLUDERNIK, MONIKA. 2003. 'Natural Narratology and the Cognitive Parameters', in *Narrative Theory and the Cognitive Sciences*, ed. by David Herman (Stanford, CA: CSLI), pp. 243–67
—— 1996. *Towards a Natural Narratology* (London and New York: Routledge)
—— 1993. 'Second Person Fiction: Narrative "You" as Addressee and/or Protagonist', *AAA: Arbeiten aus Anglistik und Amerikanistik*, 18.2: 217–47
FOUCAULT, MICHEL. 1984/1986. 'Des Espaces Autres', *Architecture-Mouvement-Continuité*, October; 'Of Other Spaces' (trans. by Jay Miskowiec), *Diacritics*, 16.1: 22–27
FRANK, JOSEPH. 1945. 'Spatial Form in Modern Literature', *Sewanee Review*, 53.2: 221–40 (Part 1), 53.3: 433–56 (Part 2), 53.4: 643–53 (Part 3)
FRAZIER, L., and K. RAYNER. 1982. 'Making and Correcting Errors during Sentence Comprehension: Eye Movements in the Analysis of Structurally Ambiguous Sentences', *Cognitive Psychology*, 14: 178–210
FRÉMONT, ARMAND. 1976. *La Règion, espace vécu* (Paris: Flammarion)
FURROW, MELISSA. 1988. 'Listening Reader and Impotent Speaker: The Role of Deixis in Literature', *Language and Style*, 21: 365–78
GADDA, CARLO EMILIO. 1957. *Quer pasticciaccio brutto de via Merulana* (Milan: Garzanti)
GALLESE, VITTORIO. 2009. 'Mirror Neurons, Embodied Simulation, and the Neural Basis of Social Identification', *Psychoanalytic Dialogues*, 19: 519–36
GALLESE, V., and G. LAKOFF. 2005. 'The Brain's Concepts: The Role of the Sensory-Motor System in Conceptual Knowledge', *Cognitive Neuropsychology*, 22.3: 455–79

GARGIULO, GIUS. 2002. 'Ra-dio, la "Theory Fiction" ipertestuale di Lorenzo Miglioli', in *Da Calvino agli ipertesti. Prospettive della postmodernità nella letteratura italiana*, ed. by Laura Rorato and Simona Storchi (Firenze: Cesati), pp. 221–32

GARRATT, PETER (ed.). 2016. *The Cognitive Humanities: Embodied Mind in Literature and Culture* (London: Palgrave Macmillan)

GARROD, S., and A. SANFORD. 1999. 'Incrementality in Discourse Understanding', in *The Construction of Mental Representations during Reading*, ed. by Herre van Oostendorp and Susan Goldman (Mahwah, NJ: Erlbaum), pp. 3–28

—— —— 1982. 'Bridging Inferences in the Extended Domain of Reference', in *Attention and Performance IX*, ed. by Alan David Baddeley and John B. Long (Hillsdale, NJ: Erlbaum), pp. 331–46

GAVINS, JOANNA. 2005. 'Scripts and Schemata', in *Routledge Encyclopedia of Narrative Theory*, ed. by David Herman, Manfred Jahn, and Marie-Laure Ryan (New York: Routledge), pp. 520–21

GENETTE, GÉRARD. 1980. *Narrative Discourse: An Essay in Method* (Ithaca: Cornell University Press)

GERRIG, RICHARD. 1993. *Experiencing Narrative Worlds: On the Psychological Activities of Reading* (London: Yale University Press)

GERRIG, R., and G. EGIDI. 2003. 'Cognitive Psychological Foundations of Narrative Experience', in *Narrative Theory and the Cognitive Sciences*, ed. by David Herman (Stanford, CA: CSLI), pp. 33–55

GIANNETTO, NELLA. 2002. *Oceano mare di Baricco: molteplicità, emozioni, confini tra Calvino e Conrad* (Milan: Arcipelago)

GIBSON, JAMES J. 1979. *The Ecological Approach to Visual Perception* (Boston: Houghton Mifflin)

GIDE, ANDRÉ. 1982. *Journal 1889–1939* (Paris: Gallimard)

GIOANOLA, ELIO. 1986. 'Modalità del fantastico nell'opera di Italo Calvino', in *Italo Calvino: la letteratura, la scienza, la città*, ed. by Giorgio Bertone (Genova: Marietti), pp. 20–35

GOFFMAN, ERVING. 1974. *Frame Analysis* (New York: Harper Colophon)

GOLDMAN, ALVIN. 2006. *Simulating Minds: The Philosophy, Psychology, and Neuroscience of Mindreading* (Oxford: Oxford University Press)

GREEN, GEOFFREY. 1986. 'Ghosts and Shadows: Reading and Writing in Italo Calvino's *If on a winter's night a traveler*', *The Review of Contemporary Fiction*, 6.2: 101–05

GREIMAS, ALGIRDAS JULIEN. 1977. 'Elements of a Narrative Grammar'. *Diacritics*, 7.1: 23–40

—— 1966/1983. *Sémantique structurale. Recherche de method* (Paris: Larousse); *Structural Semantics: An Attempt at a Method*, trans. by Daniele McDowell, Ronal Schleifer, and Alan Velie (Lincoln: Nebraska University Press)

GRISHAKOVA, M., and M. POULAKI (eds). 2020. *Narrative Complexity* (Lincoln: University of Nebraska Press)

GUGLIELMI, ANGELO. 1979. 'Domande per Italo Calvino', *Alfabeta*, 6: 12–13

GUGLIELMI, GUIDO. 2002. 'Il romanzo poliziesco', in *A Pocket Gadda Encyclopedia*, ed. by Federica Pedriali <http://www.gadda.ed.ac.uk/Pages/resources/walks/pge/poliziescguglielm.php> [accessed 1 March 2021]

GUJ, LUISA. 1988. 'The Shapeless and the Well-Designed: An Unresolved Dichotomy in Calvino's Narrative?', *Forum for Modern Language Studies*, 24.3: 206–17

—— 1987. 'The Loss of Self: "La selva oscura" of Mr Palomar', *The Modern Language Review*, 82.4: 862–68

GUTT, ERNST-AUGUST. 1991. *Translation and Relevance: Cognition and Context* (Oxford: Blackwell)

HABERMAS, JÜRGEN. 1988. *Nachmetaphysischen Denken: Philosophische Aufsätze* (Frankfurt am Main: Suhrkamp)

HADLINGTON, LEE. 2017. *Cybercognition. Brain, Behaviour and the Digital World* (London: Sage)
HARRIS, PAUL A. 2015. 'David Mitchell's Fractal Imagination: *The Bone Clocks*', *SubStance*, 44.1: 148–53
HART, ELIZABETH. 2004. 'Embodied Literature: A Cognitive-Poststructuralist Approach to Genre', in *The Work of Fiction: Cognition, Culture and Complexity*, ed. by Alan Richardson and Ellen Spolsky (Aldershot: Ashgate), pp. 85–106
—— 2001. 'The Epistemology of Cognitive Literary Studies', *Philosophy and Literature*, 25.2: 314–34
HAYLES, KATHERINE N. 2012. *How We Think. Digital Media and Contemporary Technogenesis* (Chicago: University of Chicago Press)
—— 1991. 'Introduction: Complex Dynamics in Literature and Science', in *Chaos and Order*, ed. by Katherine Hayles (Chicago: University of Chicago Press), pp. 1–33
HERMAN, DAVID. 2013A. 'Cognitive Narratology', in *the living handbook of narratology*, ed. by Peter Hühn et al. (Hamburg: Universität Hamburg), pp. 30–44
—— 2013B. *Storytelling and the Sciences of Mind* (Cambridge, MA: MIT Press)
—— 2012. 'Formal Models in Narrative Analysis', in *Circles Disturbed: The Interplay of Mathematics and Narrative*, ed. by Apostolos Doxiadis and Barry Mazur (Princeton: Princeton University Press), pp. 447–80
—— 2011. 'Introduction', in *The Emergence of Mind. Representations of Consciousness in Narrative Discourse in English*, ed. by David Herman (Lincoln: University of Nebraska Press), pp. 1–40
—— 2010. 'Narrative Theory after the Second Cognitive Revolution', in *Introduction to Cognitive Cultural Studies*, ed. by Lisa Zunshine (Baltimore: Johns Hopkins University Press), pp. 155–75
—— 2009. *Basic Elements of Narrative* (Oxford: Wiley-Blackwell)
—— 2003. 'Stories as a Tool for Thinking', in *Narrative Theory and the Cognitive Sciences*, ed. by David Herman (Stanford, CA: CSLI), pp. 163–92
—— 2002. *Story Logic: Problems and Possibilities of Narrative* (Lincoln: University of Nebraska Press)
—— 1997. 'Scripts, Sequences, and Stories: Elements of a Postclassical Narratology', *PMLA*, 112.5: 1046–59
HERMAN, D., J. PHELAN, P. J. RABINOWITZ, B. RICHARDSON, and R. WARHOL. 2012. *Narrative Theories. Core Concepts and Critical Debates* (Columbus: Ohio State University Press)
HOGAN, PATRICK COLM. 2014. *Ulysses and the Poetics of Cognition* (New York: Routledge)
—— 2004. 'Stories and Morals: Emotion, Cognitive Exempla, and the Arabic Aristotelians', in *The Work of Fiction: Cognition, Culture and Complexity*, ed. by Alan Richardson and Ellen Spolsky (Aldershot: Ashgate), pp. 31–50
HOWELL, PHILIP. 1998. 'Crime and the City Solution: Crime Fiction, Urban Knowledge, and Radical Geography', *Antipode*, 30.4: 357–78
HRUSHOVSKI, BENJAMIN. 1984. 'Fictionality and Fields of Reference: Remarks on a Theoretical Framework', *Poetics Today*, 5.2: 227–51
HÜHN, PETER. 1987. 'The Detective as Reader: Narrativity and Reading Concepts in Detective Fiction', *Modern Fiction Studies*, 33.3: 451–66
HUME, KATHRYN. 1992. *Calvino's Fictions: Cogito and Cosmos* (Oxford: Clarendon)
—— 1986. 'Calvino's Framed Narrations: Writers, Readers, and Reality', *The Review of Contemporary Italian Fiction*, 6.2: 71–80
HUTCHEON, LINDA. 1988. *A Poetics of Postmodernism: History, Theory, Fiction* (London and New York: Routledge)
INGARDEN, ROMAN. 1973. *The Literary Work of Art: An Investigation on the Borderlines of Ontology, Logic and the Theory of Literature* (Evanston, IL: Northwestern University Press)

JAÉN, I., and J. SIMON (eds). 2012. *Cognitive Literary Studies* (Austin: University of Texas Press)

JAHN, MANFRED. 1999. 'More Aspects of Focalisation: Refinements and Applications', *GRAAT*, 21: 85–110 <http://www.uni-koeln.de/~ame02/jahn99b.htm> [accessed 1 March 2021]

—— 1997. 'Frames, Preferences, and the Reading of Third Person Narratives: Towards a Cognitive Narratology', *Poetics Today*, 18.4: 442–68

JAMESON, FREDRIC. 1991. *Postmodernism, or, the Cultural Logic of Late Capitalism* (New York: Duke University Press)

JANSEN, MONICA. 2002. 'Il postmoderno in Italia, una mutazione antropologica? Da Pasolini a "Gli sfiorati" di Sandro Veronesi', in *Da Calvino agli ipertesti. Prospettiva dalla postmodernità nella letteratura italiana*, ed. by Laura Rorato and Simona Storchi (Firenze: Cesati), pp. 37–52

JOHNSON, H. M., and C. M. SEIFERT. 1999. 'Modifying Mental Representations: Comprehending Corrections', in *The Construction of Mental Representations During Reading*, ed. by Herre van Oostendorp and Susan Goldman (Mahwah, NJ: Erlbaum), pp. 303–18

JOHNSON, MARK. 2008. 'What Makes a Body?', *The Journal of Speculative Philosophy*, 22.3: 159–69

—— 1987. *The Body in the Mind. The Bodily Basis of Meaning, Imagination, and Reason* (Chicago: University of Chicago Press)

JOHNSON-LAIRD, PHILIP. 1993. *Human and Machine Thinking* (Hillsdale, NJ: Erlbaum)

—— 1983. *Mental Models: Towards a Cognitive Science of Language, Inference, and Consciousness* (Cambridge: Cambridge University Press)

—— 1981. 'Mental Models of Meaning', in *Elements of Discourse Understanding*, ed. by Joshi Aravind, Bonnie Webber, and Ivan Sag (Cambridge: Cambridge University Press), pp. 106–26

JUST, M. A., and P. A. CARPENTER. 1985. 'Cognitive Coordinate Systems: Accounts of Mental Rotation and Individual Differences in Spatial Ability', *Psychological Review*, 92: 134–46

KACANDES, IRENE. 1993. 'Are You in the Text? The "Literary Performative" in Postmodernist Fiction', *Text and Performance Quarterly*, 13: 139–53

KADONAGA, LISA. 1998. 'Strange Countries and Secret Worlds in Ruth Rendell's Crime Novels', *Geographical Review*, 88.3: 413–28

KAFALENOS, EMMA. 2006. *Narrative Causalities* (Columbus: Ohio University State Press)

KAHNEMAN, D., and D. T. MILLER. 1986. 'Norm Theory: Comparing Reality to its Alternatives', *Psychological Review*, 93.2: 136–53

KANIZSA, GAETANO. 1955. 'Margini "quasi-percettivi" in campi con stimolazione omogenea', *Rivista di psicologia*, 49.1: 7–30

KERMODE, FRANK. 1967. *The Sense of an Ending* (London: Oxford University Press)

KIMMEL, MICHAEL. 2008. 'Analyzing Image Schemas in Literature', *Cognitive Semiotics*, 5: 159–88

KITCHIN, R., and M. BLADES. 2002. *The Cognition of Geographic Space* (London: I. B. Tauris)

KNIGHT, STEPHEN. 2004. *Crime Fiction, 1800–2000: Detection, Death, Diversity* (London: Macmillan)

—— 1980. *Form and Ideology in Crime Fiction* (Bloomington: Indiana University Press)

KNOESPEL, KENNETH J. 1991. 'The Emplotment of Chaos: Instability and Narrative Order', in *Chaos and Order*, ed. by Katherine Hayles (Chicago: University of Chicago Press), pp. 100–22

KNOX, RONALD A. 1992 (1929). 'Detective Story Decalogue', in *The Art of the Mystery Story: A Collection of Critical Essays*, ed. by Howard Haycraft (New York: Carrol & Graf), pp. 194–96

KOSSLYN, S. M., G. GANIS, and W. THOMPSON. 2001. 'Neural Foundations of Imagery', *Nature Reviews Neuroscience*, 2.9: 635–42

KOTTMAN, PAUL. 1996. '*Se una notte d'inverno un viaggiatore*: L'apertura della chiusura', *Forum Italicum*, 30.1: 55–64

KUKKONEN, KARIN. 2014. 'Plot', in *the living handbook of narratology*, ed. by Peter Hühn et al. (Hamburg: Universität Hamburg) <https://www.lhn.uni-hamburg.de/node/115.html> [accessed 1 March 2021]

KUKKONEN, K., and M. CARACCIOLO (eds). 2014. *Cognitive Literary Study: Second-Generation Approaches*, a special issue of *Style*, 48.3

KUZMIČOVÁ, ANEZKA. 2014. 'Literary Narrative and Mental Imagery: A View from Embodied Cognition', *Style*, 48.3: 275–93

LABOV, WILLIAM. 1972. *Language in the Inner City* (Philadelphia: University of Pennsylvania Press)

LABOV, W., and J. WALETZKY. 1967. 'Narrative Analysis: Oral Versions of Personal Experience', in *Essays on Verbal and Visual Arts*, ed. by June Helm (Seattle: University of Washington Press), pp. 12–44

LA FAUCI, NUNZIO. 2001. 'L'italiano perenne e Andrea Camilleri', *Prometeo*, 19.75 <http://www.vigata.org/bibliografia/italianoperenne.shtml> [accessed 1 March 2021]

LAKOFF, G., and M. JOHNSON. 1999. *Philosophy in the Flesh: The Embodied Mind and its Challenge to Western Thought* (New York: Basic)

LANDO, FABIO. 1996. 'Fact and Fiction: Geography and Literature. A Bibliographic Survey', *GeoJournal*, 38.1: 3–18

LANDOW, GEORGE P. 1997. *Hypertext 2.0: The Convergence of Contemporary Critical Theory and Technology* (Baltimore: Johns Hopkins University Press)

LA PORTA, FILIPPO. 1999. *La nuova narrativa italiana* (Turin: Bollati Boringhieri)

LAU, BETH (ed.). 2018. *Jane Austen and the Sciences of the Mind* (New York: Routledge)

LAVAGETTO, MARIO. 1980. 'Per l'identità di uno scrittore di apocrifi', *Paragone*, 31.366: 71–81

LÉVI-STRAUSS, CLAUDE. 1964–71. *Mythologique*, 5 vols (Paris: Plon)

—— 1960. *La structure et la forme* (Paris: Plon)

—— 1958. *Anthropologie structurale* (Paris: Plon)

LEWIS, DAVID. 1986. *On the Plurality of Worlds* (Oxford: Blackwell)

LOGAN, MICHAEL. 1992. 'Detective Fiction and Urban Critique: Changing Perspectives of a Genre', *Journal of American Culture*, 15.3: 89–94

LOTMAN, JURIJ. 1979 (1973). 'The Origin of Plot in the Light of Typology', trans. by Julian Graffy, *Poetics Today*, 1.1: 161–84

LUTWACK, LEONARD. 1984. *The Role of Place in Literature* (Syracuse, NY: Syracuse University Press)

MACDONALD, DWIGHT. 1963. *Against the American Grain* (London: Gollancz)

MCHALE, BRIAN. 1987. *Postmodernist Fiction* (New York: Methuen)

MCLAUGHLIN, MARTIN. 1998. *Italo Calvino* (Edinburgh: Edinburgh University Press)

MCMULLEN, M., K. MARKMAN, and I. GAVANSKI. 1995. 'Living in neither the Best nor Worst of all Possible Worlds: Antecedents and Consequences of Upward and Downward Counterfactual Thinking', in *What Might Have Been: The Social Psychology of Counterfactual Thinking*, ed. by Neal Roese and James Olson (Mahwah, NJ: Erlbaum), pp. 133–68

MAGLIANO, J. P., R. A. ZWAAN, and A. GRAESSER. 1999. 'The Role of Situational Continuity in Narrative Understanding', in *The Construction of Mental Representations during Reading*, ed. by Herre van Oostendorp and Susan Goldman (Mahwah, NJ: Erlbaum), pp. 219–46

MALMGREN, CARL D. 1986. 'Romancing the Reader: Calvino's *If on a winter's night a traveler*', *The Review of Contemporary Fiction*, 6.2: 106–15

MANDELBROT, BENOIT. 1975/1977. *Les objets fractals: forme, hasard et dimension* (Paris: Flammarion); *Fractals: Form, Chance, and Dimension*, trans. and rev. edn (San Francisco: Freeman)

MARCUS, LAURA. 2003. 'Detection and Literary Fiction', in *The Cambridge Companion to Crime Fiction*, ed. by Martin Priestman (Cambridge: Cambridge University Press), pp. 245–68

MARGOLIN, URI. 2007. 'Character', in *The Cambridge Companion to Narrative*, ed. by David Herman (Cambridge: Cambridge University Press), pp. 66–79

—— 2003. 'Cognitive Science, the Thinking Mind, and Literary Narrative', in *Narrative Theory and the Cognitive Sciences*, ed. by David Herman (Stanford, CA: CSLI), pp. 271–94

—— 1990. 'Individuals in Narrative Worlds: An Ontological Perspective', *Poetics Today*, 11.4: 843–71

—— 1984. 'Narrative and Indexicality: A Tentative Framework', *Journal of Literary Semantics*, 13: 181–204

MARGOLIS, JOSEPH. 1983. 'The Logic and Structures of Fictional Narrative', *Philosophy and Literature*, 7.2: 162–81

MARKEY, CONSTANCE. 1999. *Italo Calvino: A Journey Towards Postmodernism* (Gainesville: University Press of Florida)

MARRAS, MARGHERITA. 2005. 'Leonardo Sciascia e l'affermazione del giallo nazional-regionale', *Symposium*, 59.2: 100–15

MARRONE, GIANFRANCO. 2006. 'Montalbano, eroe fra i testi', in *Le parole dei giorni. Scritti per Nino Buttitta*, ed. by Maria Teresa Ruta (Palermo: Sellerio)

—— 2003. *Montalbano: affermazioni e trasformazioni di un eroe mediatico* (Rome: RAI/ERI)

MASSEY, DOREEN. 2005. *For Space* (London: Sage)

MENARY, RICHARD. 2010. 'Introduction to the Special Issue on 4E Cognition', *Phenomenology and the Cognitive Sciences*, 9.4: 459–63

MERCADAL, DENNIS. 1990. *A Dictionary of Artificial Intelligence* (New York: Van Nostrand Reinhold)

MILANINI, CLAUDIO. 1994. 'Introduzione', in *Romanzi e racconti*, ed. by Mario Barenghi and Bruno Falcetto (Milan: Mondadori), III, pp. xi–xxxiii

—— 1991. 'Introduzione', in *Romanzi e racconti*, ed. by Mario Barenghi and Bruno Falcetto (Milan: Mondadori), I, pp. xxxvii–lix

—— 1990. *L'utopia discontinua. Saggio su Italo Calvino* (Milan: Garzanti)

MINK, LOUIS O. 1978. 'Narrative Form as Cognitive Instrument', in *The Writing of History: Literary Form and Historical Understanding*, ed. by Robert H. Canary and Henry Kozicki (Madison: University of Wisconsin Press), pp. 129–49

MINSKY, MARVIN. 1975. 'A Framework for Representing Knowledge', in *The Psychology of Computer Vision*, ed. by Patrick Henry Winston (New York: McGraw-Hill), pp. 211–77

MITCHELL, W. J. T. 1980. 'Spatial Form in Literature: Toward a General Theory', *Critical Inquiry*, 6.3: 539–67

MOORE, G. T., and R. G. GOLLEDGE. 1976. 'Environmental Knowing: Concepts and Theories', in *Environmental Knowing*, ed. by Gary Moore and Reginald George Golledge (Stroutsberg, PA: Dowden, Hutchinson and Ross), pp. 3–24

MORANTE, ELSA. 1988. *Opere*, ed. by Carlo Cecchi and Cesare Garboli, 2 vols (Milan: Mondadori)

MORRISSETTE, BRUCE. 1965. 'Narrative "You" in Contemporary Literature', *Comparative Literature Studies*, 2.1: 1–24

MOST, GLENN W. 2006. 'Urban Blues: Detective Fiction and the Metropolitan Sublime', *The Yale Review*, 94.1: 56–72

MOTTE, WARREN. 1986A. 'Calvino Combinatorics', *The Review of Contemporary Fiction*, 6.2: 81–87

—— (ed.). 1986b. *Oulipo. A Primer of Potential Literature* (Lincoln: University of Nebraska Press)

MUEHRCKE, P. C., and J. O. MUEHRCKE. 1974. 'Maps in Literature', *Geographical Review*, 64.3: 317–38
MUSARRA SCHRØDER, ULLA. 2012. 'Immagini d'architettura in Italo Calvino', *Italies*, 16: 387–410
—— 2011. *Il labirinto e la rete: percorsi moderni e postmoderni nell'opera di Italo Calvino* (Rome: Bulzoni)
NICEWICZ, EWA. 2011. 'Il caso Baricco. Lo scrittore e il panorama della super-offerta attuale', *Romanica.doc*, 2.3: 59–65
—— 2009. 'Nei labirinti dello spazio cittadino: *City* di Alessandro Baricco', *Etudes Romanes de Brno*, 30.1: 159–69
NICOLSON, MARJORIE. 1946. 'The Professor and the Detective', in *The Art of the Mystery Story*, ed. by Howard Haycraft (New York: Simon)
NELSON, TED. 1965. 'A File Structure for the Complex, the Changing, and the Indeterminate' <http://csis.pace.edu/~marchese/CS835/Lec3/nelson.pdf> [accessed 1 March 2021]
NEWEN, A., L. DE BRUIN, and S. GALLAGHER (eds). 2018. *The Oxford Handbook of 4E Cognition* (Oxford: Oxford University Press)
NOË, ALVA. 2004. *Action in Perception* (Cambridge, MA: MIT Press)
NOÉ, SIMONETTA. 1982. 'La parola ordinatrice: Italo Calvino da *Le cosmicomiche* a *Le città invisibili*', *Il cristallo*, 24.3: 79–98
NOVELLI, MAURO. 2002. 'L'isola delle voci', in *Storie di Montalbano*, ed. by Mauro Novelli (Milan: Mondadori), pp. lx–cii
NÜNNING, ANSGAR. 2003. 'Narratology or Narratologies? Taking Stocks on Recent Developments, Critique and Modest Proposal for Future Usages of the Term', in *What is Narratology? Questions and Answers Regarding the Status of a Theory*, ed. by Tom Kindt and Hans-Harald Müller (Berlin: De Gruyter), pp. 239–76
O'BRIEN, E. J., and J. L. MYERS. 1985. 'When Comprehension Difficulty Improves Memory for Text', *Journal of Experimental Psychology: Learning, Memory, and Cognition*, 11: 12–21
OCHS, E., and L. CAPPS. 2001. *Living Narrative: Creating Lives in Everyday Storytelling*. (Cambridge, MA: Harvard University Press)
OLSON, GRETA (ed.). 2011. *Current Trends in Narratology* (New York: De Gruyter)
O'REGAN, KEVIN J. 1992. 'Solving the 'Real' Mysteries of Visual Perception: The World as an Outside Memory', *Canadian Journal of Psychology*, 46.3: 461–88
ORR, MARILYN. 1985. 'Beginning in the Middle: The Story of Reading in Calvino's *If on a winter's night a traveler*', *Papers on Language and Literature*, 21.2: 210–19
OSSOLA, CARLO. 1987. 'L'invisibile e il suo "dove": "geografia interiore" di Italo Calvino', *Lettere italiane*, 39.2: 220–51
O'TOOLE, LAWRENCE. 1980. 'Dimensions of Semiotic Space in Narrative', *Poetics Today*, 1.4: 135–49
OVAN, SABRINA. 2012. 'Names, Travelers, Transindividuality: Italo Calvino in the 1970s', *Enthymema*, 7: 409–24
PADRÓN, RICARDO. 2007. 'Mapping Imaginary Worlds', in *Maps: Finding Our Place in the World*, ed. by James R. Akerman and Robert Karrow (Chicago: University of Chicago Press), pp. 255–87
PALMER, ALAN. 2004. *Fictional Minds* (Lincoln: University of Nebraska Press)
—— 2003. 'The Mind Beyond the Skin', in *Narrative Theory and the Cognitive Sciences*, ed. by David Herman (Stanford, CA: CSLI), pp. 322–48
PAOLI, MARCO. 2016. *Giorgio Scerbanenco: Urban Space, Violence and Gender Identity in Post-War Italian Crime Fiction* (Brussels: Peter Lang)
PAULSON, WILLIAM. 1991. 'Literature, Complexity, Interdisciplinarity', in *Chaos and Order*, ed. by Katherine Hayles (Chicago: University of Chicago Press), pp. 37–54

PAVEL, THOMAS. 1980. 'Narrative Domains', *Poetics Today*, 1.4: 105–14
—— 1975. 'Possible Worlds in Literary Semantics', *The Journal of Aesthetics and Art Criticism*, 34.2: 165–76
PERRY, MENAKHEM. 1979. 'Literary Dynamics: How the Order of a Text Creates its Meaning (with an Analysis of Faulkner's *A Rose for Emily*)', *Poetics Today* 1.1–2: 35–64 and 311–61
PERROUD, ROBERT. 1981. '"Se una notte d'inverno un viaggiatore" d'Italo Calvino: Combinatoire et Confession', *Revue des etudes italiennes*, 27.2/3: 237–50
PEZZIN, CLAUDIO. 2001. *Alessandro Baricco* (Verona: Cierre)
PEZZOTTI, BARBARA. 2016. *Investigating Italy's Past through Historical Crime Fiction, Films and TV Series: Murder in the Age of Chaos* (New York: Palgrave Macmillan)
—— 2012. *The Importance of Place in Contemporary Italian Crime Fiction* (Lanham, MD: Fairleigh Dickinson University Press)
PHELAN, JAMES. 2001. 'Redundant Telling, Preserving the Mimetic, and the Functions of Character Narration', *Narrative*, 9.2: 210–16
PIACENTINI, ADRIANO. 2002. *Tra il cristallo e la fiamma: le Lezioni americane di Italo Calvino* (Firenze: Atheneum)
PIAZZA, GIOVANNI. 2007. *Naufraghi del nulla* (Napoli: Guida)
PIER, JOHN. 2016. 'Metalepsis', in *the living handbook of narratology*, ed. by Peter Hühn et al. (Hamburg: Universität Hamburg) <https://www.lhn.uni-hamburg.de/node/51.html> [accessed 1 March 2021]
PIERI, GIULIANA. 2011. 'Introduction', in her *Italian Crime Fiction* (Cardiff: University of Wales Press), pp. 1–5
PILZ, KERSTIN. 2005. *Mapping Complexity. Literature and Science in the Works of Italo Calvino* (Leicester: Troubador)
—— 2003. 'Reconceptualizing Thought and Space: Labyrinths and Cities in Calvino's Fiction', *Italica*, 80.2: 229–42
PIRANDELLO, LUIGI. 2015. *Novelle per un anno* (Turin: Einaudi)
PISTELLI, MAURIZIO. 2003. *Montalbano sono. Sulle tracce del più famoso commissario di polizia italiano* (Firenze: Le Càriti)
POLACCO, MARINA. 1999. 'Andrea Camilleri, la re-invenzione del romanzo giallo', *Il Ponte*, 55.3 <http://www.vigata.org/bibliografia/reinvenzione.shtml> [accessed 1 March 2021]
POLANYI, LIVIA. 1979. 'So What's the Point?', *Semiotica*, 25: 207–41
POLVINEN, MERJA. 2016. 'Enactive Perception and Fictional Worlds', in *The Cognitive Humanities. Embodied Mind in Literature and Culture*, ed. by Peter Garratt (London: Palgrave Macmillan), pp. 19–34
POPOVA, YANNA. 2015. *Stories, Meaning and Experience: Narrativity and Enaction* (New York: Routledge)
PORTER, DENNIS. 2003. 'The Private Eye', in *The Cambridge Companion to Crime Fiction*, ed. by Martin Priestman (Cambridge: Cambridge University Press), pp. 95–114
—— 1981. *The Pursuit of Crime: Art and Ideology in Detective Fiction* (New Haven: Yale University Press)
PRIESTMAN, MARTIN. 2003. 'Introduction', in *The Cambridge Companion to Crime Fiction*, ed. by Martin Priestman (Cambridge: Cambridge University Press), pp. 1–6
—— 1998. *Crime Fiction from Poe to Present* (Plymouth: Northcote)
PRINCE, GERALD. 2008. 'Narratology', in *The Cambridge History of Literary Criticism*, VIII: *From Structuralism to Poststructuralism*, ed. by Raman Selden (Cambridge: Cambridge University Press), pp. 110–30
—— 2003 (1987). *A Dictionary of Narratology*, rev. edn (Lincoln: University of Nebraska Press)
—— 1988. 'The Disnarrated', *Style*, 22.1: 1–8

—— 1985. 'The Narratee Revisited', *Style*, 19: 299–302
—— 1982. *Narratology: The Form and Functioning of Narrative* (New York: Mouton)
PROPP, VLADIMIR. 1958 (1928). *Morphology of the Folktale* (Bloomington: Research Centre, Indiana University)
PYKETT, LYNN. 2003. 'The Newgate Novel and Sensation Fiction', in *The Cambridge Companion to Crime Fiction*, ed. by Martin Priestman (Cambridge: Cambridge University Press), pp. 19–40
PYRHÖNEN, HETA. 2005. 'Detective Fiction', in *Routledge Encyclopedia of Narrative Theory*, ed. by David Herman, Manfred Jahn, and Marie-Laure Ryan (New York: Routledge), pp. 103–04
—— 1999. *Mayhem and Murder: Narrative and Moral Problems in the Detective Story* (Toronto: University of Toronto Press)
RABINOWITZ, PETER. 2008. 'Other Reader-Oriented Theories', in *The Cambridge History of Literary Criticism*, VIII: *From Structuralism to Poststructuralism*, ed. by Raman Selden (Cambridge: Cambridge University Press), pp. 375–403
—— 1987. *Before Reading. Narrative Conventions and the Politics of Interpretation* (Columbus: Ohio State University Press)
RALL, J., and P. L. HARRIS. 2000. 'In Cinderella's Slippers? Story Comprehension from the Protagonist's Point of View', *Developmental Psychology*, 36: 202–08
RAMBELLI, LORIS. 1979. *Storia del giallo italiano* (Milan: Garzanti)
RANKIN, IAN. 1986. 'The Role of the Reader in Italo Calvino's *If on a winter's night a traveler*', *The Review of Contemporary Fiction*, 6.2: 124–29
REARDON, B. P. 1969. 'The Greek Novel', *Phoenix*, 23.3: 291–309
RELPH, EDWARD. 1976. *Place and Placelessness* (London: Pion)
RICCI, FRANCO. 1982. 'The Readers in Italo Calvino's Latest *Fabula*', *Forum Italicum*, 16.1/2: 82–102
RICHARDSON, ALAN. 2012. 'Facial Expression Theory from Romanticism to Present', in *Introduction to Cognitive Cultural Studies*, ed. by Lisa Zunshine (Baltimore: Johns Hopkins University Press), pp. 65–83
—— 2004. 'Studies in Literature and Cognition: A Field Map', in *The Work of Fiction: Cognition, Culture and Complexity*, ed. by Alan Richardson and Ellen Spolsky (Aldershot: Ashgate), pp. 1–29
RICHARDSON, A., and F. STEEN. 2002. 'Literature and the Cognitive Revolution: An Introduction', *Poetics Today*, 23.1: 1–8
RICHARDSON, BRIAN. 2006. *Unnatural Voices: Extreme Narration in Modern and Contemporary Fiction* (Columbus: Ohio State University Press)
—— 1997. *Unlikely Stories: Causality and the Nature of Modern Narrative* (Newark: University of Delaware Press)
RICOEUR, PAUL. 1982/1984. *Temps et Récit* (Paris: Seuil); *Time and Narrative*, trans. by Kathleen McLaughlin and David Pellauer (Chicago: University of Chicago Press)
RIDDLE HARDING, JENNIFER. 2011. '"He had never written a word of that": Regret and Counterfactuals in Hemingway's "The Snows of the Kilimanjaro"', *The Hemingway Review*, 30.2: 21–35
—— 2007. 'Evaluative Stance and Counterfactuals in Language and Literature', *Language and Literature*, 16.3: 263–80
RIMMON-KENAN, SHLOMITH. 1983. *Narrative Fiction. Contemporary Poetics* (London: Methuen)
RINALDI, LUCIA. 2012. *Andrea Camilleri. A Companion to the Mystery Fiction* (Jefferson: McFarland)
—— 2011. 'Annotated Bibliography', in *Italian Crime Fiction*, ed. by Giuliana Pieri (Cardiff: University of Wales Press), pp. 151–54

ROESE, NEAL and JAMES OLSON (eds). 1995. *What Might Have Been: The Social Psychology of Counterfactual Thinking* (Mahwah, NJ: Erlbaum)

RONEN, RUTH. 1994. *Possible Worlds in Literary Theory* (Cambridge: Cambridge University Press)

—— 1990. 'Paradigm Shift in Plot Models: An Outline of the History of Narratology', *Poetics Today*, 11.4: 817–42

—— 1986. 'Space in Fiction', *Poetics Today*, 7.3: 421–38

RORATO, LAURA. 2001. 'La realtà metropolitana del duemila. *Ambaraba* di Culicchia e *City* di Baricco: due opere a confronto', *Narrativa*, 20.1: 243–61

RORATO, L., and S. STORCHI. 2004. 'Città versus City: the Globalised Habitat of Alessandro Baricco', *Romance Studies*, 22.3: 251–62

ROUBAUD, JACQUES. 2008. 'Calvino e la ricerca dell'Oulipo semantico', in *Italo Calvino. Percorsi potenziali*, ed. by Raffaele Aragona (Lecce: Manni), pp. 171–76

RUMELHART, DAVID E. 1976. 'Understanding and Summarizing Brief Stories', in *Basic Processes in Reading: Perception and Comprehension*, ed. by David LaBerge and Jay S. Samuels (Hillsdale, NJ: Erlbaum), pp. 265–304

RUSHING, ROBERT. 1997. 'Il cristallo e il mare: L'enumeración caótica e l'epistemologia in Calvino e Gadda', *Forum Italicum*, 31.2: 423–37

RYAN, ALEX. 2007. 'Emergence is Coupled to Scope, not Level', *InterScience*, 13.2: 67–77

RYAN, MARIE-LAURE. 2019. 'Virtuality', in *Critical Terms in Future Studies*, ed. by Paul Heike (New York: Palgrave Macmillan), pp. 335–41

—— 2016. '*The Experientiality of Narrative: An Enactivist Approach* by Marco Caracciolo (Review)', *Style*, 50.3: 377–83

—— 2014. 'Space', in *the living handbook of narratology*, ed. by Peter Hühn et al. (Hamburg: Universität Hamburg) <https://www.lhn.uni-hamburg.de/node/55.html> [accessed 1 March 2021]

—— 2010. 'Narratology and Cognitive Science', *Style*, 44.4: 469–95

—— 2005. 'Virtuality', in *Routledge Encyclopedia of Narrative Theory*, ed. by David Herman, Manfred Jahn, and Marie-Laure Ryan (New York: Routledge), pp. 627–69

—— 2003. 'Narrative Cartography: Towards a Visual Narratology', in *What is Narratology? Questions and Answers Regarding the Status of a Theory*, ed. by Tom Kindt and Hans-Harald Müller (Berlin: De Gruyter), pp. 303–64

—— 2001. *Narrative as Virtual Reality: Immersion and Interactivity in Literature and Electronic Media* (Baltimore: Johns Hopkins University Press)

—— 1999. 'Cyberage Narratology: Computers, Metaphor, and Narrative', in *Narratologies. New Perspectives on Narrative Analysis*, ed. by David Herman (Columbus: Ohio State University Press), pp. 113–41

—— 1991. *Possible Worlds, Artificial Intelligence and Narrative Theory* (Bloomington: Indiana University Press)

—— 1986. 'Embedded Narratives and Tellability', *Style*, 20.3: 319–40

—— 1985. 'The Modal Structure of Narrative Universes', *Poetics Today*, 6.4: 717–55

RYAN, M., K. FOOTE, and M. AZARYAHU. 2016. *Narrating Space/Spatializing Narrative. Where Narrative Theory and Geography Meet* (Columbus: Ohio State University Press)

SAMEK LUDOVICI, S., and I. CALVINO. 1969. *Tarocchi. Il mazzo visconteo di Bergamo e New York* (Parma: Ricci)

SANFORD, A., AND. S. GARROD. 2009. 'The Role of Scenario Mapping in Text Comprehension', *Discourse Processes*, 26.2/3: 159–90

SANTSCHI, MADELEINE. 1967. 'Italo Calvino. Je ne suis pas satisfait de la littérature actuelle en Italie', *Gazette de Lausanne*, 127, 2–4 June

SANTOVETTI, OLIVIA. 2007. *Digression. A Narrative Strategy in the Italian Novel* (Bern: Peter Lang)

SANTULLI, FRANCESCA. 2010. *Montalbano linguista. La riflessione metalinguistica nelle storie del commissario* (Milan: Archipelago)
SCAGGS, JOHN. 2005. *Crime Fiction* (London: Routledge)
SCARPA, DOMENICO. 2008. 'Potenza e coerenza: profitti e perdite', in *Italo Calvino. Percorsi potenziali*, ed. by Raffaele Aragona (Lecce: Manni), pp. 89–101
—— 1999. *Italo Calvino* (Milan: Mondadori)
SCARPETTI, R., and A. STRANO. 2004. *Commissario Montalbano. Indagine su un successo* (Arezzo: ZONA)
SCARSELLA, ALESSANDRO. 2003. *Alessandro Baricco* (Firenze: Cadmo)
SCHANK, ROGER. 1986. *Explanation Patterns. Understanding Mechanically and Creatively* (Hillsdale, NJ: Erlbaum)
SCHANK, R., and R. ABELSON. 1977. *Script Plans Goals and Understanding* (Hillsdale, NJ: Erlbaum)
SCHNEIDER, RALF. 2001. 'Toward a Cognitive Theory of Literary Character: The Dynamics of Mental Model Construction', *Style*, 35.4: 607–39
SEGRE, CESARE. 1979. 'Se una notte d'inverno uno scrittore sognasse un aleph di dieci colori', *Strumenti critici*, 30–40: 177–214
SERRA, FRANCESCA. 2006. *Calvino* (Rome: Salerno)
SHEN, YESHAYAHU. 1985. 'On Importance Hierarchies and Evaluation Devices in Narrative Texts', *Poetics Today*, 6.4: 681–98
SHKLOVSKY, VICTOR. 1965. 'Art and Technique', in *Russian Formalist Criticism: Four Essays*, ed. by Lee T. Lemon and Marion J. Reis (Lincoln: University of Nebraska Press), pp. 3–24
SINGLES, KATHLEEN. 2012. *Alternate History. Playing with Contingency and Necessity* (Berlin: De Gruyter)
SOMIGLI, LUCA. 2005. 'Form and Ideology in Italian Detective Fiction', *Symposium*, 59.2: 67–69
SORGI, MARCELLO. 2000. *La testa ci fa dire. Dialogo con Andrea Camilleri* (Palermo: Sellerio)
SPACKMAN, BARBARA. 2008. 'Calvino's Non-Knowledge', *Romance Studies*, 26.1: 7–19
SPERBER, D., and D. WILSON. 1986. *Relevance: Communication and Cognition* (Oxford: Blackwell)
SPINAZZOLA, VITTORIO. 2010. *L'esperienza della lettura* (Milan: Unicopli)
—— 1987. 'L'io diviso di Italo Calvino', *Belfagor*, 42: 509–31
SPOLSKY, ELLEN. 2004. 'Women's Work is Chastity: Lucretia, *Cymbeline*, and Cognitive Impenetrability', in *The Work of Fiction: Cognition, Culture and Complexity*, ed. by Alan Richardson and Ellen Spolsky (Aldershot: Ashgate), pp. 51–84
—— 2003. 'Cognitive Literary Historicism: A Response to Adler and Gross', *Poetics Today*, 24.2: 161–83
STAROBINSKI, JEAN. 1991. 'Prefazione', in *Romanzi e racconti*, ed. by Mario Barenghi and Bruno Falcetto (Milan: Mondadori), I, pp. xi–xxxiii
STERNBERG, MEIR. 2010. 'Narrativity: From Objectivist to Functional Paradigm', *Poetics Today*, 31.3: 507–659
STILLE, ALEXANDER. 1985. 'An Interview with Italo Calvino', *Saturday Review*, April, 36–39
STOCKWELL, PETER. 2009. 'Situating Cognitive Approaches to Narrative Analysis', in *Cognitive Poetics: Goals, Gains and Gaps*, ed. by Geert Brône and Jeroen Vandaele (Berlin: De Gruyter Mouton), pp. 119–23
STOICHEFF, PETER. 1991. 'The Chaos of Metafiction', in *Chaos and Order*, ed. by Katherine Hayles (Chicago: University of Chicago Press), pp. 85–99
STURGESS, PHILIP J. M. 1992. *Narrativity: Theory and Practice* (Oxford: Oxford University Press)

SULEIMAN, SUSAN RUBIN. 1980. 'Redundancy and the "Readable" Text', *Poetics Today*, 1.3: 119–42
SVEVO, ITALO. 1923. *La coscienza di Zeno* (Bologna: Cappelli)
SWEENEY, S. E. 1990. 'Locked Rooms: Detective Fiction, Narrative Theory, and Self-Reflexivity', in *The Cunning Craft: Original Essays on Detective Fiction and Contemporary Literary Theory*, ed. by Ronald Walker and June Frazer (Macomb: Western Illinois University Press), pp. 1–14
SYMONS, JULIAN. 1972. *Bloody Murder: From the Detective Story to Crime Novel. A History* (Harmondsworth: Penguin)
TABUCCHI, A., P. GAGLIANONE, M. CASSINI, and R. SCRIVANO. 1995. *Conversazione con Antonio Tabucchi. Dove va il romanzo?* (Rome: Omicron)
TAPIERO, I., and J. OTERO. 1999. 'Distinguishing Between Textbase and Situation Model in the Processing of Inconsistent Information: Elaboration Versus Tagging', in *The Construction of Mental Representations During Reading*, ed. by Herre van Oostendorp and Susan Goldman (Mahwah, NJ: Erlbaum), pp. 341–66
TARANTINO, ELISABETTA. 2006. '*City* e *Good Will Hunting*', *Contemporanea*, 4: 149–54
THOMS, PETER. 1998. *Detection and its Designs* (Athens: Ohio University Press)
TODOROV, TZVETAN. 1971/1977. *La poétique de la prose* (Paris: Seuil); *The Poetics of Prose*, trans. by Richard Howard (Oxford: Blackwell)
―― 1969. 'Structural Analysis of Narrative', *Novel: A Forum on Fiction*, 3.1: 70–76
TOMASHEVSKY, BORIS. 1965. 'Thematics', in *Russian Formalist Criticism: Four Essays*, ed. by Lee T. and Marion Reis (Lincoln: University of Nebraska Press), pp. 61–95
TONIN, SIMONE. 2005. 'Sulle necessità spaziali del narrare calviniano', *Studi novecenteschi*, 32.70: 181–96
TROSCIANKO, EMILY. 2014. *Kafka's Cognitive Realism* (New York: Routledge)
TUAN, YI-FU. 1977. *Space and Place: The Perspective of Experience* (Minneapolis: University of Minnesota Press)
―― 1975. 'Images and Mental Maps', *Annals of the Association of American Geographers*, 65.2: 205–13
TURNER, MARK. 1996. *The Literary Mind. The Origins of Thought and Language* (Oxford: Oxford University Press)
―― 1994. 'Cognitive Science and Literary Theory', *Stanford Humanities Review*, 4.1, 110–12
TVERSKY, BARBARA. 1996. 'Spatial Perspective in Descriptions', in *Language and Space*, ed. by Paul Bloom, Mary Peterson, Lynn Nadel, and Garreth F. Merrill (Cambridge, MA: MIT Press), pp. 463–91
USHER, JONATHAN. 1996. 'From "Super-albero" to "Iper-romanzo": Lexical Continuity and Constraints in Calvino's *Se una notte d'inverno un viaggiatore*', *Italian Studies*, 51: 181–203
―― 1995. 'Calvino and the Computer as Writer/Reader', *Modern Language Review*, 90.1: 41–54
―― 1990. 'Interruptory Mechanisms in Calvino's *Se una note …*', *Italian Studies*, 45: 81–102
VAINA, LUCIA. 1977. 'Les Mondes possibles du texte', *Versus*, 17: 3–13
VAN DEN BOSSCHE, BART. 2002. 'Italo Calvino e la fiaba tra moderno e postmoderno', in *Da Calvino agli ipertesti. Prospettive della postmodernità nella letteratura italiana*, ed. by Laura Rorato and Simona Storchi (Firenze: Cesati), pp. 53–63
VAN DINE, S. S. 1992 (1928). 'Twenty Rules for Writing Detective Stories', in *The Art of the Mystery Story: A Collection of Critical Essays*, ed. by Howard Haycraft (New York: Carrol & Graf), pp. 189–93
VARELA, F., E. THOMPSON, and E. ROSCH. 1993. *The Embodied Mind. Cognitive Science and Human Experience* (Cambridge, MA: MIT Press)
VARESE, C., and I. CALVINO. 1973. 'Dialogo sulle "Città invisibili"', *Studi novecenteschi*, 2.4: 123–27

VARSAVA, JERRY. 1986. 'Calvino's Combinative Aesthetics: Theory and Practice', *The Review of Contemporary Italian Fiction*, 6.2: 11–18

VEEL, KRISTIN. 2003. 'The Irreducibility of Space: Labyrinths, Cities, Cyberspace', *Diacritics*, 33.3: 151–72

VITALE, ARMANDO. 2001. *Il mondo del commissario Montalbano* (Caltanissetta: Terzo Millennio)

VIZMULLER-ZOCCO, JANA. 2010. 'I gialli di Andrea Camilleri come occasione metalinguistica', *Italica*, 87.1: 115–30

—— 2001. 'Gli intrecci delle lingue ne *L'odore della notte* di Andrea Camilleri', *Spunti e Ricerche: Rivista d'Italianistica*, 16: 38–44

WALSH, R., and S. STEPNEY (eds). 2018. *Narrating Complexity* (New York: Springer)

WATSON, DAVID S. 1988. 'Calvino and the problem of textual referentiality', *The Italianist*, 8: 66–78

WAUGH, PATRICIA. 1984. *Metafiction. The Theory and Practice of Self-Conscious Fiction* (London: Methuen)

WERTH, PAUL. 1999. *Text Worlds. Representing Conceptual Space in Discourse* (London: Longman)

WHITE, HAYDEN. 1987. *The Content of the Form* (Baltimore: Johns Hopkins University Press)

—— 1981. 'The Value of Narrativity in the Representation of History', in *On Narrative*, ed. by William J. T. Mitchell (Chicago: Chicago University Press), pp. 1–23

WILENSKY, ROBERT. 1983. 'Story Grammar Versus Story Points', *The Behavioral and Brain Sciences*, 6.4: 579–623

WILSON, R. A., and L. FOGLIA. 2011. 'Embodied Cognition', in *The Stanford Encyclopedia of Philosophy*, ed. by Edward N. Zalta <https://plato.stanford.edu/archives/fall2011/entries/embodied-cognition/> [accessed 1 March 2021]

YOUNG, KATHARINE. 2005. 'Frame Theory', in *Routledge Encyclopedia of Narrative Theory*, ed. by David Herman, Manfred Jahn, and Marie-Laure Ryan (New York: Routledge), pp. 185–86

—— 1986. *Taleworlds and Storyrealms: The Phenomenology of Narrative* (Dordrecht: Nijhoff)

ZADEH, LOFTI. 1965. 'Fuzzy Sets', *Information and Control*, 8: 338–53

ZANGIROLAMI, DANIELE. 2008. *Alessandro Baricco. Il destino e le sue traiettorie* (Venice: Cafoscarina)

ZORAN, GABRIEL. 1984. 'Towards a Theory of Space in Narrative', *Poetics Today*, 5.2: 309–35

ZUBIN, D., and L. E. HEWITT. 1995. 'The Deictic Center: A Theory of Deixis in Narrative', in *Deixis in Narrative: A Cognitive Science Perspective*, ed. by Judith Duchan, Gail Bruder, and Lynne E. Hewitt (Hillsdale, NJ: Erlbaum)

ZUNSHINE, LISA. 2008. 'Theory of Mind and Fictions of Embodied Transparency', *Narrative*, 16.1: 65–92

—— 2006. *Why We Read Fiction. Theory of Mind and the Novel* (Columbus: Ohio State Press University)

ZWAAN, ROLF. 2004. 'The Immersed Experiencer: Toward an Embodied Theory of Language Comprehension', in *The Psychology of Learning and Motivation*, ed. by Brian Ross (San Diego and London: Elsevier), pp. 35–63

INDEX

Abbott, Edwin 94
absence/void 13, 38, 101, 106, 108, 114–21, 123, 127, 165, 168 n. 20, 21, 24 & 26, 174
accessibility 37–39, 57 n. 21, 69–70, 75
affordance 7, 19, 32, 35, 45, 167 n. 8
Augé, Marc, non-place 21–22, 56 n. 5, 57 n. 23

background knowledge 5, 19, 23, 36–37, 41–43, 48, 57 n. 21, 89
Barenghi, Mario 115, 132, 133, 167 n. 13
Baricco, Alessandro 17–18
    Castelli di rabbia 17, 40
    City 1–2, 9, 11, 17–26, 30–31, 33–37, 39–55, 56 n. 5, 77, 92, 109, 152, 160–61, 164, 171
    I barbari 17, 19, 39–42, 44–46, 49–50
    Tre volte all'alba 172
Barth, Jacques 123, 139, 168 n. 18, 169 n. 35
Barthes, Roland 73–74, 125, 167 n. 15
Beaudouin, Valérie 170 n. 52
Bertoni, Clotilde 68, 89
Bertoni, Roberto 168 n. 28
Bonsaver, Guido 102, 106, 109, 112, 115–16, 119, 128, 130, 132, 134, 137, 161, 164, 165, 167 n. 10, 169 n. 42, 170 n. 53
Borsellino, Nino 86, 88, 91
Bruner, Jerome 8, 47
Bunge, Mario 130–31

Calvino, Italo 1, 3, 6, 8–9, 13, 57 n. 19, 91, 101–66
    Il castello dei destini incrociati 103, 106–07, 112–13, 115, 125, 127, 130, 162, 167 n. 3 & 6, 168 n. 23, 169 n. 35
    Il cavaliere inesistente 132, 165, 167 n. 3
    Le città invisibili 104, 106–09, 114–16, 126–27, 130, 132, 162–63, 166, 167 n. 2, 3, 8, 11 & 12
    Le cosmicomiche/cosmicomical stories 103–04, 106–08, 114–15, 122, 128, 132, 162, 165, 167 n. 3 & 11, 168 n. 20
    'Cibernetica e fantasmi' 116, 121, 125, 133, 162
    'Dall'opaco' 105–06
    Fiabe italiane 106
    Lezioni americane 104–05, 110, 112, 114, 122, 126, 128, 167 n. 4 & 13, 168 n. 24
    Marcovaldo 167 n. 11
    Palomar 103, 114, 116, 167 n. 9

    Se una notte d'inverno un viaggiatore 1, 3, 9, 13, 101–17, 119–37, 139–41, 143–48, 152–66, 167 n. 1, 3, 8, 20, 21, 22, 25, 26 & 28, 169 n. 35 & 39, 170 n. 52 & 58, 172
    Il sentiero dei nidi di ragno 167 n. 2
    Ti con zero 106, 108–09, 115, 123, 132, 165, 167 n. 3
Camilleri, Andrea 61, 67–68
    Montalbano series 1, 6, 9, 12, 55 n. 2, 59, 61–62, 70–71, 85–93, 97, 98 n. 11 & 12, 99 n. 26, 171
    Il ladro di merendine 61–62, 71, 73–74, 76–80, 82–86, 89–92, 132
Cannon, JoAnn 168 n. 21
Caracciolo, Marco 7, 9, 11, 13, 19, 33, 35, 37–38, 69, 152–53, 155, 157–58, 161
Celati, Gianni *Narratori delle pianure* 172
Chandler, Raymond 65
Chettiparamb, Angelique 130–32, 134–36, 138, 169 n. 41
Christie, Agatha 65–66
Citati, Pietro 105
cognitive framework 1, 6–7, 10, 26, 27, 59, 86, 171
cognitive literary studies 1, 14 n. 8
cognitive metaphor 11, 19, 22–24, 35, 50–51, 53, 56 n. 5
    epistemological metaphor: 56 n. 8
cognitive schemata 86–87
cognitive style 12–13, 18, 39, 41, 52, 101, 104, 107, 115, 134, 161, 166, 167 n. 8
combinatorics 13, 57 n. 19, 112, 116, 122, 124–25, 128–30, 133–34
(complex) system 13, 103, 130–38, 169 n. 39, 40 & 41, 170 n. 47
complexity 105, 130–34, 166, 169 n. 36 & 41
Conan Doyle, Arthur 65–66
conventions 8–10, 12, 14 n. 3, 60, 62, 68, 73, 89, 96–97, 110, 136, 160
Corti, Maria 113, 115, 125, 127
counterfactuality 4, 6, 9, 11–13, 49, 57 n. 21 & 32, 59, 69, 73, 75–84, 87, 89, 90, 93–96, 98 n. 16, 17, 18 & 21, 101, 108–09, 115, 124, 141–42, 144, 174
    see also disnarrated
crime fiction 6, 9, 11–13, 55, 57 n. 32, 59–70, 72–77, 83, 85–88, 93–97, 97 n. 6, 7 & 8, 98 n. 17, 171–72
Cunningham, Michael *The Hours* 172

D'Eramo, Luce 111
Dannenberg, Hilary 11, 26, 33, 51, 57 n. 21, 69, 75, 78, 85, 87, 93–96, 98 n. 18
Derrida, Jacques (Derridean) 116, 168 n. 22 & 26
detection as reading process 73–74, 80–81, 98 n. 20
digression 48, 61, 88–90, 103, 109, 111, 124, 138
disnarrated 77–80, 98 n. 21
see also counterfactuality
Doležel, Lubomír 72
Downs, Roger & David Stea 24, 81–82

Eco, Umberto 15 n. 10, 19, 56 n. 8, 64, 120, 141, 168 n. 27
embeddedness/embedded narratives or storyworlds 22, 44, 53–54, 56 n. 15 & 16, 77, 112, 119, 137, 140, 143–45, 147, 151–52, 155, 159, 162–63
embodiment/embodied cognition/mind embodiment 3–6, 8–10, 14 n. 8, 15 n. 11, 23, 33–34, 41, 161, 171–73
embodiment of comprehension strategies 4, 8, 13, 19, 32–33, 50–52, 59, 69, 157, 171–73
Emmott, Catherine 11, 19, 25–27, 31, 56 n. 10 & 11, 57 n. 27, 92, 143
enactivism 6–7, 9, 11, 15 n. 11, 19, 33–34, 37–38, 82, 174
Ende, Michael *The Neverending Story* 119, 168 n. 25
expectations 5–7, 9, 12–13, 39, 46, 49–50, 57 n. 22 & 25, 60, 68, 73–75, 80–81, 90, 94–97, 110, 112, 140–43, 148, 150, 164, 171
experimentation/experimental narrative 90, 102, 122, 130, 132, 162
extended mind 15 n. 11, 75

Falcetto, Bruno 111
Fauconnier, Gilles & Mark Turner 86, 93, 98 n. 18
Fauconnier, Gilles 5
Fois, Marcello 68
Foucault, Michel 40, 56 n. 5, 57 n. 23
fractal/fractality 3, 9, 13, 62, 101–05, 107, 121, 129–30, 134–40, 142, 145–46, 148, 152, 159, 161, 166, 169 n. 34, 41, 42 & 43, 170 n. 47, 171–72
frame (in Emmott's and Goffman's sense) 11, 21, 25–32, 34–36, 43, 50, 56 n. 14 & 15, 57 n. 24 & 27, 143, 152, 173
  frame as *cornice*: 103, 104, 106, 110, 112–13, 117, 119, 122, 127–28, 132–33, 135–38, 145, 147–49, 151–52, 154–60, 165, 167, 169
Frank, Joseph 2, 102
Frémont, Armand 63

Gadda, Carlo Emilio 60, 63, 88, 89, 90, 97 n. 1, 114
Gallese, Vittorio & George Lakoff 3–4
Garrod, Simon & Anthony Sanford 37
geography and literature 12, 63–65, 67
geometry 3, 9, 11, 38, 61, 65, 97, 101, 103–06, 115, 125, 134, 148–49, 163, 167 n. 10

Gerrig, Richard 33
  and Giovanni Egidi 46
Gibson, James 7, 19
Goffman, Erving 26–28
Greimas, Algirdas 14 n. 4, 167 n. 16, 168 n. 17
Guglielmi, Angelo 111, 122, 129, 130, 168 n. 17

Hammett, Dashiell 65
Hayles, Katherine 41, 92–93
Haynes, Todd, *I'm Not There* 1–2
Herman, David 5, 7, 9–10, 13, 14 n. 5, 25–26, 33, 43, 56 n. 12, 57 n. 25, 26 & 27, 94, 153–58, 160, 163, 170 n. 54
heterotopia 40, 56 n. 5
Hühn, Peter 73, 80–81, 98 n. 17 & 20
Hume, Kathryn 102–03, 105, 110, 113, 119, 124, 161
hypernovel 108, 122–29, 135, 162, 168 n. 30
hypertext 126, 128–29, 168 n. 30, 31 & 33

image schema/schemata 4, 8–9, 57 n. 26, 60, 62, 95–96, 101, 171, 173
incipit 110–12
indeterminacy 73–74, 76, 87, 113–15, 120–21, 130–31
information theory 124, 128, 169 n. 38
interruption 111–13, 124, 129, 145–47, 167 n. 15

Johnson, Mark, 9, 86
Johnson-Laird, Philip 26

Kadonaga, Lisa 63, 81
Kottman, Paul 116
Kukkonen, Karin 5

Lakoff, George & Mark Johnson 23, 56 n. 7, 57 n. 33
Lando, Fabio 63, 97 n. 3
Lucarelli, Carlo 67
Lutwack, Leonard 63, 97 n. 5

Malmgren, Carl 170 n. 52
Mandelbrot, Benoit 129
map (plot as) 9, 17, 24–25, 54–55, 62, 96, 171
  cognitive map/mapping: 24–25, 56 n. 16, 81–82, 98 n. 21
Margolin, Uri 154
Massey, Doreen 92
McHale, Brian 69, 72
McLaughlin, Martin 102, 109, 167 n. 2, 169 n. 42
mental model 7, 14 n. 6, 25, 56 n. 18, 57 n. 28, 153, 165
mental representation 25–26
metanarrativity 6, 13, 34, 53, 79–80, 101–02, 109–10, 114, 119, 122–23, 130, 132–34, 141–42, 144–45, 147, 152, 156, 159–60, 162, 164–65, 167 n. 3, 168 n. 26, 169 n. 37 & 39
Micheli, Silvio 168 n. 19

Milanini, Claudio 102, 107, 115, 123, 130, 139, 166, 168 n. 23
mise en abyme 53, 57 n. 34, 61, 87, 89, 110, 134, 136–37, 140, 149
Mitchell, David, *Cloud Atlas* 1, 169 n. 34
modality 4, 6, 11, 14 n. 4, 15 n. 10, 33 59–62, 68–74, 93–95, 98 n. 13, 155
Montalbàn Vàzquez, Manuel 67
multiplicity 103, 105, 107, 109–17, 121, 123, 127–28, 147, 163, 166

narratee 119, 141, 143, 153, 156–57, 170 n. 53
narrative understanding/comprehension 5, 8–9, 11–13, 19, 24–26, 32, 37–39, 41, 53, 55, 61–62, 81, 85, 96, 103, 153, 171–74
narrativity 15, 21, 24, 41, 44, 47–48, 50, 52, 69–70, 80, 96–97, 121, 125, 132
Nelson, Ted 168 n. 31
Nicewicz, Ewa 20–21, 56 n. 5
Noë, Alva 7, 37–39
Noé, Simonetta 163
non-linearity 51, 55, 103, 126–27, 129–35, 168 n. 31

order 2, 11, 61, 66–67, 69, 85, 88, 97, 102–07, 111, 119–20, 124, 131, 133, 136, 138, 151, 166, 169 n. 39, 172
Oulipo/Oulipian 103, 125, 131, 166, 167 n. 5
Ovan, Sabrina 167 n. 15

Pavel, Thomas 72
Perec, Georges 104, 125
Pezzotti, Barbara, 63–64, 66, 68, 88–89, 97 n. 8
Pilz, Kerstin 103–05, 125, 127, 131, 134, 136, 168 n. 33
plot 2, 15 n. 10
   spatial 1–3, 7–9, 10, 13, 14 n. 7, 18–19, 24, 34, 39, 55, 60
   understanding/comprehension/apprehension 4–6, 8–10, 12, 24–26, 32, 34–35, 39, 50, 55, 60, 62, 74–75 87, 90, 94–97, 101, 103, 134, 137, 140, 152, 160, 171–73
Poe, Edgar Allan 65–66
points of divergence 82–85
possible worlds 4, 9, 11, 33, 60, 62, 68–72, 74–75, 82–83, 93–95, 97 n. 10, 98 n. 17, 131–32, 173
postclassical approach 5, 14 n. 8, 153
postmodern 11, 18, 19–21, 40
potentiality 4, 13, 101, 107–14, 117, 127, 130, 174
Prigogine, Ilya & Isabelle Stengers 131
Prince, Gerald 42, 48, 57 n. 24 & 34, 77–78
private world of characters 5, 11, 59, 71–73, 75, 77, 81–82, 85, 87, 93–94, 96, 98 n. 14, 132, 152
Pyrhönen, Heta 80, 81

Queneau, Raymond 125

Rankin, Ian 143, 169 n. 46

reader's virtual body 3, 8, 13, 33–36, 50, 101, 152, 155–64, 173–74
readers' engagement 7, 9, 19, 34, 36, 46, 49–50, 101, 123, 140, 157–58, 160–62, 174
Ricci, Franco 103
Ricoeur, Paul 15 n. 9
Ronen, Ruth 2, 11, 14 n. 4 & 5, 65, 97 n. 10
Rorato, Laura & Simona Storchi 20–21
Rorato, Laura 20
Roubaud, Jacques 103
Ryan, Alex 130, 135, 165, 169 n. 40
Ryan, Marie-Laure 4–5, 7, 9, 11, 14 n. 5 & 6, 25, 33, 35, 38, 41, 56 n. 17, 57 n. 21, 59, 69–73, 75, 77, 80, 93–96, 98 n. 14 & 18, 99 n. 25

Sanford, Anthony, *see* Simon Garrod 37, 43
Santovetti, Olivia 103, 109, 111, 124, 138, 162, 169 n. 42, 170 n. 58
Scaggs, John, 64–66, 69, 97 n. 9
Scarpa, Domenico 108, 123, 138
Scarsella, Alessandro 20, 27, 43
Schank, Robert & Robert Abelson 42–43, 45, 47–48
Schank, Robert 57 n. 24
Sciascia, Leonardo 63, 64, 67, 88, 89
script/script theory 11, 19, 21, 36–37, 39, 41–50, 52, 55, 57 n. 24, 27, 30 & 31, 77
second-person narration 140, 153–59, 170 n. 53
Segre, Cesare 117, 138–39, 143, 157–58, 164–65, 169 n. 43
self-reflexivity 8, 9, 13, 91, 102, 129, 132–36, 156, 161, 164, 169 n. 39 & 43, 173
Serra, Francesca 114, 123
Simenon, Georges 66, 67
Singles, Kathleen 82–83, 93
Sorgi, Marcello 67
space as mimetic setting 24–26, 64–67, 69, 81, 86, 92, 105, 167 n. 11, 172
space of narrative experience 32–34, 36, 81, 94–95, 130, 152–53, 162–63
spatiality 1–4, 7–8, 10–13, 18–19, 21, 32, 34, 37, 39, 41, 43–44, 50–55, 60–65, 67–69, 87, 93, 95–97, 99 n. 23, 101–02, 104–07, 108, 167 n. 8 & 11, 171–74
   spatially-oriented approach 8, 10–13, 35, 60, 88
   spatial mapping 7, 9, 39, 67, 86–87
   spatial metaphor 33, 40–41, 51, 81, 162, 165
   spatial plot/narrative understanding 10, 36–37, 45, 50–51, 54–55, 59, 87, 90, 96–97, 101, 103, 130, 152, 166, 173
   spatial relations 2, 19, 24, 32, 53, 81, 88, 107
   spatial thinking/cognitive style 13, 18, 134
Spolsky, Ellen 12–13
stereotypicality 43, 45–50, 57 n. 24 & 30
Stoicheff, Peter 133–34, 169 n. 37
storyworld 4–7, 10–11, 14 n. 5, 19, 21–22, 25–27, 32–39, 51, 54–55, 56 n. 12, 17 & 18, 57 n. 32,

59–60, 62, 69–73, 86–87, 93–96, 101–02, 107–10, 117–21, 132, 134–39, 143–46, 148, 151–60, 162–65, 169 n. 42, 172–74
Symons, Julian 66

Tabucchi, Antonio 64, 81, 99 n. 22
Todorov, Tzvetan 14 n. 4 & 8, 61, 68–69, 72–74, 80–81, 91, 98 n. 13
Tolman, Edward 24
Tonin, Simone 107, 167 n. 11
trajectory 9, 40, 52, 59–60, 62, 82, 92–96, 163, 171
Tversky, Barbara 163

Usher, Jonathan 109, 127–28, 137–38, 162, 165

Van den Bossche, Bart 133
Varela, Francisco, Thompson, Evan & Eleanor Rosch 3, 6, 23

Varese, Claudio 166, 167 n. 12
variation & repetition 9, 13, 101, 107, 127, 129–30, 136, 138–41, 145, 148–49, 161, 163, 166, 169 n. 42, 172
Ventavoli, Bruno 67
virtuality 1, 4–8, 10–13, 14 n. 3 & 7, 22, 34, 36, 47–48, 55, 59, 60–62, 65, 68, 71–72, 74–75, 77–78, 81, 85, 87, 93–94, 96–97, 98 n. 13 & 21, 101, 107–10, 114–15, 117–18, 122, 124–25, 127–29, 152–53, 155, 162–64, 170 n. 58, 173–74
virtual presence 9, 38–39, 49, 127
see also reader's virtual body

Waugh, Patricia 102, 143, 160, 170 n. 55
White, Hayden 2, 15 n. 9

Young, Katharine 27, 56 n. 12

www.ingramcontent.com/pod-product-compliance
Lightning Source LLC
LaVergne TN
LVHW061251060426
835507LV00017B/2010